THE WORKS OF CHARLES DARWIN

Bindings, 1845–1882

For explanation *see* pages 20–21

THE WORKS OF
CHARLES DARWIN

An Annotated Bibliographical Handlist

by

R. B. FREEMAN

Second Edition
Revised and enlarged

DAWSON · ARCHON BOOKS

First published in 1977

© R. B. Freeman 1965 & 1977

Wm Dawson & Sons Ltd, Cannon House
Folkestone, Kent, England

Archon Books, The Shoe String Press, Inc
995 Sherman Avenue, Hamden, Connecticut 06514 USA

British Library Cataloguing in Publication Data

Freeman, Richard Broke
    The works of Charles Darwin: an annotated bibliographical
    handlist.—2nd ed., revised and enlarged.
    1. Darwin, Charles—Bibliography
    I. Title
    016.575'0092'4   Z8217   LC 76-030002

ISBN 0-7129-0740-8
ISBN 0-208-01658-9   (Archon Books)

Printed in Great Britain
by W & J Mackay Limited, Chatham

CONTENTS

PART 2 PUBLICATIONS IN SERIALS

PREFACE

PREFACE

THE first part of the following list contains all the editions and issues of books, pamphlets and circulars, both British and foreign, which I have seen, or seen reliably recorded, from the first in 1835 up to the end of 1975. It also includes works which contain matter printed from manuscripts which were not published in Darwin's lifetime. For letters, I have included any that were published in his lifetime, but only the more important collections published since then. Many other works contain small collections or single letters, and a long, but incomplete, list of these is given by the late *Sir* Gavin de Beer in No. 1595.

The second part contains a list of papers, notes and letters which were originally published in serials. Many of the more important of these were translated or summarized in foreign languages in Darwin's lifetime, and more have appeared in collected editions of his works, especially in Russian, since. These have not been included.

The book does not pretend to be more than a list, giving only a brief description of each item, with, in the case of important ones, enough information to indicate what they should contain. I have used the degressive principle both for the mere reissues in Darwin's lifetime and for the less important of the later reprints. Some information is given on binders' cases, but variants are noticed only for the most important books. The difficulties of completing such a list are discussed in the first part of the Introduction. There are only fifty headings in Part I, but they produce more than 1600 entries. I am aware that, even with this number, the list is far from complete. The worst deficiencies are amongst the very numerous American reprints of the *Journal of researches* and *The origin of species*, and in the Slav language editions in the last fifteen or twenty years. Because the number of entries is more than three times that of the first edition, it has been necessary to renumber throughout, but the original numbers have been given in the right hand margin.

In the course of compiling the list, in examining the books themselves, and in reading what other people have written about them, I have come across a good deal of information which is of bibliographical interest. The general matter is placed in the Introduction, whilst that which relates to a particular work, or group of works, will be found preceding the first entry under that particular heading.

First editions, and a few others of recognized importance, are usually

7

easy to find in libraries, and all but a few are still common on the market. It is the later issues which are rare in libraries and hard to see, although many of them contain interesting introductory matter. These are of little commercial value, and will in consequence become more difficult to see as time goes on. Foreign translations are always poorly represented in libraries on both sides of the Atlantic, although, fortunately, there are a few collections, including that at Down House, which are full of them.

It is a great pleasure to acknowledge the unfailing help that has been given to me by Librarians and their staffs at many libraries throughout the world. They are too many to thank individually, and I hope that none will think it discourteous if I thank them all together. There are however three whose help has been continuing: Mr Joseph W. Scott, Librarian of University College London, whose fine library has been my day to day source of reference; Mr Peter J. Gautrey who cares for the Darwinian archive as well as the family books in the Cambridge University Library; and Mr Richard Landon of the Fisher Rare Book Library of the University of Toronto—the number of items in the list shown as held at Toronto is some indication of his help. The late John C. Wyllie, Librarian of the Alderman Library of the University of Virginia, looked at the Victorious collection and other holdings with the enthusiasm and accuracy for which he was famous.

A compilation of this sort must rely heavily on the catalogues and stock of antiquarian booksellers. Here again I have received unfailing help. I have gained more information about later issues and obscure editions from the shelves of booksellers throughout the south of England than from all the library catalogues put together. Two great bookshops stand apart: Wheldon & Wesley Ltd, where Charles and Howard Kirke Swann have let me use their vast stock and vaster knowledge; and Bernard Quaritch Ltd, where the same kindness has come from Howard Radclyffe, and earlier from John Collins who is now with Sothebys.

R. B. FREEMAN

University College London
1st June, 1976.

INTRODUCTION

DARWIN wrote sixteen books, or twenty according to how one treats them, and he contributed to a further nine, in four of which his work is long and important. There are also a number of little pieces, pamphlets or single sheets, of which he was the author or to which he gave his name with others. These together make up forty-two titles to 1882, the year of his death. There are 166 papers or notes in serials; many of these are brief, but about thirty are important contributions to the publications of learned societies. After his death there are his autobiography, his letters, publications from his manuscripts, and later editions and translations of his already published works.

A complete collection of English editions of books, pamphlets and single sheets, wholly by Darwin, or to which he contributed, excluding papers in serials, up to 1882, would amount to 116 items. To this may be added 57 American printings and 109 foreign translations, making a total of 282. With the contributions to serials, roughly 450 titles completes the printed work. The remaining items, almost three-quarters of the whole, recorded here are not to be despised as mere reprints, or late translations, of works which had been published in his lifetime. There are a few editions which were altered by Francis Darwin from his father's notes, the autobiographical matter, the letters, and the transcripts of manuscripts, all of which are important. Many later printings of the major works, both in English and in foreign translation, have introductory matter by distinguished scholars of evolution. These reflect changing knowledge and attitudes to the subject. The rest indicate that copies of his texts are still wanted and *The origin of species* and *Journal of researches* have never been out of print. Morse Peckham has written of the former that 'it would be as hopeless a task to search out all the reprints as it would be to discover those of its great—and almost as shattering—coeval, *The Rubáiyát of Omar Khayyám.*' I have tried to do just that for all of Darwin's work.

An output of sixteen books should not present any serious bibliographical difficulties, at least for those appearing in his lifetime, but even a list is not so easy to put together as might be supposed. There are two chief reasons for this. Firstly, John Murray, who was Darwin's main publisher in England, usually printed only a few thousand copies at a time, most often two thousand but sometimes less, and he changed the

9

title pages and perhaps other preliminaries at each printing. In only one instance, *The expression of the emotions*, 1872, did he print as many as seven thousand in exactly the same form including the title page. Such printings are only issues, or at most title page editions, but they exist and must be recorded. Secondly, as a result of this printing policy, Darwin was able to make small revisions between issues, even when these were printed from stereo plates, so that successive issues, in his lifetime at least and sometimes after, must not merely be seen, but must be collated. This habit of his was not confined to printings in England, but occurs in some American printings as well as in translations.

The most striking example is shown by the 1876 issue of the sixth edition of *The origin of species*, the eighteenth thousand. Neither Darwin nor John Murray ever called this an edition. Modern editors, except Morse Peckham, have also considered the first issue of the sixth edition, the eleventh thousand of 1872, to be the definitive text as Darwin left it. There is a faint hint on the title page that perhaps the text should be collated; and indeed when this is done there are found to be author's changes, small but nevertheless there. The definitive text is therefore that of 1876, and not of 1872 as is usually stated. Another good example is found in *Vegetable mould and worms*. Each of the first seven thousands has a different title page, all but the first of them stating the thousand. None of them are called editions, indeed they are not, but no mention is made of the fact that all of them, except the second, have textual differences.

It was often, but not invariably, Murray's policy to print on his title pages, except those of first printings, a statement of what total number of copies, to the nearest thousand, had been printed. This statement can sometimes be shown to be incorrect, and sometimes, though possibly correct, goes out of sequence, but on the whole it can be a useful pointer to missing entries in the list. He also prints these thousands in his advertisements, although in some cases it can be shown that the thousands stated do not exist; a list of some of these is given in the discussion of *The origin of species*. In a few cases the same thousand may be stated on title pages of different dates. In some these may be errors, but they usually represent resettings of the title pages for those books which sold slowly. In *The origin of species*, which sold quickly, the thirteenth thousand occurs with title pages dated 1872 or 1873; as these are preceded by the eleventh thousand of 1872 and are followed by the fifteenth of 1875 both are presumably correct. The thirteenth of 1872 is not shown in Murray's accounts for this printing, but it nevertheless exists. The third thousand of *Climbing plants*, which sold slowly, may have dates of 1882, 1885, or 1888.

The twenty-third thousand of *The descent of man* appeared in one volume in 1888, and the same thousand is given on the title page of the second issue of the two volume Library Edition of 1891. The latter, which goes out of sequence, is presumably a misprint. In *Vegetable mould and worms*, the editions of 1897 and 1904 are both called thirteenth thousand. The latter cannot be merely a new title page for unsold stock because the text is entirely reset. Thirteenth is presumably a misprint in 1904. The opposite situation occurs in the thirty-seventh thousand of *The origin of species*, some copies of which are dated 1883 on the title page. The list of other works, on the verso of the title leaf, shows clearly that the correct date is 1889, as in most copies of this issue, or possibly 1888, the inserted advertisements being dated September 1888. The '3' in 1883 is in a wrong fount.

However, the compilation of a list is comparatively easy, and is free from the problems which beset the bibliographers of many nineteenth-century authors. Such things as trial issues, author's editions, large or special paper, or colonial editions seem to be absent, although there are a few freaks. The appearance of the second edition text of *The origin of species* dated 1859 instead of 1860, and of Volume I only of *The descent of man* dated 1870 instead of 1871, is odd; although both are extremely rare. The 1848 printing of *Journal of researches* which is dated 1845 on the title page is however a common book; as is the *Manual of scientific enquiry* dated 1886 but clearly printed in 1906. Only two English editions were printed in parts. The second edition, 1845, of the *Journal of researches* appeared in three parts, and the *Zoology of the voyage of the Beagle* in nineteen numbers making up five parts. The former was a popular and cheap edition, not likely to have been bought by libraries, and I have seen only parts one and two; the second, expensive and full of fine plates, presents no difficulties.

Darwin had only five publishers for his own books, and three of these published one work each. One, *Letters on geology*, was privately printed, not published. Henry Colburn published the first edition of *Journal of researches* and its two subsequent reissues. The Ray Society published the *Living Cirripedia*, and the Palaeontographical Society the *Fossil Cirripedia of Great Britain*. Of the rest, Smith Elder published the geological works, which can be treated as one or as three separate books, and continued to do so until 1891. John Murray published the remaining eleven, as well as the second and subsequent editions of the *Journal*. Murray produced over 150 editions and issues, and Smith Elder eight,

All Murray Darwins have an octavo leaf shape in various paper sizes, but may be signed and sewn in eights or twelves. The first four editions of *The origin of species* are usually stated to be duodecimos. They are certainly gathered in twelves, and they are signed on the first, second and fifth leaves, the signature of leaf five being A3 *etc*. The leaf height is 197.5 mm in the first three and 195 mm in the fourth. There are no watermarks. The same format, with a page height of 195 mm, is also found in the first edition of *The fertilisation of orchids*. Such a format is consistent with a large duodecimo or with an octavo imposed in sheet and a half, but the page shape is wrong for a duodecimo and Murray's accounts state that the paper bought was 'Sht. ½ Post Spalding'. This shows that they were imposed on sheet and a half and are all octavos. After imposition, the bottom third of each sheet and a half was cut off, folded by two vertical folds, and placed as four leaves between the larger portion which was folded as an octavo. The signature A3 *etc*. is on the first leaf of the inserted portion which is the fifth of the bolt.

A gathering in twelves is found again in several other, shorter, Murray Darwins. These include the 1875, 1876, 1878 and 1880 issues of *The origin of species*, and five consecutive issues of *The descent of man* between 1874 and 1881. In these cases the preceding and succeeding issues are all octavos gathered in eights, but in every other respect they resemble those in twelves, all being printed from the same stereos and having the same page heights. They are all crown octavos, the twelves being imposed on sheet and a half paper, the eights on sheets.

Francis Darwin in *Life and letters* (Vol. III, pp. 35–36), writing of the year 1865, refers to his father's dislike of heavy books and books with the folds unopened. He states that 'the presentation copies, however, of all his later books were sent out with the edges cut'. This may be so, but it was not invariable and I have not seen enough copies to make any firm statement. What is undoubtedly true is that copies of the first editions, and others, of his Murray books, from *The descent of man* in 1871, and including some family copies, do occur with two different page heights, about 190 and 185 mm, and the cases, not being stilted, are also shorter. I have compared a number of pairs of otherwise identical copies and have found that the folds of the shorter copies are just as likely to be unopened at the top as those of the taller. Mr Murray seems to have honoured Darwin's dislike more in the breach than in the observance, but the matter needs further enquiry.

Three of Darwin's works have received serious bibliographical treatment. *The origin of species* has been surveyed in great detail by Morse Peckham in his comparative edition of the texts of 1959. He covers all English editions and issues up to 1890, and his formal descriptions include consideration of paper, type and binding cases, as well as summaries of Murray's accounts. That I have been able to add three issues in Darwin's lifetime and make a few small corrections only indicates the difficulties involved in seeing copies of all issues, especially in America. H. D. Horblit, in the Grolier Club volume *One hundred books famous in science*, 1964, has also given a full description of the first edition of the same work. Lady Barlow has considered the *Journal of researches* in her *Charles Darwin and the voyage of the Beagle*, 1945. She covers six editions and issues from the first in 1839 up to 1870, but omits that of 1852. She also covers *Letters on geology*, and some of the papers in serials which relate to the voyage. A full bibliographical description of *Living Cirripedia* is available in Curle's *The Ray Society a bibliographical history*, 1954.

I have not seen a full description of any other of Darwin's books, and information about them has been gathered not only from copies seen, but from various reference sources. A useful source of information is in Darwin's own writings. He was a meticulous man of business and usually noticed the dates of publication and the numbers of copies printed. The facts he gives are sometimes at variance with information from other sources and from the books themselves, and he never refers to mere re-issues; indeed in neither *Variation under domestication* nor *The descent of man* does he mention that there are two printings of the first edition. He also surveys the foreign editions of *The origin of species* in his auto-biography.

Another useful source is to be found in the lists which Murray printed in the preliminary matter of issues in this century. Such lists are only available in a few cases and these do not include full ones for *The origin of species* nor for the *Journal of researches*, the two most difficult. Neither do the dates given always agree with the dates given on the title pages. Lists of first, and important later editions are given in *Life and letters*. An independent list is available in Bettany's *Life of Charles Darwin*, 1887, which was compiled by John P. Anderson, mostly from material in the British Museum.

Other important sources are the catalogues of great libraries and, where they exist, union catalogues. The Library of Congress *National Union Catalog. Pre-1956 imprints*, by far the greatest of them, enters about 700 holdings for *The origin of species* and 500 for the *Journal of researches* alone. I have relied heavily on it for the more obscure American editions. National bibliographies are essential, but often un-reliable and incomplete, especially in their earlier volumes. Many recent foreign translations would have been missed but for *Index translationum*.

But the final evidence is from the books themselves, in the hand. I have examined all the copies in the British Library Reference Division, the British Museum (Natural History), the University Library Cambridge including Darwin's own copies, and Down House. The only overseas holding which I have examined is the majority of the 450 volumes in the University of Toronto. Copies of particular interest have been looked at, either by me, or for me, in many other libraries both in England and abroad. Finally booksellers stock is important. I have thanked the booksellers elsewhere; but a wise one once said that nobody ever threw away a Darwin. If for example one needs to see all the printings in Everyman, or the World's Classics, or those lesser library series which have become extinct, the bookseller is the only hope. Those firms which specialize in natural history have, by seeing many copies over the years, built up a lore about points, and this is much more often right than wrong. In the first edition of this book, I destroyed one of these sacred cows, the existence of two English editions, or issues, of *The origin of species* both dated 1859. All booksellers who have a copy of the first edition, a common book, now never hint, as they did in the past, that there might be a second. But there is: they were right in the first place and I was wrong, although it is extremely rare.

There are two English issues which stand apart from all the rest because, although they appeared within the copyright period, they were not published by the copyright holders. These are the George Routledge editions of *The origin of species*, dated 1895 and 1899, which were issued as No. 88 of *Sir* John Lubbock's Hundred Books. The first appeared either in the red cloth used for the uncut issue of the series or in the blue of the cut issue. The publishers inform me that they bought the sheets in 1895, but they are only those of the John Murray issue of 1894, the forty-fifth thousand, including the usual half-title and title leaves. The second, of 1899, is the fifty-sixth thousand, and both can be distinguished from the Murray issues by the series bindings. *Sir* John was a personal friend of both Darwin and Murray.

All English language editions, whatever their country of origin, have been incorporated in the following list in a single date sequence. Most of those not printed in Great Britain are from the United States and the *Pre-1956 imprints* reveals what a large number there are, although it by no means lists them all. There are no Canadian imprints and the only one from South America is a polyglot pamphlet *Bar of sandstone off Pernambuco*, from Recife, Brazil (No. 269). In the early days, up to 1860, the American editions seem to have been independent of the English, Harper producing eight issues of the *Journal of researches*, the first in 1846 from the second English of the previous year. By 1860, Appleton became the standard publisher and, from the fourth issue of *The origin of species* of that year, Darwin was able to gain some financial advantage as well as to send corrections for future editions. Later, from at least *The expression of the emotions*, 1873, Murray provided stereos from which the Appleton editions were printed. Appleton, like Murray, printed in small numbers at a time, and there are in consequence a large number of title page issues. These are usually dated, but he did not print the thousands on the title pages as Murray did, so that the separate printings are harder to identify. There are several other American publishers in the early days, although most of their books were produced after their Copyright Act of 1891.

There are a few printings in European countries in English, mostly school or university texts, which have also been incorporated in the list. One recent printing of the *Journal of researches* (No. 160) was published in Geneva, but distributed as a book club volume in England. Another *Journal of researches* (No. 146) and a *Descent of man* (No. 1043) have been printed, by a scholar printer, in Adelaide but distributed as a book club volume in America. Many of the modern facsimilies have been produced in Europe. A few editions in English braille have been entered at the end of the English sequence.

Almost all of Darwin's main works and many of the little things have been translated. (Only his taxonomic work on barnacles is found in English alone.) They are found in at least thirty-three languages, including eleven in his lifetime. *The origin of species* has appeared in twenty-nine, eleven in his lifetime; *Journal of researches* in twenty-two, six in his lifetime; and the *Descent of man* in eighteen, eight in his lifetime. I have entered here all that I have seen recorded, but they are notoriously difficult to track down and holdings in English and American libraries are thin. It was Darwin's habit, as has been mentioned above, to enter into correspondence with his translators and to send them amendments, so that some foreign texts may be as important as the English ones. In one case at least, the Russian *Variation under domestication*, he sent corrected proofs to the translator, who published in parts so that some of the text of his edition pre-dates the first English. In entering foreign language editions in the list, I have omitted titles to obviate errors, except where these are conspicuously different from the originals.

Collected Works of Darwin have appeared in a number of countries, although never in England. The nearest attempt here was the Grant Richards edition of *The origin of species* in the World's Classics series, 1902. It is called 'Works of Charles Darwin Vol. 1' but no more appeared. In America, the nearest is Appleton's 'Selected Works', the Westminster Edition limited to 1000 copies, which contains twelve titles. There are more or less complete sets in Dutch and German, but the only fully comprehensive one is the Russian collection edited by S. L. Sobol'. These are not set out in the lists, but will be found entered in the Index under Collected Works.

After Darwin's death, both Murray and Smith Elder continued to

keep most of the books in print and there were some new editions over-
seen by his son Francis. Smith Elder stopped in 1891, but Murray continued with some titles into the period when the copyrights expired.
His last printing was of *The origin of species* in 1929. In general, the less
enduring works ceased to be available by the end of the Edwardian
period, and there was then a long gap during which only *The origin of
species* and the *Journal of researches* were in print. Since the end of World
War II, with the increase in interest in the history of science, every book
has appeared in facsimile. It is unfortunate that the editors, or publishers,
of some of these have not considered carefully enough what it was that
needed to be reproduced. The only facsimile of *Fertilisation of orchids* is
taken from an Appleton printing of 1895. Several works have also
appeared in editions with scholarly introductory matter. Much manuscript material has also been printed, and a reprint of all the papers in
serials is to appear. A comprehensive edition of letters is projected.

A collection of Darwins on the shelf presents, with a few exceptions,
a green, monotonous, appearance. I am concerned here only with the
cases of Murray and Smith Elder, although a few others have to be
referred to in the list. A general degressive approach has been made to
late and to foreign editions and issues many of which occur in variant
cases. These may indicate later casing, or, where the work is undated,
later issues.

The cases of works before 1871 fit no particular pattern, but from the
first edition of *The descent of man*, in that year, until the end of the century
almost every edition and issue are crown octavos with a page height of
about 195 mm, or less for the cut copies referred to above. In 1900 and
later the size of Murray printings is increased to large crown octavo.
With six exceptions, they are all bound in green cloth, usually a rough
royal green, although changing to grey-green for the Library Editions
and the illustrated edition of the *Journal*, 1890, and a leaf green for almost
all the issues in this century. The six exceptions are the three issues in
cloth, 1845, [1848] and 1852, of the second edition of the *Journal*, which
were in the scarlet cloth of the Colonial and Home Library, the first
edition of *Fertilisation of orchids* which is in plum cloth, and two late
issues of The origin of species, 1910 and 1917, which are in the red cloth
of Murray's Library. The three parts of the first issue of the second
edition of the *Journal*, 1845, were in grey card. Smith Elder's later
editions of the geological works were also usually in green cloth,
although all four also occur in brown. There are a few issues in this
century which are in the traditional royal green and not leaf green: these
include the twelfth thousand of *The expression of the emotions* of 1901 and
the 1915 reprint of *Cross and self fertilisation*.

INTRODUCTION

itling, by which a book can be most easily recognized on
the shelf, shows, at least from 1871, a fairly consistent pattern, although
there are several minor variations. I have never yet been able to see all
twelve Murray Darwins in bindings with entirely uniform spine gilding.
The commonest form carries an ornamental roll at top and bottom of a
series of circles with central dots and tangential lines. The title is followed
by a plain, or slightly ornamented, rule between it and the author's
name. It is this rule which makes it impossible to find a uniform set. In
some works, all editions and issues have it plain; in others all have it
decorated. In *The expression of the emotions* alone some issues have it
plain and some decorated. The author's name is in roman in all cases
except *Variation under domestication*, where it is in italic in all editions and
issues, and in two of the four variant cases of the fifth edition of *The
origin of species*, 1869.

Below the author's name there is a pendant which is present not only
on Murrays, but also on Smith Elders. This device varies slightly and it
is clear that the case makers, usually Edmonds and Remnants, had more
than one cutting of it. In Murrays, the base of the spine bears the imprint
LONDON/JOHN MURRAY. This case appears first on the first
edition of *The descent of man*. But on this and the succeeding, two volume,
issues of it, as well as on the first edition, and the tenth thousand, of *The
expression of the emotions*, 1872, the cloth is smooth, whilst that of all
later ones is patterned. Every Murray Darwin, which first appeared in
the author's lifetime, can be found in a case of this style, as also can
Krause's biography of Erasmus Darwin. In the list I have called it the
standard binding. The three Smith Elders are similar in general appearance, but they lack the ornamental roll at top and bottom, bearing instead a broad gilt band.

There is a Murray case similar to the standard one in which the rolls
of circles are replaced by rolls of arches, but the rest of the style is the
same. This occurs on the second and later editions of *Variation under
domestication* as well as on the second and later editions of *Climbing plants*.
I have seen copies of late editions of the former in which the first volume
was in this casing and the second in a standard case. In some of these, it
was clear that the two volumes had been together since publication. I
have called this the arches style in the list. A third very similar form is
found on four issues of *The origin of species* from 1875 to 1878; in these
the rolls are of leaf form, and the device is slightly different.

From 1900 onwards, the usual Murray binding is a leaf green cloth
with an art nouveau dark green stamping on the front cover and the
rolls at the top and bottom of the spine also in dark green. The lettering
is gilt except for a few late ones which were cased just after the 1914–18

war. All Murray Darwins can be found in this case except *Forms of flowers*, *Movement in plants* and *Cross and self fertilisation*; the one volume abridged version of *Life and letters* also occurs in it. A special Library Edition of *The origin of species* and *The descent of man* was produced, each in two volumes, in grey-green cloth, and the same cloth was used for *Life and letters*, although this is a demy octavo. Both the leaf green and these grey-greens have faded badly, but the royal greens have on the whole survived well. Darwin's own copies of his books are all in the usual cases as issued, except for the second edition of *Journal of researches*. This has the usual gilt and blind stamping of the Colonial and Home Library but is of red leather instead of scarlet cloth. His copy of the first volume of *The descent of man*, the only one known which is dated 1870, has slightly different gilding from the usual standard case, and is perhaps a trial binding.

I have excluded one work from this list because I do not believe that it is by Darwin. This is the preface, called 'An appreciation', to Dent's Everyman Library edition of H. W. Bates' *The naturalist on the river Amazons*, 1910 and later printings, No. 446 in the series, (pp. vii–xii). This originally appeared as an unsigned review of Bates' book in *The natural History Review*, Vol. III for 1863 (pp. 385–89). It is entered under Darwin in the printed catalogue of the British Museum, but it is not given in *Life and letters* nor in the list in G. T. Bettany's *Life of Charles Darwin*, 1887. Mr E. F. Bozman, Editorial Director of the Everyman Library in 1964, very kindly examined the original documents connected with their edition and concluded 'We have nothing to authenticate our claim that the essay is by Charles Darwin'. In the latest printing, of 1969, the appreciation has been relegated to the end of the book, and Darwin's name does not appear. The mistake probably arose because Darwin did write an unsigned review of another of Bates' works and did publish it in the same journal earlier in the same year, (pp. 219–24). This is No. 1725 in the present list.

I have also omitted one other title which has been stated to be that of a work by Darwin, because I do not believe that the work exists or ever did exist. Its title is *My apology for my unformed ideas* and its putative date 1881 or 1882. The evidence for its existence is an article, of which I have a photocopy, 'Evolution: Darwin's other book', in *Truth and Liberty*, May 1970, p. 5 (69), which purports to be reprinted from *The Advocate of Truth*. Both these serials seem to be published by some fundamentalist organization; the former comes from Wentworthville, New South Wales and the latter from England; but I have failed to trace runs of either. The book is said to be a denial of everything that he had written in *The origin of species*, and one quotation from it is given 'I became like

King Nebuchadnezzar, of the Book of Daniel, a wild and insane creature.
God punished me by making me senseless and when I came to I realized
I must write and correct the wrongs I had committed'. The editor of
The Advocate of Truth writes 'As to the book (by Darwin) it is out of
print. It can be found only in second hand book stores. I believe the
enemy of truth has tried his best to destroy this information. My father
brought a copy with him from Seminary in Germany and has kept it as
a rare treasure'.

The article also refers to a meeting between Darwin and Lady Hope
of Northfield, in which he expressed similar views, and of which she
published recollections. The only Lady Hope who might fit is Elizabeth
Reid Hope, wife of Admiral of the Fleet *Sir* James Hope, who was
associated with national temperance and published tracts and religious
tales for children, but I have not taken the matter further. The story of
Darwin's deathbed conversion is an old one and the facts have been
summarized recently by *Sir* Hedley Atkins in *Down. The home of the
Darwins*, 1974, pp. 51–52, but he does not mention the book. Both the
conversion and the book are absurd fabrications, but the origin of the
invention of the latter needs further investigation.

It is usually stated that Darwin's first published work, whether in
periodical literature or in a book, is the *Letters on geology*, of 1835, which
is No. 1 below. Strictly however his first printed words occur six years
earlier in 1829. Whilst he was an undergraduate at Cambridge, Darwin
had sent records of insects that he had captured to James Francis Stephens,
and some of these were published in *Illustrations of British entomology*.
He refers to the pleasure that he got from seeing his name in print against
his records of beetles in his autobiography (*Life and letters*, Vol. I, p. 5)
although he gets both the title of the work and the method of citation
wrong. Stephens' classic work was published in parts between 1 May
1827 and November 1845, with a supplement in August 1846. The
following is a short description of it:

> *Illustrations of British entomology; or, a synopsis of indigenous insects* etc.
> 8vo, 245 mm, 11 vols, 80 coloured plates, Baldwin and Cradock for
> the author, London [1827–]1828–1835[–1845]; supplement, vi + 32
> pp, 15 coloured plates, 1846.

The main work is divided into four volumes of Haustellata and seven
of Mandibulata. The beetles occur in the first five volumes of the latter,
and there are about thirty records bearing Darwin's name, the earliest
being in an appendix to Volume II, which is dated June 15, 1829. The
localities include Cambridge, North Wales and Shrewsbury. There is
one further record which is earlier than this. In Haustellata, Volume II,
p. 200, Darwin records the occurrence of the common noctuid moth

Graphiphora plecta at 'Cambridge', and the date of this part is June 1, 1829. The modern scientific name of this moth is *Ochropleura plecta* (L.), and its common name the flame shoulder. In most cases these records are given in quotation marks, and therefore represent genuine publications by Darwin in a book.

Darwin's beetle records occur again in another of Stephens' works which is a revision of the relevant parts of the *Illustrations*, in an abridged form with the plates omitted. Darwin's name, like those of other correspondents, is however not printed. The following is a short description of it:

A manual of British Coleoptera or beetles etc. 8vo, 197 mm, vii + 443 pp, Longman, London 1839.

The first work published under his own name, if the reprints of parts of the *Letters on geology* which appeared in serials are ignored, is the long letter on missionaries in the Pacific, which he and Captain Robert Fitzroy sent to the *South African Christian Recorder*, and which was published there in September 1836, No. 1640 in this list. *Letters on geology* was printed for private circulation only, so that the first published work in book form which bore his name was the *Journal of researches*, 1839, although it was preceded, in 1838, by the earliest parts of the *Zoology of the Beagle*, of which he was editor.

One other minute piece of Darwin's works, which was presumably written by him and is undoubtedly printed, is the notice expressing thanks for a letter sent to him which he was unable to answer personally. There is a copy at Cambridge (Darwin Mss 133(1)), and the published catalogue of the archive remarks that it appears to have been only rarely used. It cannot be dated more accurately than later than 1868, which is the date when Downe village ceased to be in Bromley and became part of Beckenham. It does not seem to have been reprinted, and is given here to show Darwin's extreme punctiliousness towards his many correspondents:

DOWN, BECKENHAM,
KENT.

Mr. DARWIN is much obliged for the letter just received. Owing to the large number of communications which daily arrive, he regrets to say that it is almost impossible for him to do more than to acknowledge their receipt and express his thanks.

DESCRIPTION OF FRONTISPIECE

The cloth is royal green in all cases except No. 7, in which it is plum, and Nos 8 and 9, in which it is scarlet.

1 *On the origin of species.* First edition, 1859. The same style is found on the Fifth thousand, 1860, and on the Third edition, 1861, as well as on *Journal of researches,* Tenth thousand, 1860 which is No. 10 below, and early cased copies of Fritz Müller's *Facts and arguments for Darwin,* 1869.

2 *On the origin of species.* Fourth edition, 1866. Eighth thousand. Similar to No. 1, but *Origin* and *species* in italic. Peculiar to this edition.

3 *On the origin of species.* Fifth edition, 1869. Tenth thousand. Variant b. Issues of *Journal of researches* from 1870 to 1879 are similar, as are later copies of Fritz Müller's *Facts and arguments for Darwin,* 1869.

4 *The origin of species.* Sixth edition, 1872. Eleventh thousand. Found on this first issue of the sixth edition, as well as on the twelfth and thirteenth thousands.

5 *The origin of species.* Sixth edition, 1875. Fifteenth thousand. Leaf style. Also found on the eighteenth (the final text), twentieth and twenty-second thousands.

6 *The origin of species.* Sixth edition, 1882. Twenty-fourth thousand. Standard case, with the rule below the title slightly decorated, rough cloth. Compare with Nos 12–14.

7 *Fertilisation of orchids.* First edition, 1862. Plum cloth, variant a. Peculiar to this edition.

8 *Journal of researches.* Second edition, 1845. Scarlet cloth of the Colonial and Home Library. Peculiar to this edition.

9 *Journal of researches.* Second edition, second issue, 1845 [? = 1848]. Also occurs on the 'New edition' of 1852.

10 *Journal of researches.* Second edition, 1860. Tenth thousand. First issue of definitive text. Compare with No. 1 above.

11 *Journal of researches.* Second edition, 1873. Twelfth thousand. Found on all issues of this work from 1870 to 1879. Compare with No. 3 above.

12–13 *The descent of man.* First edition, 1871. First issue. Standard case, with rule below the title plain, but cloth smooth. Found on all four issues of the first edition, and on *Expression of the emotions.* First edition, 1872, and tenth thousand, 1873, but not elsewhere.

14 *The descent of man.* Second edition, 1874. Tenth thousand. Standard case, rough cloth, with rule below the title plain. Compare with No. 6 and Nos 12–13.

15–16 *Variation under domestication.* First edition, 1868. First issue. Imprint in one line. Usually peculiar to this issue, but also on the second occasionally.

17–18 *Variation under domestication*. First edition, 1868. Second issue. Imprint in two lines. Peculiar to this issue.

19–20 *Variation under domestication*. Second edition, 1875. Fourth thousand. Arches style, with author in italic. Also found on later issues of this edition, but not elsewhere.

21 *Climbing plants*. Second edition, 1874. Arches style, with author in roman. Found on later issues, but not elsewhere. Compare with Nos 19–20.

22 *Coral reefs*. Second edition, 1874. A Smith Elder case similar to those of Murray. Also found on later Smith Elder editions of the geological works.

LIBRARY HOLDINGS AND SYMBOLS

For British libraries, only the collections in the British Library Reference Division, University Library Cambridge, Darwin family collection at Cambridge, and the Down House collection have been fully entered. Other libraries are only referred to for special copies not present in the above four, or where very few copies are known. A few items in the Bibliothèque Nationale, Paris, are noticed.

For American libraries, the *National Union Catalog. Pre-1956 imprints* number, using the last three figures only, is given where possible, followed, in parentheses, by the number of libraries holding any particular item. The large holdings of the University of Toronto, which are not listed there, are entered throughout. Here again, other libraries are only referred to for special copies or for items which are not listed, or not distinguished, in the National Union Catalog. A semi-colon represents the Atlantic Ocean.

Library holdings for publications in serials are not entered.

BS	British Library, Lending Division, Boston Spa, Yorkshire.
C	University Library, Cambridge.
CD	Darwin Collection, University Library, Cambridge.
CLSU	University of Southern California, Los Angeles.
CtY	Yale University, New Haven, Connecticut.
D	Down House, Downe, Kent.
DLC	Library of Congress, Washington, District of Columbia.
ICF	Field Museum of Natural History, Chicago, Illinois.
L	British Library, Reference Division, London.
LB	Royal National Institute for the Blind, London.
LLS	Linnean Society of London.
LNH	British Museum (Natural History), London.
LU	Senate House, University of London.

LUC   University College London.
LUI   Imperial College of Science and Technology, London.
LZ   Zoological Society of London.
PBN   Bibliothèque Nationale, Paris.
PPAmP   American Philosophical Society, Philadelphia.
T   University of Toronto, Ontario.
ViU   University of Virginia, Charlottesville.

Items recorded from booksellers' catalogues, but not seen, are given the symbol BSC.

PART 1 · BOOKS AND PAMPHLETS

Letters on Geology

The preface to these extracts from Darwin's letters is dated Dec. 1, but the work itself is not dated. It has always been assumed that it was issued, to members of the Cambridge Philosophical Society, in December 1835 and this is probably so, but I have not seen a copy with a dated ownership inscription, or accession stamp, for that year. The earliest record of it seems to be in a letter from his youngest sister, Emily Catherine, dated January 1836, which he received at the Cape of Good Hope on June 1st of the same year. In his reply to it, dated June 3rd, he writes that he has been 'a good deal horrified' that 'what has been written without care or accuracy' should have been printed. 'But, as the Spaniard says "No hay remedio"' (letter in No. 1594, pp. 140–42).

The pamphlet contains extracts, not always accurately transcribed, from ten letters to John Stevens Henslow (1796–1861), Professor of Botany, mentor in natural history and life-long friend of Darwin. Three of them were printed in full in *Life and letters*, Vol. 1., and three more in *More letters*, Vol. 1. The whole set, with others, is printed in No. 1598.

A page proof copy, 255 mm, with twenty corrections, perhaps in Henslow's hand, was sold at Sotheby's on January 19, 1973. Two corrections which escaped were the spelling of the Abrolhos archipelago in the letters of May 18 and Aug. 15, 1832, as 'Abrothos'. The original pamphlet has become rare and it was reprinted in 1960, again for private circulation in the Cambridge Philosophical Society and for friends of that Society. The reprint, which is in type facsimile, retains correctly the 'Abrothos' misprint, but the error is corrected in the full transcript in No. 1598, and the name also occurs correctly in a letter by Darwin to his father, dated Feb. 8, 1832 (*Life and letters*, Vol. 1, p. 232).

The 1960 reprint has a preface by Dr Sydney Smith, Biological Secretary to the Society, in which he gives extracts from the minutes of Nov. 16 and Nov. 30 concerning the reading and the printing. It states that the pamphlet was 'the first writing of Charles Darwin ever to be published.' It was not however published, and in any case this honour belongs to his records of beetles and a moth in 1829 which are referred to earlier (p. 19). His first published work under his own name is that on missionaries, with Captain Robert Fitzroy, in the *South African Christian Recorder* for September 1836 (No. 1640). His first published work by himself alone and submitted by himself is that on recent elevation on the coast of Chile, read on Jan. 4, 1837, and published in *Proc.Geol.Soc.* for that year (No. 1645).

ENGLISH

1. [?1835] Cambridge, [University Press], for the Cambridge Philosophical Society. Dropped title. *For private distribution. The following pages contain extracts from letters addressed to Professor Henslow by C. Darwin, Esq. They are printed for distribution among the members of the Cambridge Philosophical Society, in consequence of the interest which has been excited by some of the geological notices which they contain, and which were read at a meeting of the Society on the 16th of November 1835.* 8vo, 220 mm, t.p. + 31 pp. Preface dated Dec. 1, 1835. Binding: pale grey plain wrappers. C, L; T, 906(7).   [1

2. 1836 Extracts of letters from C. Darwin, Esq., to Professor Henslow. Printed for private distribution. *Entomological Magazine*, Vol. 3, No. V, Art. XLIII, pp. 457–460. Entomological extracts only from No. 1.

3. 1836 Geological notes made during a survey of the east and west coasts of S. America, in the years 1832, 1833, 1834 and 1835, with an account of a transverse section of the Cordilleras of the Andes between Valparaiso and Mendoza. *Proceedings of the Geological Society of London*, Vol. 2, pp. 210–212. Communicated by Prof. A. Sedgwick. Read Nov. 18, 1835. Described as by Francis Darwin, but correctly indexed.

4. 1960 Cambridge, University Press. for the Cambridge Philosophical Society. *Extracts from letters addressed to Professor Henslow.* 8vo, 215 mm, v + 31 pp. Foreword by Sydney Smith. Printed not published. Type facsimile of No. 1, but omitting the signatures. Binding: brown printed paper wrappers. C, L; T, 908(1) misdated 1860.
          [2

5. [1967] In No. 1598. The letters, with others, are here published in full, pp. 52–117, letters 19–42.

GERMAN

6. 1891   In *Deutsche Rundschau*   June. Translated by
            Wilhelm Preyer.   [382

RUSSIAN

7. 1959   Moscow, Academy of Sciences, U.S.S.R. pp. 71–86.
            Translated, introduced and annotated by S. L. Sobol'.
            Collected Works, Vol. 9. L; DLC.

The Zoology of the Voyage of H.M.S. Beagle

Darwin edited this sumptuous work, which appeared in five parts,
made up of nineteen numbers, between February 1838 and October
1843. Early in 1837, he was considering asking for government help to
publish the zoological results of the voyage as a book. In May that year
he received the support of the Duke of Somerset, President of the
Linnean Society, as well as of the Earl of Derby and of Professor William
Whewell. On August 16, he called on the Chancellor of the Exchequer,
Thomas Spring Rice, who told him that the Lords Commissioners of
the Treasury had granted £1,000 towards the cost. Even so this was not
enough, and the preface to *Geological observations on South America,* p.
[iii], states that the publishers and he himself had advanced further sums.
A prospectus, a single sheet 214 × 134 mm printed on both sides, was
issued between August 16 and November 4. It gives the names of the
five experts who were to cover the vertebrate groups, but states that 'a
description of some of the invertebrate animals procured during the
voyage will also be given. At the conclusion of the work Mr. Darwin
will incorporate the materials which have been collected, in a general
sketch of the Zoology of the southern parts of South America'. Neither
of these intentions was realized.

Darwin contributed a geological introduction to Part I, the *Fossil
Mammalia* (pp. 3–12), and a geographical introduction to Part II, the
Mammalia (pp. i–iv). He also contributed notices of habits and ranges
throughout the text of *Mammalia* and *Birds*, and there are frequent notes,
mostly from his labels, in the text of the *Fish* and the *Reptiles*. The
authors of the parts were Richard Owen (*Fossil Mammalia*), George
Robert Waterhouse (*Mammalia*), John Gould (*Birds*), Leonard Jenyns
(*Fish*) and Thomas Bell (*Reptiles*). One issue only; it has not been translated, but there is a facsimile of Part V. reptiles.

The numbers were issued as they were ready, the first, by Professor
Owen, being announced for January 1st 1838, but not appearing until
February. The original intention, given in the prospectus, was to

publish 'on the first day of every alternate month; and the whole, when completed, will comprise about six hundred pages of letter-press, and from two hundred to two hundred and fifty engravings'. The final result was 632 pages, but only 166 plates. Darwin seems to have had some difficulty in keeping his authors up to time; indeed Professor Bell took almost five years to produce fifty pages, thus delaying the completion of the work for eighteen months. John Gould went to Australia in the spring of 1838, and the remaining text and the corrigenda of the *Birds* were written by George Robert Gray, of the British Museum. This is explained on a preliminary leaf issued with No. III, *Birds*, I. Parts title leaves, with half titles, preliminaries, indices and lists of plates, were issued with the last number of each part, except for a cancel title to *Mammalia* which was issued, with an errata slip, with No. XI, *Birds, IV*, the cancelland lacking the author's name. In volume form, the note about Gould is transferred to the rest of the preliminaries which were issued with No. XV, *Birds*, V. The editing is excellent: there is only one cancel, the title leaf to *Mammalia*, noticed above; there are few errata noticed and no *bis* plates. I have seen a temporary title leaf for *Birds*, issued with No. III, *Birds*, I., and those for the other four parts may exist.

C. D. Sherborn (*Ann.Mag.nat.Hist.* Vol. 20, p. 483, 1897) has listed the dates of issue of the numbers as given to him by the publishers, and these correspond to the dates printed on the numbers themselves. Unfortunately, he calls each number a part, whereas the set, as mentioned above, consists of nineteen numbers, which together make up the five parts. The full details of the issue in numbers are given in No. 8, and those for the parts issue and the same in volume form in No. 9. Inserted advertisements may vary from set to set, but there are usually four pages of publisher's general advertisements in Numbers III and IV; an advertisement for the forthcoming geological results, in a form in which these never appeared, in Number V; and a notice to subscribers to Sir Andrew Smith's *Zoology of South Africa* in Number XV. I have however seen the geological advertisement in Number VII.

The unbound parts cost £8. 15s. and the publishers advertised the completed work as available 'in half russia or cloth binding, at small addition'. The *English Catalogue* gives a price of £9. 2s. for the bound work. I have not identified the publisher's half russia, but the original cloth casing was in five volumes, one part in each. Copies also occur in publisher's cloth in three, *Fossil Mammalia* and *Mammalia* in the first, *Birds* in the second and *Fish* and *Reptiles* in the third. This form was, presumably, later than that in five, but no volume titles seem to have been issued for it.

8. 1838–1843 [Issue in numbers] London, Smith Elder and Co., [Temporary title.] *The zoology of the voyage of H.M.S. Beagle, under the command of Captain Fitzroy, during the years 1832 to 1836. Published with the approval of the Lords Commissioners of Her Majesty's Treasury.* Edited and superintended by Charles Darwin 4to, 327 mm, 19 numbers making 5 parts. Wrappers: buff printed card, plain grey-green cloth spines: front wrapper, print within a border of 3 plain rules, ornamental corners; top left, part and number within part (latter absent in No. I); top right, price (absent in No. I and replaced by number within part); bottom left, serial number (absent in Nos I & II); bottom right, month of issue (absent in Nos I & II): back wrapper, plain in No. I, publisher's advertisements Nos II–XIX. Price in numbers £8. 15s. LU; T, 1316(19) part.

I. Part I *Fossil Mammalia*, No. I. 1838 [Feb.] by Richard Owen. Temporary title leaf to whole work; preface [to whole work, by Darwin] pp. [i]–iv; half-title pp. [1–2]; geological introduction, by Darwin pp. 3–12; text [13]–40. Plain lithograph plates I–VII (I & V folding), G. Scharf del. et lith. Price: [8s.]

II. Part II *Mammalia*, No. I. 1838 [May] by George R. Waterhouse, with *A notice of their habits and ranges* by Charles Darwin, half-title [a cancelland, see No. X]; geographical introduction by Darwin pp. [i]–v; text pp. [1]–8. Coloured lithograph plates 1–10 unsigned. 8 pp publisher's advertisements undated, at end. Price 10s.

III. Part III *Birds*, No. 1 1838 Jul. by John Gould. Temporary title leaf to part. Advertisement [i]–ii [by Darwin]; text 3–16; coloured lithograph plates 1–10 unsigned. 4 pp publisher's advertisements undated, at front. Price: 10s.

IV. Part II *Mammalia*, No. II. 1838 Sep. pp. 9–32, coloured lithograph plates 11–17 unsigned, plain plate [of skulls] 35, drawn by C. M. Curtis, engraved by J. Swaine, 4 text figs. 4 pp publisher's advertisements undated, at front. Price: 10s.

V. Part II *Mammalia*, No. III, 1838 Nov. pp. 33–48,

coloured lithograph plates 18–24 unsigned, plain plate 33 [osteology], G. R. Waterhouse & C. M. Curtis del. Inserted slip for Darwin's projected geological works at beginning, in some copies. Price: 8s.

VI. Part III *Birds*, No. II. 1839 Jan. pp. 17–32, coloured lithograph plates 11–20, unsigned. Price: 10s.

VII. Part I *Fossil Mammalia*, No. II, 1839 Mar. pp. 41–64. Plain lithograph plates VIII–XVII. Inserted slip as No. V, in some copies. Price: 8s.

VIII. Part I *Fossil Mammalia*, No. III. 1839 May. pp. 65–80. Plain lithograph plates XVIII–XXVII (XX double page). Price: 8s.

IX. Part III *Birds*, No. III. 1839 Jul. pp. 33–56. Coloured lithograph plates 21–30, unsigned. Price: 10s.

X. Part II *Mammalia*, No. IV. 1839 Sep. pp. 49–97. Coloured lithograph plates 25–32, unsigned, plain plate [osteology] 34. New half-title leaf, with tipped in notice to binder to cancel one issued with Part II, No. I, cancellans has 'Illustrated by numerous coloured engravings' added. Title page dated 1839, without author's name [a cancelland, see No. XI]. List of plates pp. [vii]–ix. Index of species, 1 leaf. 'Completion of Mammalia' on front wrapper. Price: 10s.

XI. Part III *Birds*, No. IV. 1839 Nov. pp. 57–96. Coloured lithograph plates 31–40, unsigned. After plates, 5 line errata slip for *Mammalia*; cancellans title leaf for *Mammalia*, adding name of author, dated 1839. Price: 10s.

XII. Part IV *Fish*, No. I. 1840 Jan. by Leonard Jenyns. pp. 1–32. Plain lithograph plates 1–8, by Waterhouse Hawkins. Price: 8s.

XIII. Part I *Fossil Mammalia*, No. IV. 1840 Apr. pp. 81–111, plain lithograph plates XXVIII–XXXII. Title leaf, dated 1840. Contents p. [i], list of plates pp. [iii–iv]. 'Completion of Fossil Mammalia' on front wrapper. Price: 6s.

XIV. Part IV *Fish*, No. II. 1840 Jun. pp. 33–64. Plain lithograph plates 9–15, by Waterhouse Hawkins. Price: 8s.

XV. Part III *Birds*, No. V. 1841 Mar. pp. 97–146, appendix [on anatomy] by T. C. Eyton pp. [147]–156, coloured lithograph plates 41–50 unsigned. Half-title

'Birds, described by John Gould, with a notice of their habits and ranges by Charles Darwin and with an anatomical appendix by T. C. Eyton.' Title leaf, dated 1841. List of plates 1 leaf. Corrigenda, by G. R. Gray, 1 leaf. 'Completion of birds' on front wrapper. Inserted slip at front to subscribers to Andrew Smith's *Illustrations of the zoology of South Africa*, dated Nov. 1, 1840. Price: 15s.

XVI. Part IV *Fish*, No. III. 1841 Apr. pp. 65–96. Plain lithograph plates 16–20, by Waterhouse Hawkins. Front wrapper 'The next Number will complete the "Fishes". After the publication of the "Reptiles", which will be contained in One or Two Numbers, the present Work will be completed. The Geological Parts, which from unavoidable circumstances have been delayed, will, it is hoped, appear before long. The disposition of the remaining materials collected during the "Voyage of the Beagle" must depend on future contingencies.' Price: 6s.

XVII. Part IV *Fish*, No. IV. 1842 Apr. Half-title leaf pp. [i–ii], title leaf pp. [iii–iv] dated 1842, introduction [v]–xi dated Jan. 8, 1842, systematic table of species with their respective habits pp. [xiii]–xv, list of plates p. [xvi], text pp. 97–159, appendix [of omitted species and further remarks on some others] pp. 160–169. Plain lithograph plates 21–29. 'Completion of Fish' on front wrapper, also note much as in No. XVI, but adding 'The first Part of the Geology is in the Press'. Price: 8s.

XVIII. Part V *Reptiles*, No. 1. 1842 Aug. by Thomas Bell. pp. [1]–16, plain lithograph plates 1–10, by Waterhouse Dawkins. Front wrapper 'One more Number will complete this Work'. Price: 8s.

XIX. Part V *Reptiles* [and Amphibia], No. II. 1843 Oct. pp. 17–51. Plain lithograph plates 11–20, by Waterhouse Hawkins. Title leaf, dated 1843, pp. [i–ii], list of species p. [iii], list of plates & 2 line errata p. [iv], preface pp. [v]–vi, dated Sep. 2, 1843. Definitive title leaf for whole work issued with this number. Price: 10s.

9. [1838] 1839–1843 London, Smith Elder and Co. [Parts and volumes issues.] Title as No. 8, but omitting '[Temporary title]'. 4to, 327 mm in parts, c. 322 mm in volumes, 5 parts, [xlvii + 585 pp.], 82 coloured + 84 (3 folding)

plain plates. Bindings: *a*. parts in card wrappers as No. 8; *b*. grey-green cloth in 5 volumes; *c*. half russia in 5 volumes; *d*. ?cloth in 3 volumes; *e*. half russia in 3 volumes. Price: £8. 15s. in parts, 'or in half russia or cloth, at a small addition to the price', £9. 2s. in cloth. C, L, LNH; 1316(19) part.

Part I. 1838–1840. *Fossil Mammalia*. by Richard Owen. [iv] + 111 pp, 32 plain plates. Preface to whole work pp. [i]–iv [by Darwin], geological introduction pp. 3–12 by Darwin. Nos I, VII, VIII & XIII. Price: £1. 10s. in parts. £1. 14s. in cloth.

Part II. 1838–1839. *Mammalia*. by George R. Waterhouse. xi + 97 pp, 32 coloured & 3 plain plates, 5 line errata slip. Geographical introduction, pp. [i]–v, and distribution notes throughout by Darwin. Half-title and title leaves are cancellans. Nos II, IV, V & X. Price: £1. 18s. in parts, £2. 2s. in cloth.

Part III. 1838–1841. *Birds*. by John Gould [much written by G. R. Gray]. [x] + 156 pp, 50 coloured plates. Distribution notes throughout by Darwin, Nos III, VI, IX & XI. Price: £2. 15s. in parts, £3. in cloth.

Part IV. 1840–1842. *Fish*. by Leonard Jenyns. xvi + 170 pp. 29 plain plates, 4 line errata slip p. 170. Notes throughout from Darwin's labels. Nos XII, XIV, XVI & XVII. Price £1.14s in parts, £1. 18s. in cloth.

Part V. 1842–1843. *Reptiles* [and Amphibia]. by Thomas Bell. vi + 51 pp, 20 plain plates. Notes throughout from Darwin's labels. Nos XVIII & XIX. Price 18s. in parts, £1. 2s. in cloth.

Journal of Researches

Darwin's *Journal* has received a brief bibliographical notice from Lady Barlow in her *Charles Darwin and the voyage of the Beagle*, 1945, but this only goes up to 1870, although the illustrated edition of 1890 is mentioned in the text. His first published book is undoubtedly the most often read and stands second only to *On the origin of species* as the most often printed. It is an important travel book in its own right and its relation to the background of his evolutionary ideas has often been stressed. The manuscript diary from which it was written up and the little notebooks which formed the memoranda on which the diary was based have all been published, at least in part, in recent years. These are entered here in the section on transcripts of manuscripts, amongst Nos 1566 to 1577.

The first issue forms, as is well known, the third volume of *The narrative of the voyages of H.M. Ships Adventure and Beagle*, edited by Captain Robert Fitzroy and published, in three volumes and an appendix to Volume II, in 1839. In this form, it bears the subsidiary title *Journal and remarks*. Since then it has changed its name four times, so that today it is universally referred to as *The voyage of the Beagle*.

On its first appearance in its own right, also in 1839, it was called *Journal of researches into the geology and natural history* etc. The second edition, of 1845, transposes 'geology' and 'natural history' to read *Journal of researches into the natural history and geology* etc., and the spine title is *Naturalist's voyage*. The final definitive text of 1860 has the same wording on the title page, but the spine reads *Naturalist's voyage round the world*, and the fourteenth thousand of 1879 places *A naturalist's voyage* on the title page. *The voyage of the Beagle* first appears as a title in the Harmsworth Library edition of 1905. It is a bad title: she was only a floating home for Darwin, on which, in spite of good companionship, he was cramped and miserably sea-sick; whilst the book is almost entirely about his expeditions on land. The political and economic intentions of the voyage, on which Darwin was only a supernumerary, have been overshadowed by the success of the *Journal*. These have been stressed by George Basalla in 'The voyage of the Beagle without Darwin', *Mariner's Mirror*, Vol. 49, pp. 42–48, 1963.

Darwin's volume was ready much earlier than the rest. The manuscript of the main text was finished by June 1837, and it, with the index, was in print early in 1838. The preface was written later and in it he states that 'publication has been unavoidably delayed'. He also states 'I have given a list of those errata (partly caused by my absence from town when some of the sheets were in the press) which affect the sense; and have added an Appendix, containing some additional facts . . . which I have accidentally met with during the past year'. There is no list of errata in Darwin's volume, but several of the notes in the appendix refer to corrections. Darwin's volume has a different printer to the other three and both its maps are dated 1838. The insertion of the appendix a year after the rest was in print results in faulty pagination, with pp. 609–615 repeated, the second set being the index. The printing of the preliminaries and the appendix probably took place before January 24 1839. On that day he was elected a Fellow of the Royal Society, but the initials do not appear on the title page of Volume III.

The first reference which indicates that the work was out comes in a letter from Darwin's sister-in-law Sarah Elizabeth Wedgwood to her aunt Madame J. C. L. Simonde de Sismondi, dated June 5 1839. 'His journal is come out at last along with two other thick volumes of Capt. Fitzroy and Capt. King of the same voyage, but I have not had time to read it yet'. There is no mention of the appendix volume, and this must have been an advance copy. As usually seen, the complete set has publisher's advertisements of 16 + [8] pages, the first set dated August 1839, at the end of the appendix, the last volume to be printed. Many sets contain either advertisements of later date, or none at all. The binding is dark blue, blind-stamped, cloth which is liable to fade; each volume bears its author's name on the spine and the publisher's imprint reads COLBURN/LONDON/. Some later copies omit the authors' names and the imprint reads LONDON/COLBURN/. The top board of each volume contains a pocket for the two loose maps; these pockets should have dark blue ribbons for extracting the maps, but they are often absent today. Seven of the maps were published by Henry Colburn, but the eighth, of South America in Volume I, was by John Arrowsmith and was, presumably, a suitable map already available.

I have no information about the number of sets which were printed, but Darwin remarks, in a letter to his sister Susan dated February 1842, that 1,337 copies of his volume had been sold, and his diary states that Colburn printed 1,500. These figures probably include the two independent issues which are considered below.

I have seen undated Colburn inserted advertisements in a book dated 1849 which advertise a 'Cheaper edition, in 2 large Vols . . . price 1l., 11s. 6d. bound.' It is clear, from the description given, that the first volume was Captain King's voyage, and the second Captain Fitzroy's with the appendix bound in; Darwin's volume was not included. The advertisement has a footnote 'N.B. Mr. Darwin's Journal of the Geology and Natural History of the Voyage may be had in a single volume, 8vo, price 18s. bound.' This was four years after the publication by Murray of the second edition of the Darwin; it probably represents a remainder issue in a new binding at a remainder price of the unsold sheets of the King and the Fitzroy volumes, but I have never seen it in this form. The Darwin, which retains its original price, would presumably have been the issue with the 1840 title page, but it is interesting to note that it was still available so long after the appearance of the second edition.

It is remarkable that Colburn's inserted advertisements of August 1839 (p. 10) make no mention of Darwin's contribution to the work although they describe the rest of the contents in considerable detail. It is also remarkable that Darwin's work is advertised quite independently on page 14 of the same advertisements without any mention that it also forms part of the set. The *English Catalogue* makes it clear that the set was available, with or without Darwin's volume, at £3. 18s. or £2. 18s., and that his volume alone cost 18s. What was being advertised as three volumes was really two volumes and the appendix.

It has usually been stated that Darwin's volume was reissued in its own covers later in the same year, because the demand for it was greater than that for the other two volumes of technical narrative. That the demand for it was greater than the rest was probably true, and that it must be considered technically the later issue is certainly correct, because pp. [i–iv] of the preliminaries are cancels and [v–vi], the original volume title, is discarded; the rest, [vii]–xiv, and the text sheets are those of the main work, bearing Vol. III on the first page of each signature. Nevertheless, it is also certain that both were advertised in the same set of advertisements in August 1839. The last leaf of the preliminaries is a singleton c¹ and so is the last leaf of the appendix Q★★★1; these two may have been a conjugate pair.

It was issued in the same blind stamped boards with map pocket as the set, but with different spine titling; the cloth is usually blue but sometimes a purple which fades to brown. In some copies the maps have been inserted in the text, the Southern portion of South America facing p. 1 and the Keeling Islands p. 539; in these there is no pocket in the front cover. I have seen a copy with the track chart, proper to the Appendix of the set, inserted, but it may have been added later. Most copies have the same 16 pp. advertisements of August 1839 as are found in the Appendix; some also contain a single small inserted leaf advertising the forthcoming publication by Smith Elder of the geological works in one volume, a form in which they did not eventually appear.

The final, third, issue of the first edition is dated 1840 on the title page; it is identical to the second except that the conjugate half-title and title leaves have been reprinted. This is the scarcest of the three, but in my experience the maps are always inserted in the text. Some copies also have the 16 pp inserted advertisements of August 1839, presumably having been sewn up with them but not cased.

De Beer, in his biography 1963, has stressed that in the title of this first edition the word *Geology* preceded *Natural history* because the former was uppermost in Darwin's mind at the time, whereas in the second of 1845 the order is reversed. It is certainly true that geological observations predominate in the notebooks made during the voyage. But it is certainly worthy of notice that in the advertised title of August 1839 *Natural history* comes before *Geology*.

The second and only other edition was first published in 1845 in John Murray's Colonial and Home Library; Darwin sold the copyright for £150. The text was extensively revised and, according to Lady Barlow, reduced from about 224,000 words to 213,000. The title changes to *Natural history and geology*; the maps are omitted, to Darwin's regret, not to return until 1890; but the number of woodcuts is increased. It is a miserable piece of printing in small type with mean margins, but then the series was a cheap one.

The Colonial and Home Library, (the name seems to have been interchangeable with Home and Colonial Library from the beginning, but later on only the latter form is found), was originally issued in monthly parts and the *Journal* forms Nos XXII, XXIII and XXIV. Advertisements in *The Athenaeum* show No. XXII as 'this day is published' on June 28th (No. 922, p. 626) and the advertisement is repeated exactly on July 5th (No. 923, p. 651). No. XXIII is first advertised on August 2nd (No. 927, p. 754). On August 30th (No. 931, p. 862) a briefer form of Murray's advertisements states 'This day is published, post 8vo, A naturalist's Voyage round the world. By Charles Darwin. Second Edition, with additions'. No price is given, but it would seem that the three parts were then ready. On October 18th (No. 938, p. 1004) a price of 7s. 6d. is given, which was that for the three parts at 2s. 6d. each. Darwin must have received copies of the parts issue because he sent a copy of Part I to Lyell in July, but none now survives at Cambridge. This form, which is the first issue of the second edition, is rare. The pagination is given by Geoffrey West in *Charles Darwin, the fragmentary man*, 1937, but he does not mention the contents leaves inserted in each number. The details are given in No. 13 below. I have seen only the first two parts, Nos XXII and XXIII bound together in leather. They can however be reconstructed from others, closely contemporary, in the same series. Each had its own contents leaf, headed Part I (II, III). The covers were of thin grey-buff card cut flush, bearing the title *etc.* within a frame. The number in the series was in the top left-hand corner in roman, and the words 'Cheap literature for all classes' ran above 'Murray's Colonial and Home Library', followed by the title. At the bottom, below the imprint, was the price 'Half-a-crown' and the printer's note 'W. Clowes and Sons, Stamford Street'. There would have been advertisements for various Murray series on the other pages of the covers, including one for the Colonial and Home Library itself on the back.

The form in which the second edition is usually seen, which must be considered as the second issue, is, as Volume XII, in the scarlet cloth of the series in book form, with the three contents leaves replaced by a single leaf (pp. [vii]–viii). The earliest advertisements that I have seen for the book are dated December 1845, but the 16 pages of inserted advertisements in it are dated August or November and it probably appeared shortly after the publication of the third part on or about October 18th. In this form it was put on to plates and was the basis of a number of later issues.

There are however two quite separate issues which are both dated 1845 on the title pages: these have not usually been distinguished. In the first, the genuine second issue, there is a printer's note on the verso of the title leaf and advertisements for Darwin's other works, printed or in preparation, on p. 520 (= 2L4). In the second, the third issue, the versos of both title leaf and 2L4 are blank, and the inserted advertisements are dated May 1848. Copies in the original scarlet cloth of the series are easily distinguished by the gilding of the case. The earlier has 'Colonial and Home Library' gilt at the top of the spine, whilst the later has not. It would seem probable that the later was reprinted in 1848 without changing the date on the title page. The earlier also exists in scarlet leather with the same blind and gilt stamping of the series as the cloth form. Darwin's own copy, at Cambridge, is the only one which I have seen thus and I have not seen it mentioned in advertisements. Finally, there is a red, not scarlet, cloth blind-stamped publisher's case which gives no indication, in gilt or blind, that the work in one of a series; in this case the edges are sprinkled whereas they are white in the series cases.

It was again reprinted in the same series in 1852 and put out in the same case as the third issue, this time with changed date, an issue not mentioned by Lady Barlow. The title page now describes it as a new edition, instead of second, although there is no change. It appears again in 1860 and this is the final text as Darwin left it. The parts from the original stereos are the same, but a postscript, dated February 1st 1860, is added to the preliminaries. This is the tenth thousand and it no longer forms part of the Home and Colonial Library, but is in a green cloth case in the same style as that of the first three editions of *On the origin of species*. The page height is nearly two centimetres greater than before and the wider margins give the whole book a much better appearance. Inserted advertisements in this edition may be as late as September 1868.

It was reprinted in this form from 1870, although with the preliminaries reset, until the eighteenth thousand of 1888, when it was reset, but the postscript is retained in this new edition. This postscript contains three references to pages in the text and these have not been altered to suit the new setting of type so that all three are wrong. The cases continue to follow those of *The Origin*, ending up in standard green cloth in 1882. What is called a new edition appeared in 1890. The type was again reset and this time the matter of the postscript, as well as a note on the last page of text which had been there since 1845, is incorporated in footnotes in the proper places in the text.

In the same year, a large paper illustrated edition appeared which also incorporates the additions as footnotes. This is a fine edition, with eleven plates, two maps, and a much increased number of text figures. Some of these illustrations are based on original drawings made by members of the expedition, including one (p. 427) by Darwin himself which has not been reproduced elsewhere, a miserable little scribble of a cactus. Some copies contain an additional plate with two diagrams of the layout of the Beagle. These, although not acknowledged, are by Philip Gidley King, who was a midshipman on the Beagle and a son of the commander of the Adventure on the first voyage, Captain Philip Parker King. The details of the discovery of their origin are given by Lady Barlow (q.v) who reproduces them and other drawings. They are also reproduced by Joseph Richard Slevin in 'The Galápagos Islands: a history of their exploration', (*Occ.Pap.Calif.Acad.Sci.*, No. XXV, 150 pp, 1959). Slevin also gives details of special equipment carried on the ship which is not given elsewhere. This 1890 edition is in a handsome case and has a page-marker of blue silk, one of the very few that I have seen in any Darwin. Nelson had published an illustrated edition in 1888 which was reprinted in 1890 and later; Murray's edition was presumably in competition with it.

The Murray edition of 1901 and subsequent reprints of it contain sixteen plates giving all the illustrations which are present, either in plates or as text figures, in that of 1890, including the one of the layout. The last Murray printing is in 1913; it is in the same form and a similar case to that of 1890. The verso of the half-title leaf bears a list of editions in which that of 1860 is called the first and ten subsequent ones up to 1890 are called second to eleventh editions. This list bears remarkably little relation to the facts.

The very many English editions published after the work came out of copyright are of no particular interest; most are printed from the text of 1845, with or without the postscript of 1860. None, so far as I am aware, uses the consolidated text of 1890, which would seem to be the sensible procedure. Early issues in the Everyman Library are odd in that they revert to the first title *Geology and natural history*, although the text is that of 1860. It has appeared from book clubs, both beautifully and badly produced, as well as in potted versions for children and in précis. Recently there have been facsimilies of the first edition, both of the whole *Narrative* and of Darwin's volume alone. The 1845 second edition has not appeared in facsimile, although there is one of a New York issue of 1896.

The first American edition appeared as two volumes in Harper's New Miscellany in 1846, based on Murray's 1845; it continued to be printed many times unchanged and without the postscript until the turn of the century. Because Darwin did not own the copyright after 1845 and, perhaps, because the book did not contain original work or ideas he does not seem to have been so enthusiastic about translations as he was for his other books. Nevertheless, the first edition appeared in German in 1844, at the instigation of Baron von Humbolt, and the second in Danish, French, German, Italian, Russian and Swedish, in his lifetime; also in a further sixteen languages since then. The best illustrated edition, in any language, is the Spanish of 1942, printed in Buenos Aires with 121 plates. There is no fully illustrated edition in print, but the work can be usefully supplemented by the pictures in Alan Moorehead *Darwin and the Beagle*, London 1969. It has 187 illustrations, 50 of them in colour, mostly relating to the voyage and to the book.

ENGLISH

10.   1839   London, Henry Colburn. As Volume III of Fitzroy (Robert) *editor*. *Narrative of the surveying voyages of His Majesty's Ships Adventure and Beagle* etc. 8vo, 233 mm, 3 vols and appendix to Vol. II, 44 plates, 4 charts and maps inserted, 8 charts and maps loose in pockets in top boards, 6 text woodcuts. Binding: blue cloth, variant *a*. spine imprint COLBURN/LONDON, authors' names on spines; variant *b*. spine imprint LONDON/ COLBURN, and names omitted. Price: £3. 18s.

Vol. I. *Proceedings of the first expedition, 1826–30, under the command of Captain P. Parker King, R.N., F.R.S.* xxviii + [4] + 597 pp, 44 errata on p. [3], 17 plates, charts in pocket, *South America* published by John Arrowsmith 18th May 1839, *The strait Magalhaens commonly called Magellan* published by Henry Colburn 1839. Magnetic observations by Edward Sabine, pp. 497–528. Descriptions of Cirrhipedia, Conchifera, and Mollusca by Phillip P. King assisted by W. J. Broderip (from the *Zoological Journal*) pp. 545–56. Some observations relating to the southern extremity of South America, Tierra del Fuego, and the Strait of Magalhaens. Reprinted from the *Journal of the Geographical Society*, 1831, by Phillip Parker King.

Vol. II. *Proceedings of the second expedition, 1831–36, under the command of Captain Robert Fitz-Roy, R.N.* xiv + [2] + 694 + [2] pp, 25 plates, charts in pocket *Part of Tierra del Fuego, Chiloe and parts of the adjacent coast*, both published by Henry Colburn 1839. Vol. II Appendix. viii + 352 pp, 6 plates, charts in pocket *General chart showing the principal tracks*, published by Henry Colburn 1839, *Dangerous Archipelago of the Paamuto or Low Islands*, published by Henry Colburn 1838.

Vol. III. *Journal and remarks. 1832–1836.* xiv + 615 + pp. 609–629 addenda, charts in pocket *Southern portion of South America, Keeling Islands*, both published by Henry Colburn 1839. CD, C, L, LNH; T, 1002(4).   [4

11. 1839   London, Henry Colburn. *Journal of researches into the geology and natural history of the various countries visited by H.M.S. Beagle etc.* 8vo, 233 mm, [i–iv] [vii] viii–xiv + 615 + pp. 609–629 addenda, 2 charts loose in pocket in top board, or inserted at p. xiv and p. 538, 4 text woodcuts. Same sheets as Vol. III of No. 10 but preliminaries pp [i–iv] cancelled and pp [v–vi] discarded. Binding: variant *a*. dark blue cloth as variant *a*. of No. 10 but different spine titling; variant *b*. brownish purple cloth. Price: 18s. CD, L; T, 1004(1), 1005(13).   [5

12. 1840   London, Henry Colburn. As No. 11 but with cancel title leaf. Charts usually inserted at p. xiv and p. 538. Binding: as No. 11 variant *a*. T, 1006(7).   [6

13. 1845   London, John Murray. *Journal of researches into the natural history and geology of the countries visited during the voyage of H.M.S. Beagle round the world, under the Command of Capt. Fitz Roy, R.N.* Second edition. [Parts issue.] 8vo, 180 mm, 3 parts [1]–176, 177–336, 337–519[520] pp, 14 text woodcuts, Colonial and Home Library Nos XXII–XXIV. Binding: grey-buff card of the series. Price 7s. 6d. Not seen in parts, and all preliminaries not seen; probably one contents leaf to each part. T (Parts 1 & 2 only, in leather).   [7

14. 1845   London, John Murray. Issue of No. 13 in book form. 8vo, 180 mm, viii + 519 [520] pp, 14 text woodcuts. Printer's note on verso of title leaf, advertisements on verso of 2L4 = p. [520]. Inserted advertisements dated August or November 1845. Colonial and Home

Library Vol. XII. Binding: variant *a*. red morocco with blind and gilt stamping of the series, Colonial and Home Library gilt on spine [CD copy only seen]; variant *b*. scarlet cloth of the series, edges white, otherwise as *a*.; variant *c*. red cloth, blind stamped central ornamental device and ornamental corners on both boards, edges sprinkled, not Colonial and Home Library. Price: 8*s*. 6*d*. CD, C, L; T, 1007(12) part.
                                                                    [8 part

15. 1845 [= ?1848] London, John Murray. As No. 14, but with series half-title, and verso of title leaf and of 2L4 blank. Inserted advertisements dated 1848. Home and Colonial Library Vol. XII. Binding: as No. 14 variant *b*. but no library imprint on spine. T, 1007(12) part.   [8 part

16. 1846   New York, Harper & Brothers. 2 vols. Harper's New Miscellany Vols X & XI. Binding: black cloth of the series. L; T, 1010(21)   [383

17. 1852   London, John Murray. As No. 15, but called new edition. Home and Colonial Library Vol. XII. T, 1011(3).   [9

18. 1855   New York, Harper & Brothers. 2 vols. As No. 16. Harper's New Miscellany Vols X & XI. 1013(3).   [384

19. 1859   New York, Harper & Brothers. 2 vols. As No. 18. Harper's New Miscellany Vols X & XI. 1013(1).

20. 1860   London, John Murray. 8vo, Tenth thousand, 198 mm, xv + 519 pp. From stereos of No. 17 but with new preliminaries and a postscript on p. vii. Final definitive text. Binding: green cloth identical with *On the origin of species* editions 1–3. CD, D; T, 1014(12).   [10

21. 1864   New York, Harper & Brothers. 2 vols. As No. 19. Harper's New Miscellany Vols X & XI. 1016(4).   [385

22. 1870   London, John Murray. 8vo, called new edition. 190 mm, x + 519 pp, As No. 20, but with preliminaries reset. Binding: green cloth similar to *On the origin of species* edition 5. T, 1017(1)   [11

23. 1871   New York, Harper & Brothers. 2 vols. As No. 21. Harper's New Miscellany Vols X & XI. 1019(1).

24. 1871   New York, D. Appleton. 8vo, x + 519 pp. From stereos of No. 22. 1018(12).   [386

25. 1872   London, John Murray. Given in publisher's list. Not seen; perhaps equals No. 27.

26. 1872   New York, D. Appleton. As No. 24. 1020(7).

27. 1873   London, John Murray. Twelfth thousand. As No. 22, but 188 mm. L; T, 1021(1).   [12

28. 1873   New York, D. Appleton. As No. 26. 1022(3).   [387

29. 1874   New York, Harper & Brothers. 2 vols. As No. 23. 1023(1).

30. 1875   New York, D. Appleton. As No. 28, 1024(1).

31. 1876   London, John Murray. Eleventh thousand [sic]. As No. 27. D; T, 1025(4).   [14

32. 1876   New York, D. Appleton. As No. 30. 1026(4).

33. 1878   New York, D. Appleton. As No. 32. 1027(2).

34. 1879   London, John Murray. Fourteenth thousand. As No. 31 but title *A naturalist's voyage. Journal of researches* etc. CD; T.   [15

35. (1879) New York, Harper & Brothers. 8vo, 228 pp, Extracts adapted for juvenile readers with title *What Mr. Darwin saw in his voyage round the world in the ship 'Beagle'*. Introduced by Wendell Phillips Garrison. L; 1311(7).

36. 1880   New York, Harper & Brothers. As No. 35. 1312(6).

37. 1880   New York, D. Appleton. As No. 33. 1028(1).

38. 1882   London, John Murray. Fifteenth thousand. As No. 34. Binding: standard green cloth. L, LNH; T, 1142(2)   [16

39. 1882   New York, D. Appleton. As No. 37.

40. 1883   New York, D. Appleton. As No. 39. 1029(5).   [388

41. 1884   London, John Murray. Sixteenth thousand. As No. 38. L; T.   [17

42. 1884   New York, D. Appleton. As No. 40. 1030(3).

43. 1886   London, John Murray. Seventeenth thousand. As No. 41.   [18

44. 1887   New York, D. Appleton. As No. 42. 1031(4).   [389

45. 1888   London, John Murray. Seventeenth thousand. As No. 43.

46. 1888   London, John Murray. xii + 615 pp, Eighteenth thousand. T, 1032(2).   [19

47. 1888   New York, D. Appleton. As No. 44. 1033(6).

48. 1888   London, Thomas Nelson. 8vo, x–615 pp, 20 pls. L.   [20

49. 1889   London, John Murray. No thousand given. x + 519 pp. As No. 43, not as No. 46, i.e. reversion to older set of stereos. P. [iv] has advertisement for 28th thousand of this work, ?in error for 18th. Binding: green cloth with rhea hunt gilt on front board, 3/6 gilt on spine in some copies. L; T, 1034(13) part.   [21

50. 1889   London, John Murray. Twentieth thousand. As No. 46.

Advertisements read 20th thousand. Binding: green cloth; variant *a*. with rhea hunt gilt on front cover; variant *b*. without rhea hunt; neither *a* nor *b*. have price on spines. 1034(13) part.   [22

51. 1889 New York, D. Appleton. As No. 47. 1037(2).

52. 1889 London, Ward Lock. 8vo, xix + 381 pp, 15 pls, portrait. Edited by G. T. Bettany. Minerva Library No. 1. Binding: variant *a*. grey-brown cloth of the series; variant *b*. grey-green cloth of the series. Later reprints probably also occur in both cloths. T.   [23

53. 1889 London, Ward Lock. As No. 52, but called second edition. Minerva Library No. 1.   [24

54. 1889 London, Ward Lock. As No. 53, but called third edition. Minerva Library No. 1. T, 1035(3).   [25

55. 1889 London, Ward Lock. As No. 54, but called fourth edition. Minerva Library No. 1. C, L; T.   [26

56. 1889 London, Ward Lock. As No. 55, but called fifth edition. Minerva Library No. 1. T, 1036(4).   [27

57. 1889 London, Ward Lock. As No. 56, but called sixth edition. Minerva Library No. 1. T.   [30 misdated

58. 1890 London, John Murray. xi + 500 pp, portrait. New edition, no thousand given. Postscript now incorporated in text. Advertisements p [iv] give 38th thousand. Binding: green cloth with rhea hunt on front cover gilt. T.   [28

59. 1890 London, John Murray. 223 mm, xvi + 551 pp, 12 pls, 2 maps, 93 text woodcuts. Prefatory notice by John Murray. First Murray illustrated edition. Plate of layout of H.M.S. *Beagle* at p. xii is not present in all copies, and not entered in list of illustrations. R. & R. Clarke, Edinburgh, printed, see No. 122. Binding: grey-green cloth with bolas gilt on spine. C.D. in circle of porpoises, with scallop shell below, all gilt, on front cover, see No. 122. C, L; T, 1038(10).   [29

60. 1890 London, Ward Lock. As No. 57, but called seventh edition. Minerva Library No. 1. T.   [31

61. 1890 London, Ward Lock. As No. 60, but called eighth edition. Minerva Library No. 1. 1040(1)   [32

62. 1890 London, Ward Lock. As No. 61, but called ninth edition. Minerva Library No. 1.   [33

63. 1890 London, Thomas Nelson. As No. 48. Binding: red or blue cloth. C, L; T, 1039(5).   [34

64. 1890 New York, D. Appleton. 8vo, xv + 551 pp, 11 pls. An U.S.A. edition of No. 59. 1041(15). [390

65. 1891 London, John Murray. ?As No. 58, not seen. BSC. [35

66. 1891 London, Ward Lock. 492 pp, Tenth edition. Minerva Library No. 1. L; T. [36

67. 1891 London, Ward Lock. 492 pp. Biographical introduction by G. T. Bettany. From stereos of No. 66. Macaulay Library No. 3. T, 1042(2), 1045(5). [37

68. 1891 London, Thomas Nelson. As No. 63. L; T, 1043(3). [38

69. 1891 London, George Routledge. 8vo, xiii + 381 pp. *Sir* John Lubbock's Hundred Books No. 2. No list of titles on verso of title leaf, see No. 70. Bindings: red cloth uncut, spine number in gilt roman II; blue cloth cut. L; T. [39 part

70. 1891 London, George Routledge. As No. 69, but 5 titles on verso of title leaf. Bindings: as No. 69, but spine number of red binding gilt arabic 2. T. [39 part

71. 1892 London, Ward Lock Bowden. As No. 67 but called eleventh edition. T. [40

72. 1892 London, George Routledge. As No. 70. *Sir* John Lubbock's Hundred Books, No. 2. [41

73. 1892 London & Manchester, W. K. White. 8vo, viii + 194 + 1 unpaginated leaf. The Manchester Library. T, 1046(1). [42

74. 1893 London, John Murray. As No. 58. [43

75. 1893 New York, D. Appleton. As No. 47. 1048(2).

76. 1893 London, Thomas Nelson. As No. 68. 1047(1). [44

77. 1894 London, Ward Lock Bowden. As No. 71, but called twelfth edition. Title page, Captain Fitz Roy, R.A. misprint for R. N. Minerva Library No. 1. T. [45

78. [c.1895] Glasgow, Grand Colosseum Warehouse Company. pp. 17–492. From Stereos of No. 77, and with same plates but preliminaries omitted. Binding: plum cloth. T. [46

79. 1895 New York, D. Appleton. As No. 75. 1049(1).

80. 1896 London, Ward Lock. Not seen. BSC. [47

81. 1896 London, Thomas Nelson. As No. 76. [48

82. 1896 New York, D. Appleton. As No. 79. 1050(19).

83. 1897 London, John Murray. As No. 74. T, 1051(4). [49

84. 1897 London, John Murray [George Routledge]. As No. 83. [Sir John Lubbock's Hundred Books No. 2]. Binding: green cloth of the series. This issue can only be distinguished from No. 83 by the series binding. T. [50

85. 1897   London, Ward Lock Bowden. As No. 77, still twelfth
            edition.
86. 1897   New York, D. Appleton. As No. 82 1052(6).
87. [?1897] London, George Routledge. Sir John Lubbock's
            Hundred Books No. 2. Text as No. 72. Binding: of the
            series as No. 84. T.
88. 1898   London, W. K. White. xvi + 521 pp. Sea Library. C.
                                                              [51
89. 1898   New York, D. Appleton. As No. 86. 1053(5).
90. 1898   Berlin, R. Gaertner. 140 pp. Selections with title *Modern
            travels and explorations by Charles Darwin, Edward
            Whymper* etc. Edited by Hermann Krolick. Schul-
            bibliothek Französischer und Englischer Prosaschriften
            auf der neueren Zeit No. 29.
91. [1899] London, George Routledge. Sir John Lubbock's
            Hundred Books No. 2. As No. 87. T.   [52
92. 1899   New York, D. Appleton. As No. 89. 1054(5).
93. 1900   London, Thomas Nelson. As No. 81. Title page all in
            black; see No. 103. T, 1055(2).   [53
94. 1900   New York, P. F. Collier. 587 pp, Library of Universal
            Literature, Part I Science Vol. 4. 1057(5).
95. [c.1900] London, Ward Lock. As No. 76. Minerva Library,
            New Series No. 11. Binding: red or blue cloth of the
            series. T.   [54
96. [c.1900] New York, D. Appleton. xii + 512 pp. Selected
            Works, Westminster Edition. 1,000 copies. 1009(2).
97. 1901   London, John Murray. New edition. [iii]–xvi, [15]–16–
            521 pp, 16 plates. June. Binding: leaf green cloth. C, L;
            T, 1058(6).   [55
98. 1901   New York, P. F. Collier. As No. 94. Library of Uni-
            versal Literature, Part I Science Vol. 4. T, 1059(8).
99. 1902   London, John Murray. As No. 97, but i–xiv, [15]–16–
            521 pp. June. C, L; T, 1058(6).   [56
100. 1902   New York, D. Appleton. xii + 512 pp, as No. 96, but
            not Westminster Edition. 1061(3).
101. 1902   New York, P. F. Collier. As No. 94. Library of Uni-
            versal Literature, Part I Science Vol. 4. 1062(5).
102. 1902   New York, American Home Library. From stereos of
            No. 101. 1060(8).
103. 1903   London, Thomas Nelson. As No. 93, but title page in
            red and black. T, 1063(1).
104. 1904   New York, Harper & Brothers. As No. 35 1313(2).

105. 1905 London, John Murray. xi + 500 pp. T. [57

106. 1905 London, Amalgamated Press. viii + 507 pp. Harmsworth Library. L; T.

107. 1905 New York, D. Appleton. As No. 100. 1065(1).

108. 1905 New York, P. F. Collier. As No. 101. 1066(2).

109. [1905] London, George Routledge. vi + 530 pp. New Universal Library. The Works of Charles Darwin Vol. 1 [all published]. L; T, 1304(2) [58

110. [1906] London, J. M. Dent. xvi + 496 pp. Everyman Library, Science No. 104. L; T, 1306(4). [60

111. [c.1906] London, Ward Lock. As No. 95. Minerva Library, New Series No. 11. T. [61

112. 1907 London, John Murray. As No. 99. Jan. T. [62

113. 1908 London, J. M. Dent. As No. 110. Everyman Library, Science No. 104. T, 1068(5). [63

114. [1908] London, Collins. 512 pp. Frontispiece conjugate with plate facing p. 30. Illustrated Pocket Classics No. 69. T, 1067(1). [64

115. [?1908] London, Collins. As No. 114, but frontispiece conjugate with title leaf. Illustrated Pocket Classics No. 69. T.

116. [1908] London, Collins. 428 pp. Imperial Library. T.

117. 1909 London, John Murray. As No. 112. T, 1069(1). [65

118. 1909 New York, D. Appleton. As No. 117. 1070(3).

119. (1909) New York, P. F. Collier. 547 pp, Edited by Charles W. Eliot. The Harvard Classics Vol. 29. Dr Eliot's five-foot shelf of books. Many undated reprints of this edition. T, 1307(28).

120. 1910 London, J. M. Dent. As No. 113. Everyman Library, Science No. 104. T, 1071(5). [66

121. 1910 London, Ward Lock, 492 pp. As No. 111. [World Library No. 4.] T. [67

122. 1912 London, John Murray. As No. 117, but 2 maps added. April. T.

123. 1912 London, J. M. Dent. As No. 120. Everyman Library, Science No. 104. 1072(2). [68

124. 1912 New York, D. Appleton. As No. 118.

125. 1913 London, John Murray. A reprint of No. 59 by Oliver & Boyd, Edinburgh. Binding: as No. 59, but no copies have gilt scallop shell on front cover, and some have no bolas on spine and front cover in blind. T, 1073(4). [69

126. [1914] London, Thomas Nelson. 543 pp. With half-title, but

no frontispiece, see No. 133. [Nelson's Classics]. L; T, 1015(1). [70

127. 1915   New York, D. Appleton. As No. 118. 1074(1).

128. 1916   London, J. M. Dent. As No. 123. Everyman Library, Science No. 104. 1075(1). [71

129. [1918]   London, Ward Lock. As No. 121. World Library No. 4. T. [72

130. 1920   London, J. M. Dent. As No. 128. Everyman Library, Science No. 104. T, 1076(5). [73

131. 1926   London, J. M. Dent. As No. 130. Everyman Library, Science No. 104. 1077(1). [74

132. 1926   London, Fleetway House. Précis in *The world's great books in outline*. Vol. 4, pp. 2078-82. L; T.

133. [1927]   London, Thomas Nelson. As No. 126, but without half-title and frontispiece conjugate with title leaf. Nelson's Classics. T. [75

134. 1928   London, John Murray. As No. 122. T.

135. 1930   London, J. M. Dent. As No. 131. Everyman Library, Science No. 104. T, 1078(3), 1079(7). [76

136. 1930   London, Oxford University Press. vi + 530 pp. [World's Classics]. L; 1143(4).

137. [1930]   London, Watts. Abridged edition with title *H.M.S. Beagle in South America* etc. viii + 147 pp. Adapted by Amabel Williams-Ellis, helped by Ann Stephen and Charlotte and Christopher Williams-Ellis. The World of Youth Series No. 4. L; T, 977(2). [77

138. [1931]   Philadelphia, J. B. Lippincott Co., Abridged edition with title *The voyage of the Beagle; adapted from the narratives and letters of Charles Darwin and Capt. Fitzroy*. U.S.A. edition of No. 137.

139. 1936   London, J. M. Dent. As No. 135. Everyman Library, Science No. 104. T, 1309(14). [78

140. 1937   New York, Collier. As No. 108.

141. 1945   London, J. M. Dent. As No. 139. Everyman Library, Science No. 104.

142. 1950   London, J. M. Dent. As No. 141. Everyman Library, Science No. 104.

143. 1951   London, J. M. Dent. As No. 139. Everyman Library, Science No. 104. [79

144. 1952   New York, Hafner Publishing Company. xiv + 615 + 609-629 addenda pp. Offset facsimile of No. 11 with extra illustrations, 16 plates. Pallas; a collection of offset

reprints of out-of-print and classic scientific works. 250 special copies for Book Collectors Society. 1080(23).

145. 1955 London, J. M. Dent. As No. 143. Everyman Library, Science No. 104. L.

146. 1956 [New York], Limited Editions Club. Printed by the Cambridge University Press, Cambridge (England). xvi + 486 pp. Introduction by Gavin de Beer. Engravings by Robert Gibbings. Based on second edition 1845, No. 14. 1,500 copies, 25 for presentation. Not in commerce. L; T, DLC.

147. [1957] New York, Heritage Press. xvi + 489 pp. Published edition of No. 146. DLC.

148. [1958] New York, Bantam Books. 439 pp. A Bantam Classic. DLC.

149. 1959 New York, P. F. Collier. As No. 140. Fifty-first printing.

150. [1959] New York, Harper. xxiv + 327 pp. Abridged and edited by Millicent E. Selsam. DLC, T.

151. 1960 London, J. M. Dent. As No. 145, but new introduction by H. Graham Cannon. Everyman Library, Science No. 104. T, 63–7888(2). [80

152. [1960] New York, Bantam Books. As No. 148. Second printing.

153. 1961 London, J. M. Dent. As No. 151. Everyman Library, Science No. 104. T. [81

154. 1961 New York, Collier. As No. 149. DLC.

155. 1962 New York, Harper. As No. 150.

156. [1962] Garden City, N.Y., Doubleday. xxxi + 524 pp. Annotated and introduced by Leonard Engel. Anchor Books. The Natural History Library No. 16. DLC.

157. 1965 London, J. M. Dent. As No. 153. Everyman Library, Science No. 104. T.

158. 1966 Kingswood, Tadworth, Surrey, The World's Work (1913) Ltd, and London, Heinemann. As No. 155, G.B. edition.

159. (1966) New York, Harper. As No. 155. C; DLC.

160. (1968) Geneva, Edito-Service. Distributed by Heron Books, London. xviii + 551 pp, Introduction and appreciation by H. E. L. Mellersh. Offset from No. 14. Issued 'free' to subscribers to the World's Treasury of Philosophy. Books that have changed Man's Thinking. Not in commerce. L; T.

161. 1969   Brussels, Editions Culture et Civilisation. xiv + 615 +
             609–629 pp. Facsimile of No. 11, but 218 mm. Lacks
             signature 2Q = pp. 593–608, reproduced from a
             defective copy. T.

162. 1969   New York, P. F. Collier. As No. 154. Sixty-second
             printing.

163. 1969   New York, Harper. As No. 159.

164. 1972   London, J. M. Dent. As No. 157. Everyman Library,
             Science No. 104.

165. 1972   New York, Bantam Books, As No. 152, but xviii +
             143 pp. Third issue. Introduction by Walter Sullivan.

166. 1972   New York, Abrahams Magazine Service. 3 vols in 4.
             Facsimile of No. 10. DLC.

167. 1972   New York, Abrahams Magazine Service. x + 519 pp.
             Facsimile of No. 82. DLC.

ENGLISH, BRAILLE

168. 1916   London, National Institute for the Blind. 7 vols. From
             No. 123. LB.

ARMENIAN

169. 1949   Erevan, Academy of Sciences Armenian S.S.R. 765 pp.

BULGARIAN

170. 1967   Sofia, Nauka i izkustvo. Translated by Ljuben Sečanov.
             572 pp.

CZECK

171. 1956   Prague, Miadá Fronta. 537 pp, Translated by Josef
             Wolf and Zorka Wolfova.

172. 1959   Prague, Miadá Fronta. As No. 171. D.

173. 1962   Bratislava, SPN. 406 pp. Translated by Jozef Balau.

DANISH

174. 1876   Copenhagen, Salmonsen. xxii + 570 pp, portrait, 6
             plates, 1 map. Translated by Emil Chr. Hansen and
             Alfred Jørgensen. 1226(1).   [391

175. 1881   Copenhagen, Gad.   [392

DUTCH

176. [1891]   Arnhem-Nijmegen, E. & M. Cohen, vii + 568 pp.
              Translated by H. Hartogh Heijs van Zouteveen. Col-
              lected Works Vol. 7.

177. [?1895] Arnhem-Nijmegen, E. & M. Cohen. As No. 176.
              Collected Works Vol. 7.

178. [?1909] Arnhem-Nijmegen, E. & M. Cohen. As No. 177.
              Collected Works Vol. 7. LNH.

ESTONIAN

179. 1949   Tartu, Teaduslik Kirjandus. 527 pp. Translated by A.
              Uibo.

FRENCH

180. 1860   Paris. Voyages d'un naturaliste: l'Archipel Galapagos et
              les attolls de coraux in *Le tour du monde*, pp. 139–160.
              Translated by Mademoiselle A. de Montgolfier (Galapa-
              gos) & Madame S. W. Belloc (Attolls).

181. 1875   Paris, C. Reinwald. viii + 552 pp. Translated by Éd.
              Barbier. D; 1302(3).   [393

182. 1881   Paris, C. Reinwald. As No. 181.   [394

183. 1883   Paris, C. Reinwald. As No. 182. Second edition.

184. [1959]   Paris, La Farandole. 286 pp, With 4 colour plates from
              George Cuvier. Translated by Édmond Barbier. Col-
              lection Prélude. DLC.

185. 1970   Évreux, Le Cercle du Bibliophile. xviii + 590 pp. Trans-
              lated by Édmond Barbier. Introduction and discussion
              by H. E. L. Mellersh. Collection Les Livres qui ont faite
              le Monde. A book club edition corresponding to No.
              160.

186. 1970   Geneva, Edito-Service. xviii + 590 pp. Translated by
              Édmond Barbier. Commercial edition of No. 185.

GEORGIAN

187. 1951   Tiflis, Detyunizdat. viii + 543 pp. Translated from
              Russian by Shashvili. Edited by Narikashvili.

GERMAN

188. 1844   Brunswick, Friedrich Vierweg und Sohn. 2 vols, or 2
              vols in one. Translated by Ernst Dieffenbach. Printed
              on thick or thin paper. D; T, 1146(3).   [395

189. 1875 Stuttgart, Schweizerbart. xii + 596 pp. Translated by
             J. V. Carus. Collected Works Vol. 1. D, L, LSc; 1223
             (4).   [396

190. 1881 Stuttgart, Schweizerbart. As No. 189. Translated by
             J. V. Carus. Collected Works Vol. 1. L.   [397

191. 1892 Stuttgart, Schweizerbart. x + 568 pp. Translated by
             J. V. Carus.

192. 1893 Giessen, J. Ricker. xi + 604 pp. Translated by A.
             Helrich.   [398

193. 1893 Halle-am-Saale, D. Hendel. xx + 570 pp. Translated
             by Alfred Kirchoff. Bibliothek der Gesamtlitterature
             des In- und Auslandes Nos 714–22. 833(2).   [399

194. 1899 Stuttgart, Schweizerbart. As No. 191.

195. 1909 Leipzig, A. Kröner. iv + 310 pp. Translated by Hein-
             rich Schmidt. Volkausgabe. 1224(1).

196. 1910 Stuttgart, Schweizerbart. As No. 194. Collected
             Works Vol. 1.

197. 1910 Hamburg, A. Jansen. 120 pp. Condensed by E. D.
             Ezeschka. Wissenschaftliche Volksbücher für Schule
             und Haus.

198. 1911 Halle-am-Saale, D. Hendel. xv + 178 pp. Selected for
             the young.

199. 1922 Brunswick, G. Westermann. 119 pp. Translated and
             abridged by Fritz Gansberg. Wissenschaftliche Volks-
             bücker für Schule und Haus No. 6. 1225(1).

200. [1930] Breslau, Sammlung Hirts Deutsche. 96 pp. Selected
              from the translation of J. V. Carus. Sachkundbl. Abt.
              Natur.u.Naturkunde, Gr.2, Bd 4.

201. [1931] Breslau, Sammlung Hirts Deutsche. 127 pp. Selected
              from the translation of J. V. Carus by Walter Reinhard.
              Sachkundble.Abt. Länder u.Volkerkunde, Gr.1, Bd 2.

202. 1959 Leipzig, Brockhaus. 362 pp. Adapted and edited by
             Conrad Vollmer.

203. 1962 Leipzig, Brockhaus. As No. 202.

204. 1962 Stuttgart, Steingrüben. 872 pp. Translated by J. V.
             Carus, adapted by Irma Bühler. Edited by Adolf
             Narciss. Bibliothek klass. Reise Berichte. T.

205. 1967 Stuttgart, Steingrüben. As No. 204.

GREEK

206. 1900 Athens, Society for Dissemination of Useful Books.

pp. 29–77 in Bikelas, Demetrios [*Tierra del Fuego*.] 86
pp. Translated by the author. Chapter 10 only. Publication No. 3.

HEBREW

207. 1930 Tel Aviv, Omanut. 24 pp. Translated by M. Ezraḥi.
Erez ha-Esh Chapter 10, Tierra del Fuego only. Megilot
le-vate ha-sefer [Library Scrolls] No. 63.

HUNGARIAN

208. 1913 [Budapest], Révai Kiadás. 2 vols. Translated by Fülöp
Zsigmond. Világkönyvtár Nos 17–18. 871(1).

209. 1954 Budapest, Müvelt Nép Könyvkiado. 476 pp. Translated
by Boros István. 873(1).

210. 1957 Budapest, Akadémia Kiado. 511 pp. Translated by
Fülöp Zsigmond.

ITALIAN

211. 1872 Turin, Unione. 464 pp. Translated by Michele Lessona.
L. [400

212. [*c.* 1900] Turin, Unione. As No. 211. T.

213. 1915 Milan, Bruciati, 444 pp. Translated by Michele Lessona.

214. 1925 Milan, Bellasio. 505 pp. Translated by Michele Lessona.
Preface by Luigi Montemartini. Biblioteca di Cultura
Moderna

215. 1959 Milan, A. Martello. xiii + 609 pp. Translated by Mario
Magistretti.

JAPANESE

216. (1954) Tokyo, Kawade Shobō. 347 pp. Translated by Kenji
Uchiyama. Sekai Tanken Kikō Zenshū Vol. 6.

217. (1956) Tokyo, Shinchōsha. 2 vols. Translated by Kenji Uchiyama. Shinchō Bunko.

218. 1957 Tokyo, Jitsugyô no Nihon-sha. Extracts only. Translated by Toshiko Yamanushi.

219. (1958) Tokyo, Tsukija Shokan. 189 pp. ?Extracts only. Translated by Hidetoshi Arakawa.

220. (1960–61) Tokyo Iwanami Shoten. 3 vols. Translated by Takeo
Shimaji. Iwanami Bunko.

221. 1968 Tokyo, Poplar-Sha. Translated by Mitsuishi Iwao.

LITHUANIAN

222.   1963   Vilnjus, Gospolitnaučizdat. Translated by V. Kaunec-
              kas.

POLISH

223.   1887   Warsaw, Wydawnictwo Przegladu Tygodniowego.
              412 + xviii pp. Translated by Jozef Nusbaum. D.
224.   1956   Warsaw, Academy of Sciences. xv + 559 pp. Trans-
              lated by Kasimierz Szarski. Biblioteka klasyków
              Biologii. Collected Works Vol. 1. LNH.

ROMANIAN

225.   1958   Bucharest, Editura Tineretului. Translated by Radu
              Tudoran and Dinu Bondi.

RUSSIAN

226.   1870–71 St Petersburg, Cherkesov. 2 parts, xvi–277, 279–517
              pp. Translated under the editorship of A. N. Beketov.
227.   1895   St Petersburg. 421 pp. Adapted by M. A. Lyalin.
228.   1896   St Petersburg, O. N. Popov. 312 pp. Translated by
              E. G. Beketov. Edited by A. N. Beketov. Collected
              Works Vol. 1, part 1.
229.   1896   St Petersburg, A. Porokhovshchikov printed. 2 vols,
              383 + vi pp. Translated by M. Filippov. Collected
              Works. Supplement to *Nauchnoe obozrenie* Vol. 3.
              ViU (Vol. 1.).
230.   1898   St Petersburg, O. N. Popov. Second edition, as No.
              214. Translated by E. G. Beketov. Edited by A. N.
              Beketov. Collected Works Vol. 1, part 1.
231.   1902   St Petersburg, I. I. Coikiĭ. 171 + ii pp. Translated,
              edited and with a foreword by K. Z. Yaput.
232.   1908   St Petersburg, V. I. Gubinskiĭ. 336 + ii pp. Second
              edition. Translated by M. Filippov.
233.   1908   Moscow, Yu. Lepkovskiĭ. iv + 370 + iv pp. Trans-
              lated by E. Boratinskiĭ. Edited by K. Timiryazev.
              Collected Works Vol. 2.
234.   1909   St Petersburg, V. I. Gubinskiĭ. As No. 232. Translated
              by M. Filippov.
235.   1913   St Petersburg, V. V. Bitner, 544 pp. Translated by E. A.

Serebryakov. Edited by V. V. Bitner. Collected Works
Vol. VI.

236.   1924   Moscow, State Edition. vi + 216 pp. Introduction by
A. D. Nekrasov. Biblioteka putshestvii.

237.   1925   Moscow-Leningrad, State Edition. pp. 43–428. Translated by E. G. Beketov. Edited by A. N. Beketov.
Collected Works Vol. 1, part 1.

238.   1932   Moscow, OGIZ—Molodaya gvardiya. 288 pp. Translated by E. G. Beketov. Revised by V. I. Yazvitskiĭ.
Edited by V. A. Sofronov.

239.   1935   Moscow-Leningrad, State Edition. xlvii + 605 pp.
Translated by E. G. Beketov. Edited by S. L. Sobol'.
Collected Works Vol. 1.

240.   1936   Moscow-Leningrad, Library of Juvenile Literature.
399 pp. Translated by E. G. Bekatov. Edited and with
introduction by O. Kuznetzov.

241.   1953   Moscow, Geografiz. 581 pp. Translated, introduced
and annotated by S. L. Sobol'.

242.   1954   Moscow, Geografiz. As No. 241

243.   1956   Moscow, Geografiz. As No. 242.

SERBO-CROAT

244.   1949   Belgrade, Novo Pokolenje. 577 pp. Translated by
Karla Kunc and Stanko Miholic.

245.   1951   Belgrade, Novo Pokolenje. As No. 244.

246.   1964   Zagreb, Školska Knjiga. Third edition. As No. 245.

247.   1966   Zagreb, Školska Knjiga. As No. 246.

SLOVENE

248.   1950   Ljubljana, Državna Založba Slovenije. 459 pp. Translated by Olga Grahor. Prirodoznanstvens knjižnica
No. 7. 1202(2).

SPANISH

249.   1902   Valencia, A. López, Prometeo. 2 vols. Translated by
Constantino Piquer. Biblioteca Filosófica y Social.

250.   (1903)   Valencia, F. Sempere y Co. 2 vols. Translated by Constantino Piquer. 1299(1).

251.   1920   Madrid, La España Moderna. 2 vols.

252. 1922   Madrid, Antonio Marzo, edit. Calpe. 2 vols. Trans-
              lated by Juan Mateos. Viajes Clásicos Vols 9 & 10.
              842(1).

253. 1933   Madrid, Costa. 2 vols. Translated by J. Hubert. Edited
              by Joaquin Gil. Ediciones Populares Iberia No. 40.

254. 1935   Madrid, Calpe. 2 vols. As No. 252.

255. 1942   Buenos Aires, Librería El Ateneo. 617 pp, 121 pls, 2
              maps, text figs. Translated by J. Hubert. Edited and
              layout by Joaquin Gil. T, 1300(1).

256. 1944   Mexico City, Editora Intercontinental. 190 pp. Extracts
              on the animals with title *Los más curiosos animales de
              América*. Cuadernos de Cultura No. 3. 1114(2).

257. (1945) Buenos Aires, Librería El Ateneo. As No. 255. ?1301(1).

258. 1968   Montevideo, Arca. 134 pp. Extracts on Rió de la Plata
              with title *Un naturalista en el Plato*. Translated by Rafael
              Lasala. Selected and with foreword by José Pedro
              Barrán and Benjamin Nahum. Historia Viva. DLC.

259a. 1972   Barcelona, Salvat. 209 pp. Translated by Víctor Pzanco-
              yalba.

SWEDISH

259. 1872   Stockholm, Landskrifter, J. L. Törnquist. vii + 452 pp.
              Translated by G. Lindström. 1145(1).

260. 1925   Stockholm, Natur och Kultur. 445 pp. Translated by
              Torsten Pehrson. Levande Litteratur Vol. 3. T, 12227
              (1).

261. 1959   Stockholm, Natur och Kultur. As No. 260.

Questions About the Breeding of Animals

This is the first of Darwin's printed questionnaires. He bombarded his
friends and acquaintances with demands for information and specimens,
and, at least twice, perhaps three times, printed lists of questions for
wider distribution. It is an unsatisfactory method of collecting scientific
information, but, at least, his questions were on the whole objective.
The answers obtained were intended for his large book on species,
which was never published; they eventually became incorporated in
Variation under domestication, 1868.

The questions form a quarto pamphlet with no title page, just a
dropped title on the first page of the text; but it has the author's name
and address at the end of the text on p. 8, 'C. Darwin./ 12, *Upper Gower*

Street, London.' It is a single sheet, folded in quarto, sewn in the fold, with the printed surface, 90 mm wide, lying on the inner half of each page, leaving the outer half for the answers. The text consists of twenty-one numbered paragraphs, most of them containing more than one question, forty-four question marks in all. Only two copies are known to survive. One, in the University Library, Cambridge, which came with the Robin Darwin deposit and was acquired by the Library in February 1976, is in its original state uncut. The other, cut and bound, is in the Zoological Library of the British Museum (Natural History): it was bought from John Wheldon & Co. on May 19th 1909. The Cambridge copy has the answers to nineteen of the paragraphs entered on it by George Tollet, dated May 10. The Library also holds a set of five answers, not on a copy of the pamphlet, by R. S. Ford dated May 6. The British Museum (Natural History) copy is virgin. Tollet, of Betley Hall, Staffordshire, was a personal friend of the Wedgwoods and a distinguished pioneer of animal breeding; Ford was a farmer and manager of the Fitzherbert estates nearby. Both lived near Maer Hall and it is probable that Darwin gave copies to them when he stayed there with his bride between April 26 and May 13, 1839.

The facsimile edition, of 1968, is reproduced from the British Museum (Natural History) copy and has an introduction by *Sir* Gavin de Beer. He concludes, wrongly, that it should be dated 1840 and prints this date on the title page. Peter J. Vorzimmer (*Jl Hist.Biol.*, Vol. 2, pp. 269–281, 1969) and R. B. Freeman & P. J. Gautrey (*Jl Soc.Biblphy nat.Hist.*, Vol. 5, pp. 220–225, 1969) have examined the work in detail, the former printing the text. Both these papers show conclusively that it was printed between December 31st 1838, the day on which Darwin moved into 12 Upper Gower Street, and May 6th 1839, the date on R. S. Ford's answers. Vorzimmer has suggested a date between March 13th and May 5th, but Darwin arrived at Maer on April 26th; late March or early April is probably correct. It has no printer or place, but was almost certainly printed in London.

Paul H. Barrett, in Howard E. Gruber, *Darwin on man*, 1974, has transcribed another set of questions, mostly on the same subject, from a manuscript at Cambridge which is headed 'Questions for Mr Wynne'. They are brief, ungrammatical and in places illegible. They could not have been sent to Mr Wynne in this form and are either a rough draft or an aide-memoir for use when Darwin met Mr Wynne. Nothing is known of Mr Wynne except that he bred Malay fowl and was known to Darwin's father. Professor Barrett suggests that they were written earlier than the printed questions, because if the printed ones had been available Darwin would have used those.

ENGLISH

262. [1839]   [?London], no printer, not published. Dropped title *Questions about the breeding of animals*. 4to, 290 mm, 8 pp, no covers. C, LNH.   [82

263. 1968   London, Society for the Bibliography of Natural History. *Questions about the breeding of animals [1840]*. 4to, 280 mm, xi + 8 pp. Facsimile of No. 262, with introduction by *Sir* Gavin de Beer. Sherborn Fund Facsimile No. 3. Binding: black cloth or yellow paper wrappers. Price: £1. 15s. or £1. 5s. C, L; T.

264. 1969   Cambridge, Mass., Belknap Press of Harvard University Press. pp. 277–281 in Vorzimmer, Peter J. Darwin's Questions about the breeding of animals. *Journal of the History of Biology*, Vol. 2, pp. 269–281.

265. 1974   London, Wildwood House. pp. 423–425 in Gruber, Howard E. *Darwin on man*. No. 1582. Title Questions for Mr Wynne. An earlier set of questions not previously printed. (For two sets of answers to these questions *see* Freeman, R. B. & Gautrey, P. J. 1969. *J.Soc.Biblphy nat.Hist*. Vol. 5, pp. 220–25).

Bar of Sandstone Off Pernambuco

The original English edition of this appeared in a serial (No. 1659), but, because the three language edition (No. 269) appeared as a pamphlet, an entry is needed here.

ENGLISH

266. 1841   On a remarkable bar of sandstone off Pernambuco, on the coast of Brazil. *Philosophical Magazine*, Vol. 19, pp. 257–260, 1 text figure. October. Reprinted in No. 269. = No. 1659.

FRENCH

267.   Translated by Édmond Barbier. Not traced. Reprinted in No. 269.

PORTUGUESE

268. 1904   In *Rev.Inst.Archaeol.Geogr.Pernambucono*, Recife, No. 60, pp. 196–200. Translated by Alfredo de Carvalho. Reprinted in No. 269.

PORTUGUESE, ENGLISH, FRENCH

269. [1959] Recife, Universidade Rural de Pernambuco, Ministério
de Agricultura. *Memoria de Charles Darwin sôbre os
arrecifes de arenito do pôrto de Parnambuco* [por] *João de
Deus de Oliviera Dias*, 8vo, 60 pp, portrait, maps, text
figs. Translated by Alfredo de Carvalho. Also contains
a facsimile of the original English, No. 266, and the
French translation by Édmond Barbier, No. 267. The
Portuguese is a reprint of No. 268. DLC.

RUSSIAN

270. 1936 Moscow, Academy of Sciences. pp. 443–445. Translated by L. S. Davitashvili. Collected Works Vol. 2.

Geology of The Voyage of The Beagle

The three parts of Darwin's geological results of the Beagle voyage
were separately published over a period of five years, but they were
intended, and described on the title pages, as parts of one work. They
were all published by Smith Elder, with the approval of the Lords
Commissioners of the Treasury, some of the £1,000 given for the
publication of the results of the voyage going towards the cost of at
least the first part. Darwin notes, in May 1842, that the cost of *Coral
reefs* was £130–140 and that 'the government money has gone much
quicker than I thought'. By that date there were only two parts of the
Zoology of the Beagle still to come out. Smith Elder also published the
important later editions.

A publisher's advertisement of 1838 announced the preparation of a
work in one volume octavo entitled *Geological observations on volcanic
islands and coral formations*, but this plan was abandoned and the first part,
Coral reefs, appeared in May 1842, at a cost of 15s. The second part,
Volcanic islands, was published in November 1844, at a cost of 10s. 6d.
The one folding map is of Ascension Island and is dated 1825. The third,
South America, was published late in 1846, at a cost of 12s. *Coral reefs*
has two lines of errata on p. [206] and *South America* three lines on p. viii.

In *Coral reefs*, the last leaf (Q2) advertises the two other projected
parts on the recto and the, then unfinished, *Zoology of the Beagle* on the
verso. There are sixteen pages of inserted publisher's advertisements,
dated May 1842, in some copies. *Volcanic islands* may have twenty-four
pages of inserted publisher's advertisements, dated January 1844, and
South America thirty-two pages dated 1846. The last text page of the latter

[p. 280] advertises the, now completed, *Geology* and *Zoology*. All three parts were published in blue or purple cloth, the latter fading to brown. The blue bindings, which are probably earlier, usually, perhaps always, have the price in gilt on the spine, and this is sometimes present on the purple cloth.

In 1851, the three parts were reissued in one volume. The old pagination was retained although the title and half-title leaves of the parts were discarded and replaced by a new general title leaf. This issue is clearly a remainder made up from unsold sheets and priced at 10s. 6d. I have seen it in both blue and purple cloth with sixteen pages of inserted advertisements dated June 1851, and in purple cloth with slightly different spine lettering with advertisements, dated September 18th, 1856 or May 1st, 1858.

A second edition of *Coral reefs* appeared in 1874; it was extensively revised and largely rewritten in the light of the findings of Dana and of Jukes. The other two parts appeared in a single volume in 1876 which is called a second edition. The text however was not altered although a few new references are given in the preface. No further editions or issues were published in Darwin's lifetime, but a third edition of *Coral reefs* appeared in 1889, and a third edition of the other two parts in 1891. The text of the former was edited by T. G. Bonney to the extent of adding footnotes as well as a large appendix bringing the matter up to date. The latter is only a title page edition with some resetting. These four volumes all appeared in a green cloth binding, closely resembling that of Murray Darwins and with the same device on the spine. I have also seen the second in brown cloth, with the same gilt stampings, and it is possible that the others also occur in this form.

All three parts of the first edition were reprinted in Ward Lock's Minerva Series, later World Series, but have not appeared since 1910. *Coral reefs* alone was republished from the first edition in 1962 and a facsimile edition appeared in 1969. Facsimile editions of late American printings, 1896 and 1897, appeared in 1972. These geological works have been little translated. In Darwin's lifetime, all three appeared in German and *Coral reefs* in French and in a Russian précis.

ENGLISH

271.   1842   London, Smith Elder and Co. *The structure and distribu-*
                tion of coral reefs. Being the first part of the geology of the
                voyage of the Beagle, under the command of Capt. Fitzroy,
                R.N. during the years 1832 to 1836. 8vo, 225 mm, xii +
                214 pp, 3 folding maps, 6 text woodcuts, 2 errata on

1. [206]. Inserted advertisements May 1842 in some copies. Binding: blue or purple cloth. Price: 15s. C, L, LNH; T, 1235(16). [83

272. 1844 London, Smith Elder and Co. *Geological observations on the volcanic islands visited during the voyage of H.M.S. Beagle, together with some brief notices of the geology of Australia and the Cape of Good Hope. Being the second part of the geology of the voyage of the Beagle, under the command of Capt. Fitzroy, R.N. during the years 1832 to 1836.* 8vo, 225 mm, vii + 175 pp, folding map, 14 text woodcuts. Appendix by G. B. Sowerby [I], pp. [153] 154–160. Description of six species of corals from the Palaeozoic formation of Van Diemen's Land, by W. Lonsdale, pp. 161–169. Inserted advertisements Jan. 1844 in some copies. Binding: blue or purple cloth. Price: 10s. 6d. CD, C, D, L; T, 960(14). [84

273. 1846 London, Smith Elder and Co. *Geological observations on South America. Being the third part of the geology of the voyage of the Beagle, under the command of Capt. Fitzroy, R.N. during the years 1832 to 1836.* 8vo, 225 mm, vii + 279 pp, 5 plates (one coloured), one folding map. 3 errata on p. [viii]. Appendix. Descriptions of tertiary fossil shells from South America, by G. B. Sowerby [I], pp. [249] 250–264. Descriptions of secondary fossil shells from South America, by Edward Forbes, pp. [265] 266–268. Binding: purple, or blue, cloth. Price: 12s. CD, C, L, LNH; T, 958(15). [85

274. 1851 London, Smith Elder and Co. *Geological observations on coral reefs, volcanic islands, and on South America etc.* 8vo, 223 mm. Combined edition made up from the original sheets of Nos 220–222, but title leaves discarded and new general title added. Inserted advertisements of several dates. Binding: as Nos 271–273. Price: 10s. 6d. ?A remainder. LNH; T, 957(13). [86

275. 1874 London, Smith Elder and Co. *The Structure and distribution of coral reefs.* Second edition. 8vo, 188 mm, xx + 278 pp, 3 folding maps (2 coloured), 14 text woodcuts. Binding: green or brown cloth as Nos 276 & 277. CD, C, L; T, 1236(10) [87

276. 1876 London, Smith Elder and Co. *Geological observations on the volcanic islands and parts of South America. etc.* Second edition. 8vo, 190 mm, xiii + 647 pp, 5 folding plates

(one coloured), 2 folding maps, 40 text woodcuts. Binding: green or brown cloth as Nos 275 & 277. CD, C, L, LNH; T, 962(10).   [88

277. 1889 London, Smith Elder and Co. *The structure and distribution of coral reefs*. Third edition. 8vo, 190 mm, xx + 344 pp, 3 folding maps (2 coloured), 8 text woodcuts. With an appendix by T. G. Bonney. Binding: green cloth as Nos 275 & 276. C. L, LNH; T, 1237(12).   [89

278. 1889 D. Appleton, New York. *Coral reefs* only. Third edition. With an appendix by T. G. Bonney. From stereos of No. 277.

279. 1890 London, Ward Lock. 8vo, xx + 549 pp. Contains all three parts. Introduction by John W. Judd. Minerva Library No. 18. Binding: variant *a*. grey green cloth of the series, 178 mm; variant *b*. peacock blue cloth of the series, 185 mm. L; T, 1174(10).   [90

280. 1890 London, Walter Scott, Newcastle-on-Tyne printed. *Coral reefs* only. 8vo, xxiv + 278 pp. Introduction by Joseph W. Williams. Also contains No. 1647. T, ?1173(9).   [91

281. [?1890] Glasgow, Grand Colosseum Warehouse Company. 549 pp. From sheets of No. 279 with preliminaries omitted. Binding: pale blue cloth. T.

282. 1891 London, Smith Elder & Co. *Volcanic islands and South America* only. Third edition. As No. 276 but xiii + 648 pp. Binding: as No. 260 etc. T, 963(11).

283. 1891 New York, D. Appleton. *Volcanic islands and South America* only. Third edition. From stereos of No. 282 T, 964(1).

284. [?1891] London, Ward Lock. As No. 279 and from stereos, but undated. Minerva Library No. 18. Binding: as No. 279. T.

285. [1894] London, Ward Lock. As No. 284. Minerva Library No. 18. Binding: brown-green cloth of the series. T.

286. 1896 New York, D. Appleton. *Coral reefs* only. Third edition, As No. 278. 1240(15).   [401

287. 1896 New York, D. Appleton. *Volcanic islands and South America* only. Third edition. As No. 283. 966(17). [402

288. 1897 New York, D. Appleton. *Coral reefs* only. As No. 286. 1241(18).   [403

289. 1897 New York, D. Appleton. *Volcanic islands and South America* only. As No. 287. 967(13).

290. 1898   New York, D. Appleton. *Coral reefs* only. As No. 288.
               1242(4).

291. 1898   New York, D. Appleton. *Volcanic islands and South
               America* only. As No. 289. 968(1).

292. 1900   New York, D. Appleton. *Volcanic islands and South
               America* only. As No. 291. 971(8).

293. [c. 1900] London, Walter Scott, Newcastle-on-Tyne printed.
               Coral reefs only. As No. 280. Also contains No. 1647.
               Scott Library No. 64. L; T.

294. [c. 1900] London, Ward Lock. As No. 285. Minerva Library,
               New Series No. 8. Binding: red cloth of the series, gilt
               on front cover. T.   [92

295. [c. 1900] New York, D. Appleton. *Coral reefs* only. As No. 290,
               but Selected Works, Westminster Edition. 1,000
               copies. T, 1239(1).

296. [c. 1900] New York, D. Appleton. *Volcanic islands and South
               America* only. As No. 292, but Selected Works, West-
               minster Edition. 1,000 copies. T, 969(6).

297. 1900   New York, D. Appleton. *Volcanic islands and South
               America* only. As No. 292.

298. [c. 1906] London, Ward Lock. As No. 294. Minerva Library,
               New Series No. 8. Binding: red cloth of the series, no
               gilt on front cover. T.

299. [1907]   London and Felling-on-Tyne, Walter Scott. *Coral reefs*
               only. As No. 293. Also contains No. 1647. Scott
               Library No. 64. T.   [93

300. 1910   London, Ward Lock, As No. 298. World Library. T,
               822(4).   [94

301. [c. 1910] New York, Harper. xx + 549 pp. As No. 298 and from
               stereos. World Library.

302. 1915   New York, D. Appleton. *Coral reefs* only. As No. 295.

303. 1915   New York, D. Appleton. *Volcanic islands and South
               America* only. As No. 297. 972(1).

304. 1962   Berkeley and Los Angeles, University of California
               Press. *Coral reefs* only. xii + 214 pp. Foreword by
               H. W. Menard. L: T, DLC.   [95

305. [1962]   Gloucester, Mass., Peter Smith [University of Cali-
               fornia Press]. *Coral reefs* only. As No. 304.

306. 1969   Brussels, Editions Culture et Civilisation. *Coral reefs*
               only. Facsimile of No. 271, but 218 mm.

307. 1972   New York, Abrahams Magazine Service. *Volcanic*

islands and South America only. Facsimile of No. 286 (1896). DLC.

308. 1972   New York, Abrahams Magazine Service. *Coral reefs* only. Facsimile of No. 288 (1897). DLC.

FRENCH

309. 1878   Paris, Germer Baillière. *Coral reefs* only. xx + 347 pp. Translated by L. Cosserat. D; T, 1222(2).   [404

310. 1902   Paris, C. Reinwald, Schleicher Frères. *Volcanic islands* only. xxii + 218 pp. Translated by A. F. Renard. LNH, BS; T, 1152(2).

GERMAN

311. 1876   Stuttgart, Schweizerbart. *Coral reefs* only. xiv + 213 pp. Translated by J. V. Carus. Collected Works, Vol. 11, part 1. D, L, BS; T, 1250(1).   [405

312. 1877   Stuttgart, Schweizerbart. *Volcanic islands* only. viii + 176 pp. Translated by J. V. Carus. Collected Works, Vol. 11, part 2. D, L, BS; T, 973(4).   [406

313. 1878   Stuttgart, Schweizerbart. *South America* only. x + 400 pp. Translated by J. V. Carus. Collected Works, Vol. 12, part 1. D, L; T, DLC.   [407

314. 1879   Stuttgart, Schweizerbart. *Coral reefs* only. As No. 311. T.

315. 1899   Stuttgart, Schweizerbart. *Coral reefs* only. As No. 314. Collected Works, Vol. 11, part 1.

316. 1899   Stuttgart, Schweizerbart. *Volcanic islands* only. As No. 312. Collected Works, Vol. 11, part 2.

317. 1899   Stuttgart, Schweizerbart. *South America* only. As No. 313. Collected Works, Vol. 12, part 1.

ITALIAN

318. 1888   Turin, Unione. *Coral reefs* only. 210 pp. Translated by Giovanni & Riccardo Canestrini. Works of Darwin. D.   [408

JAPANESE

319. 1949   Tokyo, Kaizōsha. *Coral reefs* only. Collected Works, Vol. 2.

RUSSIAN

320. 1846   *Journal of Mining Information*, I. Glazunov, St Peters-
                burg. Vol. 4, part 1, pp. 1–67. *Coral reefs* summary
                only. Translated by Lieut. Beka.

321. 1936   Moscow, Academy of Sciences U.S.S.R. *Coral reefs*
                only. pp. 285–448. Translated by L. S. Davitashvili &
                N. M. Kelevich. Annotated by L. S. Davitashvili &
                N. S. Shatskiĭ. Collected Works, Vol. 2.

323. 1936   Moscow, Academy of Sciences U.S.S.R. *Volcanic islands
                and South America* only. pp. 449–562. Translated by
                V. G. Epifanov. Introduced and annotated by N. S.
                Shatskiĭ. Collected Works, Vol 2.

SPANISH

324. 1906   Santiago de Chile, Imprenta Cervantes. *South America*
                only. viii + 417 pp. Translated by Alfredo Escuti
                Orrego. Annexo a los *Anales de la Universidad de Chile*.
                1001(11).

Brayley Testimonials

It was customary, through much of the nineteenth century and indeed
until later, for applicants for Chairs to send printed letters with supporting testimonials. These confidential pamphlets were submitted to
governors and members of selecting bodies. Few copies were printed
and they tend to survive, if at all, only in the archives of the Universities
concerned. I know of three to which Darwin contributed testimonial
letters, T. H. Huxley applying to Toronto in 1851 (No. 344), W. Boyd
Dawkins applying to Cambridge in 1873 (No. 1216), and this one, the
earliest. There may be more. Darwin refused to supply one to Alfred
Newton, on the foundation of the Chair of Comparative Anatomy at
Cambridge in 1865, on the ground that a specialized knowledge of
birds was not what was wanted in the interests of zoology (in No. 1595,
p. 45): Newton was appointed in 1866 and retained the Chair until his
death. He also declined to provide one for George Robert Gray, of the
British Museum, who was applying, in 1869, for an unspecified post, on
the ground that he did not know enough of Gray's work (in No. 1596,
pp. 92–93).

Brayley had applied in 1841, on the foundation of the Chair, but it
went to Thomas Webster. On Webster's death in 1844, he applied
again with these additional testimonials, but owing to a lack of funds,

the post was not filled. The only copy of these additions, as well as of the originals of 1841, known to me is in private hands: University College London is without them.

ENGLISH

324. 1845   London, Richard & John E. Taylor. In Brayley, Edward William *Additional testimonials submitted to the Council of University College, London, by Edward William Brayley . . . a candidate for the Professorship of Geology.* 4to, 215 mm, 19 pp. Darwin's letter p. [7]. No covers. LUC (xerox); T (xerox).

Manual of Scientific Enquiry

This useful book, edited by *Sir* John Herschel, went through six editions, remaining in print until 1906. Professor James Geikie's high opinion of Darwin's article on geology is given in *Life and letters*, Vol. 1, pp. 328–29. The first edition is found in three forms. In some copies there is a serious transposition of about two pages in the text of Darwin's article, although no matter is missing. This starts on page 178 at lines 2–4 which read 'Most bold coasts/are fronted by sharp promontories and even isolated/found by removing earth and birds' dung'. The transposition ends on page 180 where lines 2–3 read 'the now deeply submerged portions of the cliff have been/pinnacles:'. This transposition, of course, causes a third disjointed sentence at the point where the correct text begins again, on page 190 where lines 4–5 read 'these may be sometimes/simply worn away by the currents'. It would look as if the compositor had one sheet of the manuscript out of order. Some copies occur in this form with no cancel, although I have not seen one in publisher's cloth; some, including Darwin's own at Cambridge, have a cancel for his whole article in a pocket in the back board. The most frequent form, in my experience, has the cancel inserted in its correct place and no pocket. The correct text reads 'Most bold coasts/are fronted by sharp promontories and even isolated/pinnacles'; 'the now deeply submerged portions of the cliff have been/simply worn away by the currents' and 'these may be sometimes/found by removing earth and birds' dung'. In the good text the lines differ from those of the bad because the whole has been reset.

This edition was issued in blue cloth with foul-anchors on both boards; in some copies, but not all, the anchor on the top board is gilt.

Darwin's articles from the first, third and fourth editions also occur

as separate offprints; those from the others may exist but I have not
seen them. A facsimile of the second edition appeared in 1974.

ENGLISH

325. 1849 London, John Murray. In Herschel, *Sir* John F. W.
           *Bart. editor A manual of scientific enquiry; prepared for the
           use of Her Majesty's Navy: and adapted for travellers in
           general.* 8vo in 12s, 203 mm, xi + 488 pp + 96a, 96b +
           inserted leaf unnumbered at p. 98, 2 folding charts, 16
           text woodcuts. Darwin's contribution is Section VI,
           Geology pp 156–95, no illustrations. Text transposed
           on p. 178 line 2, p. 180 line 2, and p. 190 line 4. With a
           20 pp cancel, pp. 171–190. Binding: blue cloth, with a
           pocket in bottom board to hold the cancel section.
           Price 10s. 6d. CD. Note: copies may have been issued
           without the cancellans, and without the pocket in
           bottom board; such a copy, in leather, is in LUC.
                                                            [96 part

326. 1849 London, John Murray. [First edition, second issue.] All
           as No. 325, but cancelland discarded and replaced by
           cancellans. Binding: as No. 307, but no pocket in
           bottom board. L; LNH; T, 2002(12).   [96 part

327. [1849] London, William Clowes printed. *Geology.* 8vo in 12s.
           200 mm, 42 pp. Signatures $B^{12}C^8D^2$. A reprint of
           Darwin's contribution to No. 326, the text being in
           corrected form. Binding: pale fawn printed wrappers.
           LUC; T.   [97

328. 1851 London, John Murray. Second edition. 8vo in 12s, xi +
           503 pp + inserted leaf unnumbered at p. 98. Darwin's
           contribution pp. 166–204. L; T, 2004(14).   [98

329. 1859 London, John Murray. Third edition. 8vo, xviii + 429
           pp. Superintended by R. Main. Darwin's contribution
           pp. 268–99. L, LNH; 2005(9)   [99

330. [1859] London, William Clowes printed. *Manual of geology.*
           (*Extracted from the Admiralty manual of scientific enquiry,
           Third edition, 1859*). 8vo, 195 mm, 34 pp. A reprint of
           Darwin's contribution to No. 319. Binding: printed
           drab card, cloth spine. L; 1113(1).   [100

331. 1871 London, John Murray. Fourth edition. xvi + 392 pp.
           Revised by J. Phillips. Darwin's contribution pp. 248–
           75. L, LNH; T, 2006(8).   [101

332. [1871] [London]. *Geology; revised by Professor J. Phillips*. 200 mm, 29 pp. A reprint of Darwin's contribution to No. 331. 974(1).

333. 1886 London, John Murray. Fifth edition. xii + 450 pp. Edited by *Sir* Robert S. Ball. Darwin's contribution Article X, pp. 272–299, revised by A. Geikie. Title page with 3 wavy and 2 straight rules. Printed by Eyre & Spottiswoode. See No. 334. LNH; T, 2007(8).   [102

334. 1886 [= 1906] London, John Murray. Fifth [= sixth] edition. As No. 333, but with erratum leaf dated May 1906 at p. 62. Printed by Darling & Son [see p. 450] in spite of Eyre & Spottiswoode on title page. Title page with 5 straight rules. Darwin's contribution unaltered. T.

335. 1974 London, Dawsons of Pall Mall. Second edition. Facsimile of No. 328. Introduction by David Knight.

RUSSIAN

336. 1860 In *Morskoi Sbornik*, Maritime Ministry, St Petersburg. Vol, No. 13, suppl. 1–31. Darwin's article only.

337. 1860 St Petersburg, Maritime Ministry. An edition of the whole book.

338. 1935 Moscow, Academy of Sciences U.S.S.R. Darwin's article only. pp. 613–637. Translated by D. L. Weiss. Annotated by N. S. Shatskiĭ. Collected Works Vol. 2.

Living Cirripedia

A detailed bibliography of this is given by Richard Curle *A bibliographical history of the Ray Society*, 1954. There is no indication that the two volumes are parts of the same work. Robert Hardwicke was publisher to the Society, and advertisements for this work, in later Darwins, often give his name alone as publisher. Curle states that the number of copies printed may not have been more than 800, that is about fifty more than the number of members of the Society at the time. He does not give the original price, but the *English catalogue* gives £2. 2s. for the set. It appeared in facsimile in 1965, and it is also available on microfiches from the International Documentation Centre. Darwin spent much of his time for eight years, beginning in 1846, on this work and on the corresponding volume of the British fossil forms. They are his only contributions to formal taxonomy and are still held in high regard.

339. 1851, 1854 London, The Ray Society. [Vol. I] *A monograph of the sub-class Cirripedia, with figures of all the species. The Lepadidæ; or, pedunculated cirripedes.* [Vol. II.] . . . *The Balanidæ, (or sessile cirripedes); the Verrucidæ, etc., etc., etc.* 8vo, 215 mm, 2 vols, xii + 400 pp. + p. 3* [folding]; viii + 684 pp. + p. 3*, 40 pls (3 partly coloured), 24 text woodcuts (1–7, 1–11; [I–III[3]]). Vol. [I] 4 errata on p. xii. Society's Publications No. 21 for 1851 and No. 25 for 1853. Binding: blue cloth of the series. Price £2. 2s. CD, C, D, L, LNH; T, 1121(19).   [103

340. 1964 Weinheim, J. Cramer. 2 vols in one. Facsimile reprint of No. 339. Historiæ Naturalis Classica, Vol. 38. 67–31685(13).   [104

RUSSIAN

341. 1936 Moscow, Academy of Sciences U.S.S.R. Extracts only, without the systematic matter. pp. 47–87. Translated by N. I. Tarasov. Collected Works Vol. 2. L.

Fossil Cirripedia of Great Britain

As with the *Living Cirripedia*, there is no indication on the title pages that the two volumes are parts of the same work, but the preface to Volume II states that this completes the work. In a circular to members of the Palæontographical Society, dated June 1863, the Secretary, Thomas Wiltshire, gives 'the dates of the years *for which* the volume containing the Monograph was issued' as 1851, 1854, 1858a (the 'a' refers to a footnote which states that the index came out in that year); he also gives 'the dates of the years *in which* the Monograph was published' as 1851, 1855, 1861. What Wiltshire meant was that the complete volumes 5, 8 and 12, were published in those years. Each of the two parts contains its own index; that for the first part was issued with it; that for the second was apparently forgotten and this omission was not set right until the issue of a single leaf in 1858. The Geological Society of London holds a set bound up as issued and this single leaf occurs in its correct place.

Darwin had assisted John Morris with the cirripedes in the second edition of his *A catalogue of British fossils*, 1854. On page 97 of this work, the author writes 'Mr. Darwin has kindly supplied the following references to the above species which will be figured in his forthcoming Memoir on the fossil Balanidae'. He then refers to fifteen plates and to the figures given in each, whereas Darwin's work has only two plates. In fact, the first six species named occur in the first plate, the seventh, *Balanus tulipa* in both plates, and the rest in the second. The species given by Morris as *B. tulipa* O. F. Müller 1776 eventually appeared in Darwin's work as *B. hameri* Ascanius 1767.

A complete set of the Palæontographical Society's monograph volumes appeared in facsimile in 1966, but Darwin's work was not available alone.

ENGLISH

342. 1851, 1854, 1858 London, Palæontographical Society. [Vol. I] *A monograph of the fossil Lepadidæ, or pedunculated cirripedes of Great Britain.* [Vol. II] *A monograph of the fossil Balanidæ and Verrucidæ of Great Britain.* [*Index* to Vol. II, 1858]. 4to, 275 mm, [Vol. I] vi + 88 pp, 5 plates each with content leaf, 4 text woodcuts; [Vol. II] [iv] + 44 pp. 2 plates each with content leaf, 8 text woodcuts; Index [to Vol. II] 2 pp. Being Vol. 5, No. 13, the volume published June 1851 for 1850; Vol. 8, No. 30, the volume published May 1855; and Vol. 12, the volume published 1861. Binding: fawn printed paper boards of the series. C, L, LNH; T, 1119(18), 1120(18).

[105

343. 1966 New York and London, Johnson Reprint Corporation. In Vols 5 & 8 of the Palæontographical Society's Annual Volumes, the numbers not available separately. Facsimile reprint of No. 342.

Huxley Testimonials

Thomas Henry Huxley, at the age of twenty six, was applying for the chair of Natural History at the University of Toronto. Darwin's letter, of five lines, occurs on page 4. In spite of excellent testimonials, Huxley did not get the post; it went to William Hincks, brother of *Sir* Francis Hincks, Prime Minister of Upper Canada.

The pamphlet appeared late in 1851. Huxley's letter of application, printed in it, is dated October 17th, and the copy in the Huxley archive at the Imperial College of Science and Technology, London, was authenticated in manuscript by Richard Taylor, the printer, on October 16th. For a general note on these printed testimonials see No. 324, *Brayley Testimonials*.

ENGLISH

344. [1851] London, Richard Taylor printed. *Testimonials for Thomas H. Huxley, F.R.S., candidate for the Chair of Natural History at the University of Toronto.* 8vo, 245 mm [cut], 10 pp, Darwin's testimonial p. 4. No binding. LUI; T. Note: the LUI copy has a certification note in ms by Richard Taylor dated Oct. 16, 1851.

Enquiry by the Trustees of the British Museum

ENGLISH

345. 1848 *Enquiry by the Trustees of the British Museum.* Not seen. [Contains a letter by Darwin to R. I. Murchison which is also published in *More letters* Vol. 1, pp. 109–10, dated Jun. 19 [1858]. Letter in *More letters* Vol. 1, pp. 452–453 to J. D. Hooker dated March 30, 1859, refers.]

On the Tendency of Species to form Varieties

This famous paper originally appeared in the *Journal of the Linnean Society of London, Zoology,* but has been printed in books, in part or in whole, several times since. The events and correspondence, between June 18th, when Darwin received Wallace's letter, and August 30th, when it appeared in print, are given in *Life and letters,* Vol. II, pp. 115–131. The paper was communicated to the Society by *Sir* Charles Lyell and *Sir* Joseph Hooker, on the evening of Tuesday, July 1st, 1858. Darwin was not present because of serious illness amongst his children. The meeting was largely concerned with the death of Robert Brown and it aroused little interest.

There are five different forms in which the original edition can be found, but they are all from the same setting of type. Four of these are the results of the publishing customs of the Linnean Society of London and the fifth is the authors' offprints. The *Journal* came out in parts and was available to Fellows of the Society with *Zoology* and *Botany* together in each part, *Zoology* alone, or *Botany* alone. Later it appeared in volume form made up from reserved stock of the parts with new title pages, dated in the year of completion of the volume, and indexes. This again was available complete or as *Zoology* or *Botany* alone. The *Zoology* was signed with numbers and the *Botany* with letters. The Darwin-Wallace paper occurs in the complete part in blue wrappers, or in the *Zoology* part in pink wrappers; the *Botany* parts were in green. The Linnean Society has all the forms in its reference files, although it does not hold the offprint.

The authors' offprints were issued in buff printed wrappers with the original pagination retained. They have 'From the Journal of the Proceedings of the Linnean Society for August 1858.' on page [45]. They were printed from the standing type but, presumably, after the copies of the number had been run off. The only copies which I have seen have been inscribed personally by Darwin, but *Life and letters*, Vol. II, p. 138, notes that Darwin had sent eight copies to Wallace, still in the far-east, and had kept others for him.

Life and letters, Vol. II, p. 120, states, in a footnote, that the date of Darwin's letter to Asa Gray 'is given as October in the "Linnean Journal".' This is not so; the date is given correctly in the *Journal* as 'September 5th, 1857'. However, in the *Proceedings* for 1857–58 (pp. liv–lv) it is given as 'in October 1857'.

It has never been reprinted as a pamphlet, but occurs on several occasions in books and papers, first in 1908 in the Linnean Society's celebrations of Darwin's birth, and in 1930 in facsimile in Sarton's paper in *Isis*. It was translated into German in Darwin's lifetime and into Italian and Russian since his death.

ENGLISH

346.   1858   On the tendency of species to form varieties, and on the perpetuation of varieties and species by natural means of selection. By Charles Darwin . . . and Alfred Wallace . . . Communicated by Sir Charles Lyell . . . and J. D. Hooker etc. pp. 45–62 in first pagination in *Journal of the Proceedings of the Linnean Society of London*, Longman, Brown, Green, Longmans & Roberts, and Williams and Norgate [for the Society] Vol. III, No. 9, pp. 1–62 [63–64, a blank leaf], 8vo, 223 mm. Darwin's contributions: I. Extract from an unpublished work on species . . . consisting of a portion of a chapter entitled 'On the variation of organic beings in a state of nature; on the natural means of selection; on the comparison of domestic races and true species' pp. 46–50: II. Abstract of a letter from C. Darwin Esq., to Prof. Asa Gray, Boston, U.S. dated Down, September 5th 1857, pp. 50–53. Dated August 30 1858. Binding: blue printed wrappers of the part. Price 3s. LLS. Note: This is Part 9 as issued to Fellows of the Society who took both the zoological and the botanical parts of the *Journal*. The signatures of the Part are 1–4⁸B–E⁸.   [106 part

347. 1858 Identical with No. 346 except: pp. 45–62 in: *Journal of the Proceedings of the Linnean Society of London, Zoology*. Vol. III No. 9, pp. 1–62 [63–64 a blank leaf]. Binding: pink printed wrappers of the part. Price 2s. Note: This is Part 9 as issued to Fellows who took only the zoological parts of the *Journal*. The signatures of Part 9 Zoology are 1–4^8, and it is printed from the same standing type as No. 346.   [106 part

348. 1858 The Darwin Wallace paper as an offprint. pp. 45–62. Binding: buff printed wrappers. C, L; 1080(4).   [107

349. 1858 Three papers on the tendency of species to form varieties; and on the perpetuation of varieties and species by natural means of selection. *Zoologist* Vol. 16, pp. 6263–6308. Reprinted complete from No. 346 = No. 1700.

350. 1859 [= 1858–1859] The Darwin Wallace paper contained in the whole volume of the *Journal*, being pp. 45–62 of Zoology iv + 204 pp, *Botany* iv + 214 pp, *Supplement to Botany* 171 pp.

351. 1859 [= 1858–1859] The Darwin Wallace paper contained in the whole volume of the *Journal, Zoology*, pp. 45–62, iv + 204 pp.

352. 1887– In *Life and letters* (No. 1452–) Vol. II, pp. 120–125. The letter to Asa Gray is printed in full.

353. 1908 London, Linnean Society of London. In *The Darwin-Wallace celebrations held on Thursday, 1st July, 1908, by the Linnean Society of London*. 8vo, 220 mm, viii + 139 pp, 8 portraits, 2 plates. The reprint is pp. 89–107. Darwin's contributions pp. 89–98. C, L; T.   [108

354. 1930 In Sarton, George Discovery of the theory of natural selection. *Isis*, Bruges, Vol. 14, pp. 133–136, 45–62. Facsimile of No. 348.   [109

355. 1951 New York, McGraw Hill. in Thomas J. Hall *A source book in animal biology*. xv + 716 pp, pp. 607–627.

356. [1956] New York, Scribner. In *The Darwin reader* (No. 1613). pp. 103–119. Darwin's contribution pp. 105–110.

357. 1957 London, Macmillan. In The Darwin reader (No. 1614). As No. 337.   [110

358. 1957 New Haven, Conn., G. E. Cinnamon. In Loewenberg Bert James *Darwin, Wallace, and the theory of natural selection including the Linnean Society papers*. C, L; DLC.

359. 1958 Cambridge, University Press for the International

Congress of Zoology. In de Beer, *Sir* Gavin *editor*
Evolution by natural selection. (No. 1557). pp. 257–79.
Darwin's contribution pp. 259–267.   [111

360. 1960   San Francisco, Wadsworth. in Bernard R. Kogan
Darwin and his critics. The darwinian revolution. xii + 180
pp.

361. 1963   London, Deutsch. in H. M. Jones & I. B. Cohen
Science before Darwin, a nineteenth century anthology. vi +
372 pp. With the assistance of Everett Mendelsohn.

362. 1964   New York, Hafner. As No. 355.

363. 1964   New York, Blaisdell. in Bern Dibner *Darwin of the
Beagle*. ix + 143 pp.

364. 1970   New York, W. W. Norton. Appleman, Philip *editor*
Darwin (No. 1624). pp. 81–97. Darwin's contribution
pp. 83–89.

GERMAN

365. 1870   Erlangen, Eduard Besold. In *Charles Darwin und Alfred
Russel Wallace. Ihre ersten Publicationen über die Entste-
hung der Arten* etc. 8vo, xxxiii + 56 pp. Mit Autorisa-
tion herausgegeben von Dr. Adolf Mayer. Darwin's
contribution pp. 1–13. T.

366. 1886   Leipzig, E. Günther. In *Gesammelte kleinere Schriften von
Charles Darwin. Ein Supplement zu seinen grosseren
Werken*. (No. 1601). Darwin's contribution only pp.
3–8.

367. 1959   Stuttgart, G. Fischer. In Heberer, Gerhard editor *Darwin–
Wallace Dokumente zur Begründung der Abstammungs-
lehre vor 100 Jahren 1858/59–1958–59*. 71 pp. Translated
by Gerhard Heberer. DLC.

ITALIAN

368. 1960   Turin, R. Baringhieri. 125 pp. *Enciclopedia di Autori
Classici*, No. 34. Also contains No. 1562.

369. 1974   Rome, Newton Compton. in *Charles Darwin, introduzione all'evoluzionismo*. 302 pp, pp. 274–299. Introduction by Giuseppe Montalenti. Also includes No.
1563.

RUSSIAN

370. 1939   Moscow, Academy of Sciences U.S.S.R. pp. 239–255.

Translated by A. D. Nekrasov, S. L. Solol' & K. A.
Timiryazev. Annotated by S. L. Sobol'. Collected
Works Vol. 3. L.

Public Natural History Collections

ENGLISH

371. (1858)   [No place, no publisher.] [dropped title] *Public natural
history collections. Copy of a memorial addressed to the
Right Honourable the Chancellor of the Exchequer.* [Benjamin Disraeli.] 4to, 260 mm, 4 pp. Dated November 18,
1858 at end. Signed by Darwin, George Bentham,
W. H. Harvey, Arthur Henfrey, J. S. Henslow, John
Lindley, George Busk, William B. Carpenter and
Thomas Huxley. C, LIC; T.

372. 1858   Memorial. *Gardeners' Chronicle*, No. 48, p. 861. Nov.
27. A reprint of No. 371 and with the same signatories.
= No. 1702.

On the Origin of Species

This, certainly the most important biological book ever written, has
received detailed bibliographical treatment in Morse Peckham's variorum edition, 1959. The first edition also has a full bibliographic
description in H. D. Horblit *One hundred books famous in science*, 1964,
Grolier Club. Peckham considers all editions and issues published in
England of which he was aware, from the first of 1859 up to the thirty-ninth thousand of 1890. His work includes consideration of paper, type
and bindings, as well as giving summaries of John Murray's accounts
for each printing. The bibliography is an adjunct to the variorum text
which shows the great changes which Darwin made to the five editions
which follow the first. The author's minor changes in the printing of
1876, which seem to have been ignored by all subsequent editors and
even by the publisher's themselves, are brought to light, although
Peckham was only able to see the issue of 1878.

Since Peckham's list is likely to remain the standard bibliography of
the work for a long time, it is worth while to summarise here the few
apparent errors which I have noticed in it. These are not surprising in
view of the great difficulties involved, even in England, of sighting
copies of all of the many issues. Within Darwin's lifetime he misses, so
far as I am aware, only three, the 1859 issue of the fifth thousand and the
twelfth and thirteenth thousands of 1872. He refers to the thirteenth

thousand of 1873, but the same issue occurs with an earlier title page. None of these three is mentioned in Murray's accounts. The 1872 thirteenth is the same as that of 1873 except for the date on the title page and the advertisements of Darwin's works. He describes the fifteenth thousand of 1875 and the twentieth of 1878, both of which he had seen, as being identical in format with the thirteenth of 1873. Whereas the latter is an octavo in eights, the former two, as well as the eighteenth of 1876, are octavos in twelves. He treats all the octavos in twelves as duodecimos, when Murray's accounts make it clear that they are octavos imposed in sheet and a half.

He states (p. 9) that editions since 1898 have not contained the summary of differences. Murray Darwins after this date occur in three forms, the standard, in cloth, those in Murray's Library series in cloth, and the cheap in paper covers. All the issues are listed in the printing of 1920, and all that I have seen do contain the summary of differences. Indeed I have never seen a Murray Darwin without it after 1861, when it first appeared. He also states that issues after 1898 are printed from the stereos of the two volume Library Edition repaginated. This is true of the issues which are paginated xxxi + 703 pp., but there are also issues in both cloth and paper with a pagination of xxi + 432 pp; these are the cheap ones which tend not to be found in libraries. His statement on page [792] that in the later issues, from the thirty-fifth thousand of 1888, the thousands given on the title pages are correct is not true because he has ignored the two volume Library Edition of 1888 which is the thirty-third thousand. Finally, he considers only the editions and issues printed in England. Darwin was extremely keen that his ideas should be disseminated as widely as possible by translation, and that the changes in these ideas should also reach foreign editions. To this end, he corresponded with translators and with publishers. Certainly, the fourth American printing of 1860 and the first Spanish of 1877 contain matter not present in any English printing. The early German and French editions also need examination. Although Peckham describes and illustrates the bindings, he does not seem to have seen enough copies to notice even striking variations in them.

Darwin had intended to write a much larger work on transmutation and had made considerable progress towards it when he received, on June 18th 1858, the letter from Wallace which led to the publication of their joint paper in August. His 'big book' as he called it was never published as such, but *Variation under domestication* (1868) represents the first part of it, and his surviving manuscript of most of the second part, *Natural selection*, although far from prepared for the printer, has appeared recently, edited by Robert C. Stauffer (No. 1583). Hooker wrote to Darwin, late in 1859 after the publication of *On the origin of species*, 'I am all the more glad that you have published in this form, for the three volumes, unprefaced by this, would have choked any naturalist of the nineteenth century'.

He started work on the book on Tuesday July 20th, 1858, whilst on holiday at Sandown in the Isle of Wight. The details of its composition and publishing are given in *Life and letters* (Vol. II, pp. 126–178). To begin with, he expected it to be an abstract of perhaps as little as thirty pages, published in the *Journal of the Linnean Society*, but by the winter it was clear that it would have to be a book. In March Lyell mentioned it to John Murray who accepted it in April, after seeing the first three chapters. It was all, except the index, in corrected proof by September 11th. Darwin was still calling it an abstract up until the end of March, and he roughed out a title page which Lyell showed to Murray. This is printed in *Life and letters* (Vol. II, p. 152), but in upper case throughout whilst the original, now at the American Philosophical Society, Philadelphia, reads 'An abstract of an Essay/on the/Origin/of/Species and Varieties/Through natural selection/. Murray thought it too long.

Darwin received a copy early in November; Peckham says that Murray sent it on Wednesday 2nd. The overseas presentation copies were sent out before Friday 11th, and the home ones must have gone out at about the same time because he received a letter of thanks from *Sir* John Lubbock on Tuesday 15th, or earlier. Twenty-three author's presentation copies are recorded, but there were probably more; the twelve which I have seen are all inscribed by one of Murray's clerks and I know of no record of one inscribed by Darwin himself. It was offered to the trade at Murray's autumn sale a week later, on 22nd; most sources say that 1,500 were taken up, others 1,493. Only 1,250 had however been printed of which 1,192 were available for sale, the rest being twelve for the author, forty-one for review and five for Stationers' Hall copyright. As Darwin took at least another twenty for presentation, the final number available for the trade was about 1,170. These facts are at variance with the often-printed statement that all the 1,250 copies were sold to the public on publication day, Thursday 24th; indeed once copies had reached the bookshops, up and down the country, how could any-one know whether they were sold or not. The origin of this mistake is in Darwin's diary '1250 copies printed. The first edition was published on November 24th, and all copies sold first day.'

There is only one issue of the first edition, the text being identical in all copies. There are, however, small differences in the cases and in the inserted advertisements; these points have been considered in detail in *The Book collector*, Vol. 16, pp. 340–344. The book cannot be recognized from the date on the title page, because as discussed below, there are copies of the second edition which are also dated 1859; nor can it be recognized by the misspelling 'LINNÆAN' on the title page. The presence of two quotations only, from Whewell and Bacon, on the verso of the half-title leaf (p. [ii]) is however diagnostic; the only other edition with two is the first issue of the first American and that is dated 1860. Two other points are usually made, the misprint 'speceies' on page 20, line 11, and the whale-bear story in full on page 184; these are not necessary for its recognition, and many more differences can be found in Peckham's edition. Indeed the whale-bear story in full is not peculiar to the first edition, but occurs in all the four American printings of 1860. The single folded lithographic diagram, by William West, is inserted facing page 117. It indicates Darwin's views of possible sequences of evolution, and continued to be used in all subsequent editions. Philip D. Gingerich has used it recently in a discussion of the speed and pattern of evolution at a species level (*Amer. J. Sci.*, Vol. 276, pp. 1–28, 1976).

The book is signed and sewn in twelves and is often described as a duodecimo. The page shape is that of an octavo and Murray's ledger shows that the paper used was sheet and a half crown. In the bolts the folded half sheet is inserted in the middle of the folded sheet; the first and second leaves are signed A1, A2 etc. and the fifth leaf is signed A3 etc.

The identification of original variants of the case is bedevilled by the habit of transferring the text of copies in original, but worn, cases into better cases taken off copies of the second or third editions, which are closely similar. However, examination of copies with impeccable antecedents has shown two variants. These are described under No. 349 and are illustrated in my paper in *The Book collector* (*loc. cit.*); no priority can be assigned.

The first edition, when in the cloth, has, almost invariably, thirty-two pages of inserted advertisements of Murray's general list dated June 1859 and with the edges uncut. I have seen a copy in commerce with [4] pages of Murray's popular works, dated July 1859, following the general works. The copy gave no indication of being sophisticated and was probably a freak. The general list occurs in three forms:

1 With the text of each page surrounded by a frame of a single rule; page [1] signed B; on page 2 the fourth item of Admiralty publications retains the numeral 4, and on page 3 in item 22 the name HARRISON's retains the genitive S.

2 The text of each page is not surrounded by a frame, but page [1] is signed B; on page 2 the numeral 4 is retained, but on page 3 the genitive S has dropped out, reading HARRISON'.

3 There is no frame, and signature B has dropped out on page [1]; 4 has dropped out on page 2, and the genitive S is still absent on page 3.

The other anomalies in the Admiralty list, that is the repetition of number 17, and the number 22 coming before 21, are the same in all issues. This situation would seem to suggest that the advertisements were printed from standing type at least three times, in the order given. I have seen only two copies of the first, Darwin's own, at Cambridge, and one at the University of Toronto, bought in Cambridge but not an author's presentation. Both the other two are found in author's presentation copies, the third more commonly.

Although John Murray was more than 250 copies short of the orders received at his autumn sale, he did not reprint, but asked Darwin to start revising at once. Murray's letter reached the author on November 24th, while he was on a long water cure at Ilkley, Yorkshire. On November 25th, he writes 'I have been going over the sheets'; on December 14th 'I have been busy in getting a reprint (with a very few corrections) through the press . . . Murray is now printing 3000 copies'; and on December 21st 'my publisher is printing off, as *rapidly as possible* . . . The new edition is only a reprint, yet I have made a *few* important corrections'. It was advertised as now ready in *The Times* on Christmas eve and in *The Athenaeum* and *The Saturday Review* on New Year's eve. This would have been quite normal practice for a book which was to have an official publication date early in the new year, nevertheless there are two copies known which are dated 1859 on the title page. The existence of such copies has long been known to the trade, although, from their extreme rarity, few booksellers can ever have seen one. It was customary, for many years, for anyone offering a copy of the first edition to describe it as 'first edition, first issue', and Casey A. Wood *An introduction to the literature of vertebrate zoology*, 1931, claimed that McGill University held them both. It does not and never did. The booksellers were, in a purist sense, right; the new printing was from standing type of the first edition, although with a considerable number of resettings. Darwin himself considered that it was merely corrected, but the next printing, in 1861, was called the third edition on the title page.

The title leaves are the same, and from the same setting of type, with the same misspelling 'LINNÆAN'. The quotations on the verso of the half-title are now three; the new one, from Joseph Butler's *Analogy*, is placed between those from Whewell and Bacon, and the former reads 'WHEWELL' instead of 'W. WHEWELL'. The note of date of publication, at the foot of this page, differs in the two copies seen; in one it reads '*Down, Bromley, Kent,/October 1st*, 1859.', as in the first edition but reset; in the other, the setting is so far the same but '(1st Thousand).' is added, and the whole page is exactly as it is in the usual [second] edition of 1860. The copy at Yale is in poor condition and that at the

University of Southern California bad, but both are in the original cases which are identical with one of the variants of the cases of 1860 and neither has any inserted advertisements.

The second edition, which is not so-called on the title page, was published, in the form in which it is usually seen, on January 7th, 1860. Three thousand copies were printed, perhaps including the few, considered above, which have 1859 on the title page; this was the largest printing of any edition or issue in Darwin's lifetime. It can be recognized immediately by the date, by the words 'FIFTH THOUSAND', and the correct spelling of 'LINNEAN' on the title page. There are three quotations on the verso of the half-title leaf. The misprint 'speceies' is corrected and the whale-bear story diluted, an alteration which Darwin later regretted, although he never restored the full text. This story is not found again in any printing, except in the American editions of 1860, until the end of copyright. It is to be found reprinted in full, however in James Lamont *Seasons with the sea-horses*, 1861, as part of an essay on the origin of marine mammals (pp. 271–285).

The cases are closely similar to those of the first edition, but three minor variants occur. These are entered here under No. 376 and have been described in detail in *The Book Collector*, Vol. 13, pp. 213–214, 1964; the third, with small letters in the publisher's imprint, is later than the other two. Murray's general list advertisements, dated January 1860, are present in most, but not all, copies; in some of them each page of text is surrounded by a frame of a single rule, as in variant 1 of the first edition; in others this rule is absent. The price fell to 14s. Murray sold 700 copies at his November sale 'but has not half the number to supply'; so Darwin started revising again. Darwin received six free copies; one, inscribed to an unknown recipient 'With the kind regards of the Author' in his own hand, was sold at Sotheby's in 1974; this is the only inscribed copy of any edition of the *Origin*, other than family copies, known to me.

The third edition appeared in April 1861, 2,000 copies being printed. The case is the same as that of the two previous editions, but again differing in small details. It was extensively altered, and is of interest for the addition of a table of differences between it and the second edition, a table which occurs in each subsequent edition, and also for the addition of the historical sketch. This sketch, which was written to satisfy complaints that Darwin had not sufficiently considered his predecessors in the general theory of evolution, had already appeared in a shorter form in the first German edition, as well as in the fourth American printing where it is called a preface; both of these appeared in 1860. There is also a postscript on page xii. This concerns a review of the earlier editions by Asa Gray which had appeared in the *Atlantic Monthly* in 1860, and as a pamphlet paid for by Darwin, in 1861. This edition has one leaf of advertisements which is part of the book (2A6).

The fourth edition of 1866 was of 1,500 copies. It was again extensively altered, and it is in this one that the date of the first edition, as given on the verso of the half title, is corrected from *October 1st* to *November 24th*. Darwin's own copy, at Cambridge, is in a case of the same pattern as those of the first three editions, but all other copies, although the same in general, have ORIGIN and SPECIES in italic; the blind stamping on both boards is new and the whole volume is a little shorter. There are two minor variations of this case; the earlier has the inserted advertisements dated January 1865 and the later dated April 1867.

The fifth edition of 1869 was of 2,000 copies and was again much revised. It is in this one that Darwin used the expression 'survival of the fittest', Herbert Spencer's term, for the first time; it appears first in the heading of Chapter IV. In the footnote on page xxii, the name D'Alton, which occurs twice, should read D'Alton both times, as it does in the fourth edition, but the second one has become Dalton. It remains thus until the thirty-ninth thousand of 1890, but in the forty-first of 1891, which was reset, Francis Darwin altered the first to Dalton, so that there were then two mistakes. Modern editions continue to have either D'Alton/Dalton or Dalton/Dalton. The format of this edition changes to octavo in eights; the cases, of which there are four conspicuous variants, are entirely new, and the spine title is reduced to *Origin of species*. Inserted advertisements, dated September 1868, are usually present.

The sixth edition, which is usually regarded as the last, appeared in February 1872. Murray's accounts show that 3,000 copies were printed, but this total presumably included both those with eleventh thousand on the title page and those with twelfth, the latter being notably less common. It is again extensively revised and contains a new chapter, VII. This was inserted to confute the views of the Roman Catholic biologist St George Mivart. The edition was aimed at a wider public and printed in smaller type, the volume shorter again and giving the general impression of a cheap edition, which at 7s. 6d. it was. The title changes to *The origin of species*, and a glossary, compiled by W. S. Dallas, appears. It is in this edition that the word 'evolution' occurs for the first time. It had been used in the first edition of *The descent of man* in the previous year, but not before in this work. 'Evolved' had been the last word of the text in all previous editions, but 'evolution' had been omitted, perhaps to avoid confusion with the use of the word by Herbert Spencer or with its more particular embryological meaning. The word had however been used in its transformist sense by Lyell as early as 1832 (*Principles of geology*, Vol. II, p. 11). In this edition it occurs twice on page 201 and three times on page 424. The title page reads 'Sixth edition, with additions and corrections. (*Eleventh thousand*).'

Three misprints have been noticed in this text, the first of which persists in all British and American editions, except those based on earlier texts, to this day; it is also transferred to translations. The last sentence of the third paragraph of Chapter XIV (p. 365) reads:

'I believe that this is the case, and that community of descent—the one known cause of close similarity in organic beings—is the bond, which though observed by various degrees of modification, is partially revealed to us by our classifications.'

The word 'observed' makes nonsense of this sentence and, as the previous five editions read 'hidden as it is by various degrees of modification'. is clearly a misprint for 'obscured'.

In the glossary of scientific terms, the word 'indigenes' is misprinted 'indigeens'; this persists until 1888. In the Library Edition of that year the text reads 'indigeens', but there is an inserted erratum leaf (Vol. 2, pp. [vii–viii]) which alters it to 'indigens', and it is altered in the text, from stereos, for the second edition of the Library Edition of 1891. The one volume thirty-third thousand of 1888 has 'indigeens', but the thirty-fifth, of the same year, has 'indigens'; this latter form continues in all further Murray printings. Darwin himself uses 'indigenes' several times in the fourth chapter of the first and all later editions. 'Indigens' was used by Sir Thomas Browne and is allowable, but 'indigenes' is what Darwin would have written. Both forms are found in editions in print today.

Finally, in this edition, the opening words of the Historical Sketch read 'I will here a give a brief sketch . . .'. This continues unnoticed through seventeen printings from the same stereos; but it was corrected when the whole book was reset for the forty-first thousand of 1891.

This edition was reprinted, from stereos, later in the same year as the thirteenth thousand, and, again as the thirteenth, in 1873. On the verso of the title leaf of that of 1872 there are advertisements for nine of Darwin's works, whereas the 1873 reprint has ten. The addition is the *Expression of the emotions* in its tenth thousand of 1873. As the first edition of the *Expression of the emotions* came out in November 1872, the first issue of the thirteenth thousand must have been in press before this time, or else the new book would have been added. The issue has no inserted advertisements, but copies of 1873 may have them dated April 1874.

The printing of 1876 is the final text as Darwin left it. Peckham drew attention to the little known fact that there are small differences between the text of 1878 and that of 1872. He knew that the printings of 1873 and 1875 were from unaltered stereos of 1872, but was unable to see a copy of 1876 and had therefore to leave it uncertain whether these differences occur for the first time in that printing or in that of 1878 which he used for collation.

The issue was of 1,250 copies only. This number is as small as any, being equalled only by that of the first edition; and, whilst the latter has been carefully conserved in libraries, no attention seems to have been paid to this one. It does not seem to have been previously recognized as the first printing of the final text, and is remarkably hard to come by. It was, incidentally, this edition which Samuel Butler had beside him when writing *Evolution old and new* in 1879.

This printing is the eighteenth thousand, but, as it is important to know what was the first issue of the final text, it should be noticed that advertisements for *The origin of species* in other works by Darwin around 1876 mention the existence of both sixteenth and seventeenth thousands as well as this one. These may be summarized as follows:

1875	*Insectivorous plants*	advertises the sixteenth
1875	*Variation under domestication*	„ „ seventeenth
1876	*Cross and self fertilisation*	„ „ sixteenth
1876	*Geological observations*	„ „ seventeenth
1876	*Journal of researches*	„ „ eighteenth
1876	*Climbing plants*	„ „ eighteenth
1877	*Fertilisation of orchids*	„ „ sixteenth
1877	*The descent of man*	„ „ sixteenth
1877	*Forms of flowers*	„ „ sixteenth

No copies of the sixteenth or seventeenth thousands have ever been recorded; it is difficult to see from the printing records how they can exist, although they may. We know that the eighteenth was in print in 1876, yet the sixteenth is advertised three times in the following year. It is more likely that the compositor was making up from bad copy.

The title page of this issue bears 'Sixth edition, with additions and corrections to 1872. *Eighteenth thousand*.' What the intention of this change of inscription was must remain doubtful. There are no additions to the text and the pagination, from stereos, is unchanged. There are however corrections, slight but undoubtedly those of Darwin himself. The two most obvious of these are the change from Cape de Verde Islands to Cape Verde Islands, and the change from climax to acme. The index is not altered so that Cape de Verde is retained there in this edition and later issues and editions, including the two volume Library Edition, which was entirely reset. The reason for the change of the name of these islands is not known, and Cape de Verde is retained long afterwards in issues of the *Journal of researches* printed from stereos. However Darwin had no copyright in his *Journal* and only Cape Verde is found in *Vegetable mould and worms* which was first published in 1881. There is also one small change in sense in Chapter XIV. The details of these changes can be found in Peckham.

In 1878, and subsequently, the same stereos were used for the very many issues which appeared, in a variety of bindings. The first one to appear in a standard binding was the twenty-fourth thousand of 1882. All these issues, right up to the last in 1929, continue to include the summary of differences and the historical sketch. An entirely new setting in larger type, was made for the Library Edition of 1888 in two volumes and, after two reissues in that form, the same stereos, repaginated, were used for the standard edition of the Edwardian period. This Library Edition is uniform with a similar edition of *The descent of man*, and the same cloth was used for *Life and letters*. The cheap edition was entirely reset for the forty-first thousand of 1891. The paper covered issues, which have been referred to above, have the title embossed on the front cover, and were produced for the remarkable price of one shilling, whilst the same printing in cheap cloth cost 2s. 6d. Both of these, the latter particularly, are hard to find.

There are two issues by another publisher in the copyright period. These were by George Routledge in the bindings of *Sir* John Lubbock's 'Hundred Books', in which they were No. 88. In the first issue, the title page and text are those of the forty-fifth thousand of 1894, with a list of *Sir* John's choices tipped in before the half-title leaf. Seven hundred and fifty sets of the sheets were bought from Murray and issued in this form by Routledge and Kegan Paul in 1895. The second issue consists of Murray's fifty-sixth thousand, of 1899, and there is no printed indication that this is a part of *Sir* John's series. The green cloth binding is however uniform with the rest of the series.

The first edition came out of copyright in November 1901, and Ward Lock printed it in the same year in the Minerva Library new series. The statement by Darlington, in Watt's reprint of 1950, that his is the only reprinting of the first edition is not true. This Ward Lock, the Unit Library edition of 1902, the Hutchinson's Popular Classics of 1906, and the Ward Lock World Library of 1910 are all based on the first. Most of the other early reprints are based on the fifth thousand, but that of Collins in 1910 is based on the third edition. Modern reprints usually state that they are based on the sixth edition of 1872, but they are actually based on that of 1876.

There have been about 140 reprints in English in this century, many of them in standard library series such as Everyman and the World's Classics. Some are important because they are introduced by leading scholars of evolution and show the changing attitudes towards darwinism over the years; one, the Everyman of 1956, has even had its introduction reprinted by the Evolution Protest Movement. Almost all of them are bread and butter reprints in small type, but at a reasonable price. However there is one spacious edition, that for the Limited Editions Club of New York in 1963; this was designed and printed by the scholar-printer George Dunstan, at the Griffin Press, Adelaide. There are the usual abridged versions and extracts for schools, and even a coupon edition from Odhams Press. There have been two facsimiles of the first edition; the earlier, in 1964, omits the original index and substitutes its own; the later, in 1969, is twenty millimetres taller than the original.

In January 1860, Asa Gray was arranging for an American issue of the first edition to be published in Boston, but two New York houses, Appleton and Harpers, were also considering it. The former got their edition out in the middle of January and Harpers withdrew. Darwin wrote in his diary for May 22nd that it was of 2,500 copies, but there were four separate printings in 1860 and it is not clear whether this figure refers to the first alone. The title pages of the first two of these are identical, but the first has only two quotations on the verso of the half-title leaf whereas the second has three; the one from Butler's *Analogy* was added after Whewell and Bacon instead of between them as in the English second edition. The third has 'REVISED EDITION' in roman capitals on the title page, and the fourth '*NEW EDITION, REVISED AND AUGMENTED BY THE AUTHOR*' in italic capitals. In all four 'LINNÆAN' is wrongly spelt, but 'FAVOURED' is in the English style. The University of Virginia holds all four and their copies have been examined with a Hinman scanner. The texts of the first three are identical, in spite of the statement on the title page of the third, and follow that of the first English. The fourth is considerably altered. It includes a supplement of seven pages at the end of author's 'additions and alterations . . . received too late to be incorporated in their proper places'. It also contains the historical sketch, in its earlier and shorter form, as a preface. All four contain the whale-bear story in full.

The book was translated in Darwin's lifetime into Danish, Dutch, French, German, Hungarian, Italian, Polish, Russian, Serbian, Spanish and Swedish, and has appeared in a further eighteen languages since. This total of twenty-nine is higher than any other scientific work, except for the first books of Euclid. The *Autobiography* also gives Bohemian and Japanese; the former refers to the Serbian, but he was misinformed

about the latter; the first appeared in 1896. Darwin was not happy about
the first German translation. It was done from the second English
edition by H. G. Bronn, who had, at Darwin's suggestion, added an
appendix of the difficulties which occurred to him; but he had also
excised bits of which he did not approve. This edition also contains the
historical sketch in its shorter and earlier form. The text was tactfully
revised by J. V. Carus who remained the most faithful and punctual of
all Darwin's translators. There were also difficulties with the first
French. Mlle Royer, who Darwin described as 'one of the cleverest and
oddest women in Europe' and wished 'had known more of natural
history', added her own footnotes. He was not really happy until the
third translation by Édouard Barbier appeared in 1876. The first Spanish,
of 1877, contains two letters from Darwin which have not been printed
elsewhere.

ENGLISH

373. 1859   London, John Murray. *On the origin of species by means
of natural selection, or the preservation of favoured races
in the struggle for life.* 8vo in 12s, 198 mm, ix + 502 pp,
one folding diagram. Two quotations on p. [ii]. Inserted advertisements dated June 1859. Binding: green
cloth, variant *a.* in spine imprint, upright of L in
LONDON slightly to the right of right hand upright
of H in JOHN. Right hand upright of second N in
LONDON over upright of second R in MURRAY.
Length of LONDON 16 mm. Gap between lower
triangle and gilt rule below it 2 mm. No full point
after MURRAY; variant *b.* upright of L in LONDON
over or very slightly to the left of right hand upright
of H in JOHN. Right hand upright of second N in
LONDON well to right of upright of second R in
MURRAY. Length of LONDON 18 mm. Triangle
gap 2 mm. No full point after MURRAY. Compare
with cases of Nos 375 & 376. Note variation of inserted
advertisements described in text. CD, C, D, L, LNH;
T, 580(32).   [112

374. 1859 [= 1968] London, John Murray [Jonathan Cape]. Title
leaf and pp. 80–82 only of No. 373 in facsimile. '6'
printed in top right-hand corner of title page. This is a
part of No. 1622.

375. 1859   London, John Murray. [Second edition, first issue.] 8vo

in 12s, 198 mm, ix + 502 pp, one folding diagram. Three quotations on p. [ii]. No inserted advertisements. No thousand on title page. Binding: as variant *a.* of No. 373, gap between lower triangle and gilt rule below it 1 mm. Full point after MURRAY. = variant *a.* of No. 376. CLSU, CtY.

376. 1860   London, John Murray. [Second edition, second issue.] As No. 375, but fifth thousand on title page. Inserted advertisements dated January 1860. Binding: as No. 375, variant *a.* upright of L in LONDON over right-hand upright of H in JOHN. Gap between lower triangle and gilt rule below it 1 mm. Imprint letters 3 mm high; variant *b.* upright of L in LONDON over lefthand upright of N in JOHN. Gap and imprint letters as variant *a.*; variant *c.* triangle gap 2 mm, imprint letters 2 mm high, CD, D, L; T, 581(9).   [113

377. 1860   New York, D. Appleton. 8vo, 432 pp. Text that of No. 373. Two quotations facing title page. L; T, ViU, 583 part (19).   [409

378. 1860   New York, D. Appleton. Text as No. 377, but three quotations facing title page. ViU, 583 part (19).

379. 1860   New York, D. Appleton. Text as No. 378 and with three quotations, but 'REVISED EDITION' on title page. ViU.

380. 1860   New York, D. Appleton. 8vo, xi + 440 pp. 116*–121* pp. 'NEW EDITION, REVISED AND AUGMENTED BY THE AUTHOR' on title page, and with historical sketch called preface. Supplement, pp. [426–] 432, of author's additions and alterations. Text not that of No. 373 nor No. 376. LNH; 582(6), ViU.

381. 1861   London, John Murray. Third edition. Seventh thousand. 8vo in 12s, 198 mm, xix + 538 pp. With an historical sketch in its full form, see Nos 380 & 672. Binding: as No. 376; variant *a.* full point after MURRAY in imprint; variant *b.* no full point. CD, D, L; T, 584(8).   [114

382. 1861   New York, D. Appleton. As No. 380. 585(2).

383. 1864   New York, D. Appleton. As No. 382, but xi–5–440 pp. T.

384. 1865   New York, D. Appleton, As No. 383.

385. 1866   London, John Murray. Fourth edition. Eighth thousand. 8vo in 12s, 195 mm, xxi + 593 pp. Binding:

variant *a*. as editions 1–3, Darwin's copy only; variant *b*. as editions 1–3 but *ORIGIN* and *SPECIES* in italic, imprint L of LONDON over H of JOHN, one gilt rule below imprint, inserted advertisements dated January 1865; variant *c*. as variant *b*. but L over N of JOHN, inserted advertisements dated April 1867. CD, C, D, LNH; T, 586(13). [115

386. 1868   New York, D. Appleton. As No. 384. 587(7). [410

387. 1869   London, John Murray. Fifth edition. Tenth thousand. 8vo in 8s, 190 mm, xxiii + 596 pp. Binding: green cloth; variant *a*. spine title ORIGIN/OF/SPECIES/ DARWIN/, two gilt rules at top and bottom; variant *b*. spine title *ORIGIN/OF/SPECIES*/DARWIN/, two gilt rules at top and bottom; variant *c*. spine title as variant *a*., but three gilt rules top and bottom; variant *d*. spine title as variant *b*., but three gilt rules top and bottom. CD, C, D, L; T, 588(7). [116

388. 1869   New York, D. Appleton. As No. 386. CD.

389a. 1870   New York, D. Appleton. As No. 388.

390. 1870   New York, D. Appleton. 447 pp. Fifth edition, Text not that of No. 387. 589(4). [411

390. 1871   New York, D. Appleton. As No. 389. T, 590(10).

391. 1872   London, John Murray. *The origin of species* etc. Sixth edition; with additions and corrections. Eleventh thousand. 8vo in 8s, 183 mm, xxi + 458 pp, Glossary by W. S. Dallas. Binding: green cloth. L; T, 592 part (3). [117

392. 1872   London, John Murray. As No. 391, but twelfth thousand. CD, L; T, 592 part (3). [118

393. 1872   London, John Murray. As No. 392, but thirteenth thousand. T, 592 part (3). [119

394. 1872   New York, D. Appleton. As No. 390. 593(5).

395. 1872   Philadelphia, J. Wanamaker. 2 vols. 592(2). [Date doubtful, perhaps later.]

396. 1873   London, John Murray. As No. 393, still thirteenth thousand. T. [120

397. 1873   New York, D. Appleton. New edition from the sixth English edition. xxi + 458 pp. From stereos of No. 391. 598(7). [412

398. 1875   London, John Murray. As No. 396, but fifteenth thousand and 8vo in 12s. Binding: green cloth, top and bottom rolls leaf type. T. [121

399. 1875 New York, D. Appleton. As No. 397. 599(7).

400. 1876 New York, D. Appleton. As No. 399.

401. 1876 London, John Murray. Sixth edition, with additions and corrections to 1872. As No. 398, but eighteenth thousand, and with slight textual changes. This is the first issue of the final definitive text. Binding: as No. 398. C; T, 600(3). [122

402. 1877 New York, D. Appleton. As No. 400. 601(4).

403. 1878 London, John Murray. As No. 401, but twentieth thousand. T. [123

404. 1878 New York, D. Appleton. As No. 402. 602(7).

405. 1880 London, John Murray. As No. 403, but twenty-second thousand. T, 603(3). [124

406. 1881 New York, D. Appleton. As No. 404. 604(5). [413

407. 1882 London, John Murray. As No. 405, but twenty-fourth thousand, and 8vo in 8s. 17 titles on verso of title leaf. Binding: standard green cloth. June. T, 605 part (3).

[125

408. 1882 London, John Murray. As No. 407, and twenty-fourth thousand, but 19 titles on verso of title leaf. December. T, 605 part (3). [126

409. 1882 New York, D. Appleton. As No. 406. 606(1).

410. 1883 London, John Murray, Thirty-seventh thousand. See No. 427.

411. 1883 New York, D. Appleton. As No. 409. 607(8).

412. 1884 London, John Murray. As No. 408, but twenty-sixth thousand. LNH; T. [127

413. 1884 New York, D. Appleton. As No. 411. 608(2).

414. 1884 New York, J. Fitzgerald. 2 parts, 1–130, 131–253 pp, also paginated 441–693. Humboldt Library, Library of Popular Science Nos 58–59. Binding: blue paper wrappers. July & August. T, 609 part (5).

415. 1884 New York, Humboldt Publishing Co. As No. 414, but another issue. Binding: yellow paper wrappers. T, 609 part (5).

416. 1885 London, John Murray. As No. 412, but twenty-eighth thousand. T. [128

417. 1886 London, John Murray. As No. 416, but thirtieth thousand. T. [129

418. 1886 New York, D. Appleton. 2 vols in 1. 614(3).

419. 1886 New York, John B. Alden. With *The descent of man*. 2 vols in one. The principal works of Charles Darwin.

Spine title Darwin's Selected Works. = No. 962.
612(2), 772(4).

420. [1886] New York, John B. Alden. xix + 501 pp. 613(1) ?=
No. 419.

421. 1887 New York, D. Appleton. As No. 418. 615(3).

422. 1888 London, John Murray. 2 vols. Thirty-third thousand.
First issue of Library Edition. In spite of the thirty-
third thousand, this is a different edition from No. 423.
Binding: grey-green cloth, uniform with Nos 965 and
1452. L; T, 616(9).   [130

423. 1888 London, John Murray. As No. 417. Thirty-third
thousand. In spite of this a different edition. T.   [131

424. 1888 London, John Murray. As No. 423, but thirty-fifth
thousand. ViU.   [132

425. 1888 New York, D. Appleton. As No. 421. 617(2).

426. 1889 London, John Murray. As No. 424, but thirty-seventh
thousand. T.   [133

427. 1883 [=? 1889] London, John Murray. As No. 426, and thirty-
seventh thousand, but 1883 on title page with '3' in
wrong fount. T.

428. 1889 New York, D. Appleton. 2 vols. U.S.A. edition of No.
422 and from stereos. 619(5).

429. 1890 New York, D. Appleton. 2 vols in one. As No. 428.
626(5).   [414

430. [189-] Boston, Estes and Lauriat. xix + 501 pp. Roxburghe
Classics. 602(2).

431. [189-] New York, American Publishers Corporation. xix +
501 pp. Century Series. 621(1).

432. [189-] New York, Lovell, Coryell & Co. xix + 501 pp.
Century Series. As No. 431. 623(2).

433. [189-] New York, Merrill and Baker. 2 vols in 1. World's
Famous Books. 624(7).

434. [189-] Chicago, Henneberry. xix + 503 pp. 578(1).

435. [189-] Chicago, National Library Association. 579(6).

436. 1890 London, John Murray. As No. 426, but thirty-ninth
thousand. T.   [134

437. 1891 London, John Murray. 2 vols. As No. 422. Second
issue of Library Edition. No thousand given. T.   [135

438. 1891 London, John Murray. xxi + 432 pp. Forty-first
thousand. C; T, 628(6).   [136

439. 1892 London, John Murray. As No. 438, but forty-third
thousand. D; T, 629(2).   [137

440. 1892   New York, D. Appleton. As No. 425. 630(3).   [415

441. 1893   New York, D. Appleton. As No. 429, 2 vols in one. 631(4).

442. 1894   London, John Murray. As No. 439, but forty-fifth thousand. T.   [138

443. [?1894] New York, A. L. Burt. xxi + 538 pp. Library of the World's Best Books. ?594(2), 627(24).

444. [?1894] New York, Thomas Y. Crowell. xx + 480 pp. ViU.

445. 1894 [= 1895] London, John Murray [George Routledge]. Title page and text as No. 442, but *Sir* John Lubbock's Hundred Books No. 88. The date [1895] from publisher's records. Binding: red or blue cloth of the series. T, 632(2).   [139

446. 1895   London, John Murray. As No. 442, but forty-seventh thousand. T, 633(3).   [140

447. [?1895] Chicago, W. B. Conkey. 2 vols in one. Homewood Series No. 132. ViU.

448. 1896   New York, D. Appleton. 2 vols. As No. 428. 635(15).

449. [1896] Chicago, Weeks. 503 pp. 634(1).

450. [?1896] New York, Thomas Y. Crowell. xix + 501 pp. Standard Library Edition. 636(3).

451. 1897   London, John Murray. As No. 446, but forty-ninth thousand. T.   [141

452. 1897   London, John Murray. As No. 451, but fiftieth thousand. LUC.

453. 1897   London, John Murray. 2 vols. Third issue of Library Edition. As No. 437. No thousand given. 637(5).   [142

454. 1897   New York, D. Appleton. 2 vols. As No. 448. 636(6).

455. 1898   London, John Murray. As No. 452, but fifty-first thousand. 639(2).   [143

456. 1898   New York, D. Appleton. 2 vols. As No. 454. 640(12).

457. 1899   London, John Murray. As No. 455, but fifty-sixth thousand. T, 641 part (2).   [144

458. 1899   London, John Murray [George Routledge]. As No. 457. [*Sir* John Lubbock's Hundred Books.] Binding: green cloth of the series. From Murray sheets and can only be distinguished by the binding. T, 641 part (2).   [145

458a. 1899   New York, D. Appleton. 2 vols. As No. 456. 642(2).

459. [?1899] Chicago & New York, Rand McNally. 2 vols in one. 591(5).

460. [?1899] New York & Boston, H. M. Caldwell. xix + 501 pp. Berkeley Library. 622(1), 647(1).

461. [?1899] New York, Hurst & Co. xix + 501 pp. Library of Famous Books by Famous Authors. ?595(1), 643(4), ?669(1).

462. [?1899] New York, A. L. Burt. As No. 443. ViU.

463. [?190-] Chicago & New York, Rand McNally. xxi + 218 pp. Alpha Library, or Antique Library.

464. [?19—] Chicago, W. B. Conkey Co. 601 pp. 645(7).

465. [?190-] New York, Literary Classics Inc. viii + 375 pp.

466. [?19—] New York, A. L. Foule. 2 vols. International Science Library. T, 649(1).

467. 1900 London, John Murray. xxxi + 703 pp. From re-paginated stereos of No. 453. No statement of month of issue on p. [iv]. [September]. Binding: leaf green cloth, spine title ORIGIN/OF/SPECIES. L; T, 650 part (2).   [146

468. 1900 London, John Murray. As No. 467, but statement of month of issue on p. [iv]. November. Binding: as No. 467, but spine title THE/ORIGIN/OF/SPECIES. T, 650 part (2).   [147

469. 1900 New York, D. Appleton. 2 vols. As No. 458a. 651(5).

470. 1900 New York, P. F. Collier. 2 vols. Library of Universal Literature, Science Vols 1 & 2. 652(2).

471. [c. 1900] New York, D. Appleton. 2 vols in one. As No. 469, but Westminster Edition limited to 1000 copies.

472. [?1900] New York, Thomas Y. Crowell. xx + 480 pp. 653(1).

473. [?1900] Akron, Ohio, The Werner Company. 2 vols. International Science Library. 644(4).

474. 1901 London, John Murray. As No. 468, but imprint gives ninth to thirteenth thousand inclusive. January. T.

                                                                        [148

475. 1901 London, John Murray. 200 mm. xxi + 432 pp. As No. 457, but no thousand given on title page. November. *Binding: green printed paper wrappers, no thousand given on front cover. L; T, ViU, 654 part (2).   [149

476. 1901 London, John Murray. 195 mm. As No. 475. December. *Binding: green printed paper wrappers, twentieth thousand on front cover. T, 654 part (2).

*These issues were published in paper wrappers at 1s. Some, or all, of them were also issued in cheap green cloth cases at 2s. 6d. Copies in cloth do not give the number of copies on the front cover.

477. 1901   London, Ward Lock. 389 pp. Minerva Library, New
              Series No. XVI. Binding: blue or red cloth of the
              series. T, 656(1).   [151

478. 1901   New York, P. F. Collier. 2 vols. As No. 470. Library of
              Universal Literature, Part 1 Science Vols 1 & 2. T,
              657(8).

479. 1902   London, John Murray. As No. 474, but imprint gives
              thirteenth to eighteenth thousand on p. [vi]. January.
              L; T.   [152

480. 1902   London, John Murray. As No. 476, but title page gives
              imprint tenth to thirtieth thousand. February. *Bind-
              ing: green paper wrappers; variant *a.* twentieth
              thousand on front cover; variant *b.* thirtieth thousand
              on front cover. T.   [153 + 156

481. 1902   London, John Murray. As No. 480, but title page
              imprint gives thirtieth to thirty-fifth thousand. *Bind-
              ing: green paper wrappers, thirty-fifth thousand on
              front cover.

482. 1902   London, John Murray. As No. 481, but title page
              imprint gives thirty-fifth to fortieth thousand. April.
              *Binding: green paper wrappers, fortieth thousand on
              front cover. T.

483. 1902   London, John Murray. As No. 482, but title page
              imprint gives 40,000th to 47,500th. August. *Binding:
              green paper wrappers, forty-eighth thousand on front
              cover. T.   [156a

484. 1902   London, John Murray. As No. 479, but imprint gives
              eighteenth to twenty-third thousand on p. [iv].
              December. T.

485. 1902   London, Grant Richards. 454 pp. Introductory note by
              Grant Allen. World's Classics No. 11. Works of
              Charles Darwin Vol. 1 [all published]. January. L; T,
              658(5).   [157

486. 1902   London, Grant Richards. As No. 485, but second issue.
              World's Classics No. 11. T.   [158

487. 1902   London, Unit Library. viii + 487 pp. Biographical
              note by A. R. W[allace]. Editorial note by J. W.
              M[atthews]. Unit Library No. 3, twenty units. Bind-
              ing: cloth or paper of the series. L; T, 659(1).   [159

*These issues were published in paper wrappers at 1s. Some, or all, of them were
also issued in cheap green cloth cases at 2s. 6d. Copies in cloth do not give the
number of copies on the front cover.

488. 1902 New York, American Home Library Company. 2 vols in one. Home Library, Science Vol. 1. 660(3).

489. 1902 New York, D. Appleton. 2 vols in one. As No. 469. 561(2).

490. 1902 New York, P. F. Collier. 2 vols in one. As No. 478. Library of Universal Literature, Part 1 Science. 662(6).

491. 1903 London, Watts for the Rationalist Press Association. 208 pp. Cheap Reprints No. 11. Binding: green cloth or paper of the series. T.   [160

492. 1904 London, Grant Richards. As No. 486. World's Classics No. 11. Third issue. T.   [161

493. 1904 New York, D. Appleton. 2 vols in one. As No. 462. 663(2).

494. 1904 New York, J. A. Hill. xiv + 435 pp. De luxe edition, The New Science Library [Vol. 4]. Popular edition, Popular Science Library No. 4. 664(3), 665(4).

495. 1905 London, Oxford University Press. As No. 492, except change in publisher. World's Classics No. 11. Fourth issue. T, 666(1).   [162

496. 1905 New York, D. Appleton. 2 vols in one. As No. 493. 667(1).

497. 1905 New York, P. F. Collier. 2 vols in one. As No. 490. 668(1).

498. 1906 London, John Murray. As No. 483, no statement of numbers. March. *Binding: green paper wrappers, no statement of numbers.   [163

499. 1906 London, John Murray. As No. 484. June. T, 672(5).
                                                                    [164

500. 1906 London, Hutchinson. viii + 487 pp. Biographical note by A. R. W[allace]. Editorial note by J. W. M[atthews]. From stereos of No. 487. Hutchinson's Popular Classics. T, 671(1).   [164

501. 1906 London, Watts for the Rationalist Press Association. As No. 491.

502. 1906 New York, D. Appleton. 2 vols in one. As No. 496.

503. 1907 London, Oxford University Press. As No. 495. World's Classics No. 11. Fourth [sic] issue. T, 673(2).
                                                                    [166

*These issues were published in paper wrappers at 1s. Some, or all, of them were also issued in cheap green cloth cases at 2s. 6d. Copies in cloth do not give the number of copies on the front cover.

504. 1907   London, Watts for the Rationalist Press Association. As
              No. 501.

505. 1909   London, Cassell. 430 pp. People's Library No. 73. L;
              T, 674(4).   [167

506. 1909   London, Watts for the Rationalist Press Association. As
              No. 504 T.   [168

507. 1909   New York, D. Appleton. 2 vols in one. As No. 496. 675(1).

508. (1909) New York, P. F. Collier. 552 pp. Edited by Charles W.
              Eliot. The Harvard Classics Vol. 11. Dr Eliot's Five-
              foot Shelf of Books. T, 676(18).

509. 1910   London, John Murray. xxi + 432 pp. As No. 498, but
              Murray's Library. December. Binding: red cloth of the
              series or paper wrappers. L; T, 677(6).

510. 1910   London, Ward Lock. As No. 477, but World Library
              No. 5. T.   [170

511. 1910   New York, D. Appleton. 2 vols in one. As No. 507.
              678(3).

512. [1910] London, Collins. 524 pp. Illustrated Pocket Classics
              No. 149. T.   [171

513. [c. 1910] New York, Merrill & Baker. 2 vols in one. World's
              Famous Books. T, 694(1).

514. [?1910] New York, A. L. Burt. As No. 462. The Home
              Library. 679(8).

515. 1911   London, John Murray. As No. 499. January. T.   [172

516. 1911   London, Watts for the Rationalist Press Association. As
              No. 506. T.

517. 1912   New York, D. Appleton. 2 vols in one. As No. 511.
              681(4).

518. [?1912] New York, Hurst & Co. xix + 501 pp. Companion
              Books. 682(3).

519. 1914   London, Oxford University Press. As No. 503, but no
              issue given. World's Classics No. 11. T, 683(2).   [173

520. 1915   New York, D. Appleton. xxvi + 338 pp. As No. 413.
              Popular Uniform Edition.

521. [1915] New York, Thomas Y. Crowell Co. As No. 472. The
              Astor Prose Series. 684(10).

522. 1917 [= 1916] London, John Murray. As No. 509. Murray's
              Library. Printed October 1916. T, 685(1).   ]174

523. 1917   London, Watts for the Rationalist Press Association. As
              No. 516.

524. [?1917] Philadelphia, J. Winston Co. 524 pp. 686(1). Only copy
              recorded lacks title leaf.

525. 1919   London, Oxford University Press. As No. 519. World's Classics No. 11.   [175

526. 1920   London, John Murray. As No. 522. Murray's Library. January. T, 687(1).   [176

527. 1920   New York & London, D. Appleton. 2 vols in one. As No. 517. 688(3).

528. 1921   London, John Murray. As No. 526. Murray's Library. 689(1).

529. 1921   London, Watts for the Rationalist Press Association. As No. 523.   [177

530. 1923   London, Oxford University Press. As No. 525. World's Classics No. 11. T, 690(1).   [178

531. 1923   New York, D. Appleton. 2 vols in one. As No. 527. 691(1).

532. 1925   London, Oxford University Press. As No. 530. World's Classics No. 11.   [179

533. 1925   London, Watts for the Rationalist Press Association. As No. 529.   [180

534. 1925   New York & London, D. Appleton. 2 vols in one. As No. 531. 692(8).

535. [?1925] New York, A. L. Burt. As No. 514. Home Library. New Pocket Editions of Standard Classics.

536. 1926   London, John Murray. xxi + 430 pp. As No. 528, but pagination of glossary and index differs. Murray's Library. T.   [181

537. 1926   London, Fleetway House. Précis by C. W. Saleeby in *The World's great books in outline*. Vol. 1, pp. 206–213. L; T.

538. 1926   New York, D. Appleton. 2 vols in one. As No. 534. 693(2).

539. 1926   Bielefeld, Velhagen u. Klasing. 61 pp. Extracts, edited by Hans Marcus. Französ. u. Engl. Lesebogen Nos 112–113.

540. [1926] Frankfurt a/M., M. Diesterweg. 32 pp. Extracts, edited by H. Dohmann. Neuspracht. Lesehefte, Engl.Reihr. No. 121.

541. 1927   New York, The Macmillan Company. xxxv + 557 pp. Introduction by Edmund Beecher Wilson. The Modern Reader Series. 695(6).

542. [1928] London, J. M. Dent. xxix + 488 pp. Preface by *Sir* Arthur Keith. Everyman Library No. 811. L; T, 696(1), 697(9).   [182

543. 1929 London, John Murray. As No. 515. The last Murray printing and contains the final list of 20c. issues. T, 698(3).

544. 1929 London, Oxford University Press. As No. 532, but with foreword by Leonard Darwin, and table of differences by Irene Manton. World's Classics No. 11. L.
           [183

545. 1929 London, Watts. vi + 434 pp. Thinker's Library No. 8. Based on sixth edition, see Nos 571 & 572. L; T, 700(1).
           [184

546. 1929 London, George Routledge. 79 pp. Extracts with title *What Darwin really said. Connected extracts from the 'Origin of species'*. Introduced by Julian Huxley. Introductions to Modern Knowledge No. 8. L; 699(5). [185

547. 1929 New York, D. Appleton. 2 vols in one. As No. 538. 701(2).

548. 1929 New York, Book League of America. xxxv + 557 pp. As No. 541. 702(1).

549. 1931 New York, D. Appleton. 2 vols in one. As No. 547. 705(2).

550. 1931 New York, The Macmillan Company. As No. 541. The Modern Reader Series. 706(3).

551. 1934 London, J. M. Dent. As No. 542. Everyman Library No. 811. T, 707(5).   [186

552. 1935 London, Oxford University Press. As No. 544. World's Classics No. 11. T.   [187

553. [c. 1935] London, Odhams Press. 525 pp. A Daily Herald coupon book. Not in commerce. T.   [188

554. [1936] New York, Modern Library. xvi + 1000 pp. With *The descent of man. Origin of species* pp. 1–386. World's Best Books. Modern Library Giants. = No. 1036. See also No. 555. T, 708(38).

555. 1936 Harmondsworth, Penguin Books. xvi + 1000 pp. U.S.A. printed. British issue of No. 554 = No. 1037. L; T.   [189

556. 1936 Pasadena, Quarter Books. 112 pp. Abridged.

557. 1936 New York, Collier. 550 pp. As No. 508. Harvard Classics No. 11.

558. 1937 New York, D. Appleton. 2 vols in one. As No. 549. 710(1).

559. 1937 New York, Collier. As No. 557. Harvard Classics No. 11.

560. 1939   London, J. M. Dent. As No. 551. Everyman Library
               No. 811. T, 711(1).   [190

561. [193–]   New York, Carlton House. x + 374 pp. World's
               Great Thinkers. 703(3).

562. [193–]   New York, Literary Classics Inc. viii + 375 pp. 704(2),
               ?712(2).

563. 1942   London, J. M. Dent. As No. 560. Everyman Library
               No. 811. 713(1).

564. 1944   London, Oxford University Press. As No. 552. World's
               Classics No. 11.   [191

565. 1945   London, Watts. As No. 545. Thinker's Library No. 8.
               See also Nos 571 & 572. T.   [192

566. 1947   London, Oxford University Press. As No. 564. World's
               Classics No. 11.   [193

567. 1947   London, J. M. Dent. As No. 563. Everyman Library
               No. 811. 714(1).

568. 1948   London, Watts. As No. 565. Thinker's Library No. 8.
               See also Nos 571 & 572.

569. 1948   New York, H. Hill, Random House.

570. 1949   Chicago, Regnery for Great Books Foundation.
               270 pp. Ch. 1–6 & 15 only. Fourth Year Course.
               715(2).

571. 1950   London, Watts. 195 mm. xx + 426 pp. Foreword by
               C. D. Darlington. Same setting of type as No. 572, but
               not Thinker's Library. Based on first edition, but with
               punctuation changes, See also Nos 545 & 572. C, L; T,
               716(8).   [196

572. 1950   London, Watts. 175 mm. As No. 571, with foreword
               by C. D. Darlington, but Thinker's Library No. 8. See
               also Nos 545 & 571 .T.   [197

573. 1951   London, Oxford University Press. As No. 566, but
               with introduction by *Sir* Gavin de Beer. World's
               Classics No. 11. 717(6).   [198

574. 1951   London, J. M. Dent. As No. 567. Everyman Library
               No. 811.   [199

575. 1951   New York, Philosophical Library. xx + 426 pp. Fore-
               word by C. D. Darlington. U.S.A. issue of No. 572.
               718(7).

576. 1952   Chicago, William Benton, Encyclopaedia Britannica
               Inc. xiii + 659 pp. With *The descent of man. Origin of
               species* pp. vii–xii, 1–251, 601–610. Great Books of the
               Western World No. 49. = No. 1039. T.

577. [1955] Chicago, Encyclopaedia Britannica Inc. As No. 576. Great Books of the Western World No. 49. = No. 1040. DLC.

578. [1956] New York, F. Ungar Publishing Company. vii + 134 pp. Edited and abridged by Charlotte & William Irvine. Milestones of Thought. DLC.

579. 1956 London, J. M. Dent. xxx + 488 pp. Preface by Professor W. R. Thompson. Everyman Library No. 811. The preface has been reprinted in 1967 title *New challenging introduction to The origin of species*. 8vo, 20 pp, Evolution Protest Movement, Hayling Island, Hants. Notes by Frank W. Cousins.

580. 1956 London, Oxford University Press. As No. 573. World's Classics No. 11. ViU.   [200

581. 1957 New York, Ungar. As No. 578. Second printing. Milestones of Thought.

582. [1957] Chicago, Great Books Foundation. As No. 578.

583. 1958 London, Oxford University Press. As No. 580. World's Classics No. 11. ViU.   [203

584. 1958 London, J. M. Dent. As No. 579. Everyman Library No. 811. T.   [202

585. (1958) New York, New American Library. xv + 479 pp. Preface by *Sir* Julian Huxley. Mentor Books MG 503. LNH; DLC.

586. 1958 London, New English Library, New York printed. xv + 479 pp. Preface by *Sir* Julian Huxley. British issue of No. 585.

587. 1958 Muller. [not seen]

588. 1959 Philadelphia, University of Pennsylvania Press. 816 pp. 'Variourum text', i.e. a comparative text of the British editions 1–6 and [7]. Edited by Morse Peckham. C, L, LNH; T, ViU, DLC.

588a. 1960 New York, New American Library. As No. 585. Second printing. Feb. Mentor Books.

589. 1960 New York, New American Library. As No. 588. Third printing. Dec. Mentor Books.

590. [1960] Garden City, N.Y., Doubleday. 517 pp. A Dolphin Book. DLC.

591. 1961 New York, F. Ungar. Fourth issue. As No. 578.

592. 1961 New York, Collier. 550 pp. As No. 557. Harvard Classics Vol. 11. DLC.

593. 1962 New York, Collier-Macmillan. 512 pp. Foreword by

George Gaylord Simpson. Collier Books HS 34. T, 62–292(1).

594.   1962   Garden City, N.Y., Doubleday. As No. 590. A Dolphin Book.

595.   [?1962]   New York, Modern Library. As No. 554. With *The descent of man.* = No. 1041. C; 67–56018(2).

596.   1963   London, Oxford University Press. As No. 583, but note of editions on p. [iv] altered. World's Classics No. 11. T.   [206

597.   1963   London, J. M. Dent. As No. 584. Everyman Library No. 811.

598.   1963   [New York] at the Griffin Press, Adelaide, Limited Editions Club. xxxii + 470 pp. Preface by *Sir* Charles G. Darwin. Limited to 1500 copies. Not in commerce. Binding: quarter wallaby and wood veneer boards. T, 64–67741(4).

599.   1963   New York, Heritage Press. xxx + 470 pp. Preface by *Sir* Charles G. Darwin. Commercial edition of No. 598. 63–5353(2).

600.   1963   New York, New American Library. As No. 588a. Fifth printing. Mentor Books.

601.   (1963)   New York, Washington Square Press. xxxvii + 506 pp. Introduction by Hampton L. Carson. 64–37704(1).

602.   1964   Cambridge, Mass., Harvard University Press. xxvii + ix + 502 pp. Facsimile of first edition (No. 373), but with new index. Introduction by Ernst Mayr. L, LNH; T, 63–17196(6).

603.   1964   New York, Collier-Macmillan. As No. 593.

604.   1964   New York, New English Library. As No. 588a. Sixth printing. Mentor Books.

605.   1964   New York, Ungar. As No. 578. Fifth printing. Milestones of Thought.

606.   1966   New York, Collier-Macmillan. As No. 603. T.

607.   1966   New York, Ungar. As No. 605. Sixth printing. Milestones of Thought.

608.   1966   Cambridge Mass., Harvard University Press. As No. 602. Second printing.

609.   1967   London, J. M. Dent. As No. 597. Everyman Library No. 811.

610.   1967   New York, Atheneum Publications. xxvii + ix + 502 pp. As No. 608. Introduction by Ernst Mayr. 67–93396(1).

611. 1967   New York, New American Library. As No. 604. Seventh printing. Mentor Books.

612. 1968   Harmondsworth, Penguin Books. 477 pp. Introduction by John W. Burrow. First edition text, with glossary by W. S. Dallas, and historical sketch added, but index omitted. Pelican Classics. Also published by Penguin, Baltimore. L; T.

613. 1968   London, Oxford University Press. As No. 596. World's Classics No. 11.

614. 1969   Brussels, Editions Culture et Civilisation. ix + 502 pp. Facsimile of first edition (No. 373), but 218 mm.

615. 1969   New York, Collier. As No. 606. Fifth printing.

616. 1969   New York, New American Library. As No. 611. Eighth printing. Mentor Books.

617. 1970   Harmondsworth, Penguin Books. As No. 612.

618. 1971   London, J. M. Dent. 180 mm, xx + 488 pp, Text as No. 609 and from stereos, but new preface by L. Harrison Matthews. Everyman Library No. 811. In cloth or paperback; or 190 mm cloth in Everyman University Library.

619. [1971]   New York, New American Library, As No. 616. Ninth printing. Mentor Books.

620. 1972   Harmondsworth, Penguin Books. As No. 617.

621. 1972   New York, Collier. As No. 615. Sixth printing.

622. 1972   New York, Atheneum. As No. 610. Second printing.

623. 1972   New York, Abrahams Magazine Service. 2 vols. Facsimile of Vol. I, 1896 (No. 448), Vol. II, 1897 (No. 454).

624. [1972]   New York, New American Library. As No. 616. Tenth printing. Mentor Books.

625. [1973]   New York, New American Library. As No. 624. Eleventh printing. Mentor Books.

626. 1974   Harmondsworth, Penguin Books. As No. 620.

626a. 1974   New York, Collier. As No. 621. Seventh printing.

627. 1974   New York, New American Library. As No. 625. Twelfth printing. Mentor Books.

628. 1975   Harmondsworth, Penguin Books. As No. 626.

ENGLISH, BRAILLE

629. 1934   London, National Institute for the Blind. 9 vols. From No. 457. LB.

ARMENIAN

630.   1936   Erevan, Gosizdat. 765 pp. Translated by S. Sargsyan.
631.   1963   Erevan, Ajpetrat. Translated by K. A. Timiryazev, from Russian.

BULGARIAN

632.   1946   Sofia, Narisdat. 608 pp. Translated by K. N. Kantardzhiev from Russian. Introduction and edited by N. I. Vavilov and V. L. Komarov. Introductory essay by K. A. Timiryazev. LNH.
633.   1950   Sofia, Narisdat. 2 vols, 751 pp. Translation etc. as No. 632. L.

CHINESE

634.   1903   Shanghai. Chapters 3 & 4 only, as separate booklets. The introduction had appeared in *Xinmin congbao* No. 8, May 22, 1902, pp. 9–18. Chapter 4 may also have been published in 1902 in *Shaonian xin zhorigguo she*, [?Shanghai]. All translated by Ma Chün-wu.
635.   1904   Shanghai. Vol. 1 [i.e. preliminaries and chapters 1–5 only.] Translated by Ma Chün-wu.
636.   1906   Shanghai. Vol. 1 only. As No. 635.
637.   ?1918   Shanghai. Translated by Ma Chün-wu. No. 640 gives this date for the first appearance of their reprint.
638.   1920   Shanghai, Chunhua Press. Preliminaries and chapters 1–5 revised from No. 635, the rest new. Translated by Ma Chün-wu.
639.   1955   Peking, Science Press. v + 436 pp. Translated by Hsieh yün-chen. Edited by Wu hsien-wen & Ch'en Shih-hsiang. LNH.
640.   (1957)   Taipei, Taiwan, T'ai-wan Chung-Hua Shu-Chü. 2 vols. Translated by Ma Chün-wu. Dated 46th year, 2nd month. D, LNH.
640a.   1972   Peking, Science Press. iii + 330 pp. Reprint of No. 639, with same translators. LZ.

CZECH

641.   1914   Prague, I. L. Kobra for the translator. 388 pp. Translated by Frant. Klapálek.

642.   1953   Prague, Czechoslovak Scientific Academy. 392 pp.
              Translated by Emil Hadač and Alena Hadačová. Com-
              mentary by Emil Hadač and F. Hořavka. Sekce
              biologicka 52.2.

DANISH

643.   1872   Copenhagen, Gyldendal. xiii + 605 pp. Translated by
              J. P. Jacobsen. L; 720(3).   [416
644.   1909   Copenhagen, Gyldendal. 512 + iv pp. Second edition.
              Translated by J. P. Jacobsen. Revised by Frits Heide.
              With *Autobiography* (No. 1512). Uniform with No.
              1051. Some copies 2 vols in 1. LNH; T, 778(1).
645.   1913   Copenhagen, Gyldendal. 400 pp. Third edition. Trans-
              lated by J. P. Jacobsen. Revised by Frits Heide.
646.   1935   Copenhagen, Heides Verlag. 394 pp. Translated by
              Fritz Heide. Folkendgave.
647.   1967   Copenhagen, Christian Ejlers. 512 pp. Translated by
              J. P. Jacobsen. Revised by Ove Frydenberg. Uniform
              with No. 1052. LNH.

DUTCH (*see also* FLEMISH)

594.   1864   Haarlem. 2 vols. Translated by T. E. Winkler.   [417
595.   1869   Utrecht. 2 vols. Second edition. Translated by T. E.
              Winkler.   [418
650.   (1889) Arnhem-Nijmegen, E. & M. Cohen. viii + 718 pp.
              Third edition. Translated by T. E. Winkler. Revised by
              H. Hartogh Heijs van Zouteveen. Collected Works
              Vol. 1.
651.   [?1909] Arnhem-Nijmegen, E. & M. Cohen. As No. 650. Col-
              lected Works Vol. 1. LNH.
652.   [?1913] Amsterdam, E. & M. Cohen. 2 vols. Fourth edition.
              Translated by T. E. Winkler. Revised and with an
              introduction by Eva de Vries, assisted by Hugo de Vries.
              722(1).

FINNISH

653.   1928   Häneenlinha, Arvi A. Karisto, Osakeyhtiö. 684 pp.
              Translated by A. R. Koskimies. Kariston Klassillinen
              Kirjasto 42. LNH.

FLEMISH (*see also* DUTCH)

654.   1958   Antwerp, Wereld Bibl. Translated and with a bio-
                 graphy of Darwin by Abraham Schierbeek, 165 pp.

FRENCH

655.   1862   Paris, Guillaumin et Cie. lxiv + 712 pp. Translated and
                 with preface and notes by Mlle Clémence-Auguste
                 Royer. L, LSc; 725(2).   [419

656.   1866   Paris, V. Masson et Fils, Guillaumin. lix + 614 pp.
                 Second edition. As No. 655, but with notes by the
                 author. D, L; T, 726(3).   [420

657.   1870   Paris, V. Masson et Fils, Guillaumin. As No. 656. Third
                 edition. 727(2).   [421

658.   [   ]   Paris, C. Marpon & E. Flammarion. 1 + 650 pp.
                 Fourth edition. Translated by Mlle Clémence-Auguste
                 Royer.   [422

659.   [   ]   Paris, C. Marpon & E. Flammarion. Fifth edition. As
                 No. 658.

660.   1873   Paris, C. Reinwald. xx + 612 pp. Translated by J. J.
                 Moulinié. L; T, 728(2).   [423

661.   1876   Paris, C. Reinwald. xix + 614 pp. Translated by Éd.
                 Barbier. D.   [424

662.   1880   Paris, C. Reinwald. xxi + 604 pp. Translated by Éd.
                 Barbier. D, L, LNH, LSc. Some copies Ouvrages de
                 Darwin.   [425

663.   1882   Paris, C. Reinwald. As No. 662. 730(1).   [426

664.   [1883]   Paris, C. Reinwald. As No. 663. Les meilleurs Auteurs
                 Classiques Français et Étrangers. 731(2).

665.   1887   Paris, C. Reinwald. As No. 664. 732(1).

666.   1890   Paris, C. Reinwald. As No. 665.

667.   1896   Paris, C. Reinwald. As No. 666.

668.   1907   Paris, Schleicher Fréres. xxi + 604. Translated by É.
                 Barbier. 724(1), 733(1).

669.   1918   Paris, E. Flammarion. 2 vols. i + 675 pp. Translated
                 by Mlle Clémence-Auguste Royer. Les meilleurs
                 Auteurs Classiques Français et Étrangers.

670.   1951   Paris, Alfred Costes. xxi + 604 pp. As No. 668. Trans-
                 lated by É. Barbier. 734(1).

671.   1973   Paris et Verviers, Gérard. 571 pp. Translated by J. J.
                 Moulinié. Introduction by Pierre Paul Grassé. Marabout
                 University Serie Classique No. 234.

GERMAN

672. 1860   Stuttgart, Schweizerbart. viii + 520 pp. With an historical sketch by Darwin, in its earliest form, see Nos 380 & 381. Translated by H. G. Bronn. L, LNH; 737(1).   [427

673. [1862–] 1863 Stuttgart, Schweizerbart, viii + 551 pp. Second edition. Translated by H. G. Bronn and J. V. Carus. D; 739(1).   [428

674. 1867   Stuttgart, Schweizerbart. ix + 571 pp. Third edition. Translated by H. G. Bronn and J. V. Carus. D, LNH; T, 740(3).   [429

675. 1870   Stuttgart, Schweizerbart. viii + 530 pp. Fourth edition. LSc.; 741(1).   [430

676. 1872   Stuttgart, Schweizerbart. viii + 584 pp. Fifth edition, from the sixth English edition. LNH; 742(4).   [431

677. 1876   Stuttgart, Schweizerbart. viii + 592 pp. Sixth edition. Translated by H. G. Bronn and J. V. Carus. Collected Works Vol. 2. D, L, LSc; T, 744(3).   [432

678. 1881   Stuttgart, Schweizerbart. As No. 677. Collected Works Vol. 2, L.   [433

679. 1882   Stuttgart, Schweizerbart. vi + 578 pp. Translated by H. G. Bronn & J. V. Carus.

680. 1884   Stuttgart, Schweizerbart. As No. 679. Seventh edition. 745(1).

681. 1892   Halle am Saale, D. Hendel. xxxii + 570 pp. Translated by Georg Gärtner. Bibliothek der Gesamtlitteratur des In- und Auslandes Nos 611–621. 746(1).

682. [1892]   Leipzig, Ph. Reclam jun. 696 pp. Translated by David Haek. Universal-Bibliothek Nos 3071–3076. L; 736(6).

683. 1899   Stuttgart, Schweizerbart. As No. 680. Eighth edition. LNH; T.

684. 1899   Stuttgart, Schwiezerbart. As No. 683. Ninth edition. LNH.

685. 1902   Leipzig, Bibliograph. Institut. 2 vols. Translated by Paul Seliger. Meyers Volksbücher Nos 1292–1301.

686. [1902]   Berlin, Carl Hermann Otto. xvi + 477 pp. Translated by Richard Böhme.

687. [19--]   Berlin, A. Weichert. As No. 686.

688. [1906]   Stuttgart, A. Kröner. iv + 297 pp. Translated by J. V. Carus. Edited by Heinrich Schmidt. Volks-ausgabe. 747(1).

689.   1909   Stuttgart, A. Kröner. As No. 688. Volks-ausgabe. 16–
              20 thousand. 478(2).

690.   1910   Stuttgart, Schweizerbart. As No. 684. Collected Works
              Vol. 2 479(1).

691.   1913   Leipzig, Bibliograph. Institut. 2 vols. As No. 685.
              Meyers Volksbücher Nos 1658–1667.

692.   1915   Leipzig. Ph. Reclam jun. As No. 688. iv + 297 pp.
              Translated by J. V. Carus. Edited by Heinrich Schmidt.
              21–25 thousand.

693.   1916   Leipzig, A. Kröner. As No. 692. Translated by J. V.
              Carus. Edited by Heinrich Schmidt. 31–35 thousand.

694.   1920   Stuttgart, Schweizerbart. As No. 690. Ninth edition.

695.   (1921) Leipzig, Ph. Reclam jun. 694 pp. Translated and edited
              by Carl W. Neumann. Universal-Bibliothek Nos
              3071–3076a, b, c and d. 750(1).

696.   [1951] Leipzig, Ph. Reclam jun. 451 pp. Translated by Carl W.
              Neumann. Notes by Georg Uschmann. 751(1).

697.   1963   Stuttgart, Reclam. 693 pp. As No. 695. Translated by
              Carl Wilhelm Neumann. Notes by Gerhard Heberer.
              Universal Bibliothek 3071–80.

GREEK

698.   1915   Athens, Georgios D. Phexes. 583 pp. Translated by K.
              Kazantzake. Library of Philosophy and Sociology. T.

699.   1956   Athens, Ekdoseis Govostis. 523 pp. Translated by Andr.
              Pagkalos. LNH.

HEBREW

700.   (1960) Jerusalem, Bialik Institute. [xliv] + 375 pp. Translated
              and with introduction by Saul Adler. D; HE64–166.

701.   1965   Jerusalem, Bialik Institute. As No. 700. Second edition.
              T.

HINDI

702.   1964   Lucknow, Hindi Samiti, Information Department U.P.
              Translated by Umasankar Šrivastava.

HUNGARIAN

703.   1873–1874 Budapest, Academy of Sciences. 2 vols. Translated by
              Dapsy László. Revised by Margó Tivadar. 753(1). [436

704. 1911   Budapest, Athenæum. 2 vols. Translated by Mikes Lájos. Part of Természet tudomanyi Könyvtar. L; 754(1).

705. 1955   Budapest, Academy of Sciences. 692 pp. Translated by Mikes Lájos. With *Autobiography* (No. 1521). LNH.

705a. 1971   Bucharest, Kriterion. 207 pp. Extracts only with extracts from *Descent of man* = No. 1087a.

ITALIAN

706. 1864   Modena, Nicola Zanichelli. xv + 403 pp. Translated by G. Canestrini and L. Salimbeni. D. This was a parts issue and D also holds Part 1 alone pp. xiii + 55.   [434

707. 1875   Turin, Unione. 509 pp. Translated by Giovanni Canestrini. D, LNH; 756(2).   [435

708. 1914   Milan, Bruciati. 544 pp. New edition. Translated by G. Canestrini.

709. 1914   Milan, Istituto Editoriale Italiano. 2 vols. Translated by G. Canestrini. With two contributions by G. Brunelli.

710. 1915   Turin, Unione, 512 pp. New edition. Translated by G. Canestrini.

711. 1924   Milan, Bellasio. 469 pp. Translated by G. Canestrini. Introduction by Romeo Manzoni. Biblioteca di Coltura Moderna.

712. 1926   Sesto San Giovanni, Barian. 432 pp. Translated by G. Canestrini.

713. [c. 1930] Milan, Istituto Editoriale Italiano. 2 vols. Translated by G. Canestrini. With two contributions by G. Brunelli. Gli Immortali, Ser. 1, Vol. 3. LNH.

714. 1933   Sesto San Giovanni, Barian. 524 pp. Translated by G. Canestrini.

715. 1945   Milan, Istituto Editoriale Italiano. 480 pp. Translated by M. Lessona. DLC.

716. 1959   Turin, Einaudi. lxxi + 551 pp. Translated by Luciana Fratini. Introduction by Guiseppe Montalenti. Biblioteca di Cultura Scientifica No. 61.

717. 1967   Turin, Boringieri. 580 pp. Translated by G. Canestrini. Introduction by Guiseppe Montalenti.

JAPANESE

718. 1896   Tokyo, Keizai Zasshi. 955 pp. Translated by Senzaburo Tachibana.

719. 1905   Tokyo, Kaisekan. Translated by Senzaburo Tachibana.

720. (1916)   ?Tokyo, Translated by Sakae Ōsugi. No. 721 states that it is a reprint of an edition first published in 1916.

721. 1922   Tokyo, Shinchōsha. 2 vols, 1075 pp. Translated by Sakae Ōsugi. Dated Taishō 11. LNH.

722. (1927)   Tokyo, Shinchōsha. 2 vols. Translated and with a note by Kenji Uchiyama. Sekai Daishisō Zenshū [Complete Collection of the World's Great Ideas.] Dated Shōwa 2. LNH.

723. (1929)   ?Tokyo. Translated and with notes by Makoto Koizumi. No. 724 states that it is a reprint of an edition first published in 1929.

724. (1938)   Tokyo, Iwanami Shoten. 3 vols. Translated and with notes by Makoto Koizumi. Iwanami Series Nos 568–?574. Dated Shōwa 13. LNH (Vols 1–2 only).

725. (1949)   Tokyo, Kaizōsha. 2 vols. Translated by Kenji Uchiyama and Shūzō Ishida. Kaizō Sensho. Collected Works Vols 5 & 6.

726. (1950)   Tokyo, Kurarute-Sha. 795 pp. Translated by Nobuo Hori. Fifth impression.

727. (1952)   Tokyo and Osaka, Sōgen-sha. 3 vols. Translated by Kenji Uchiyama and Shūzō Ishida. Sōgen Bunko Vols 14–16.

728. (1958, 1959) Tokyo, Hinoki Shoten. 2 vols. Translated by Nobuo Hori.

729. (1958, ?1959) Tokyo, Maki Shoten. 2 vols. Translated by Nobuo Hori. ?Another issue of No. 728.

730. (1959)   Kyoto, San'ichi Shobō. 206 pp. Translated by Mitoshi Tokuda. Based on first edition (No. 373).

731. (1963, 1968) Tokyo, Iwanami Shoten. 3 vols. Translated by Ryūichi Yasugo. Iwanami Bunko.

731a. 1971   Tokyo, Iwanami Shoten. As No. 731.

KOREAN

732. 1957   Seoul, Ho Jig Gim. xx + 393 pp. Translated by Min-jungseogwan.

733. 1959   Seoul, Sang'mun'mun'hwa'sa. Translated by Sa'sang'-gyo'yang'yeon'gu'hoc.

734. 1961   Moscow, Foreign Language Publishing House. 616 pp. From Russian.

735. 1970   Seoul, Eulu. Translated by Lee Min Jae.

LATVIAN

736.   1914–1915 St Petersburg [Riga], Gul'bich. 2 vols in one. 708 pp.
                   Translated by V. Dermanis and V. Teikmanis. Fore-
                   word by V. Dermanis. 758(1).

737.   1953   Riga, State Publishing House. 418 pp. Translated by
                   P. Galenieks. Introduction by P. Valeskaln. With *Auto-
                   biography* (No. 1526). D.

LITHUANIAN

738.   1959   Vilnjus, State Publishing House. 591 pp. Translated by
                   K. Bechyus, I. Dalis, M. Naĭkevichaĭte-Ivanauskeie,
                   Ts. Mapyukas, I. Mantvidas & V. Povilaĭtic. Edited
                   and with notes by V. Kauietskas. Foreword by T. Ivan-
                   auskas. Introduction by K. A. Timiryazev. With *Auto-
                   biography* (No. 1527).

POLISH

739.   1873   Warsaw, *Niwa*. 228 pp. Translated by Wacław Mayzel.
                   Unfinished.

740.   1884–1885   Warsaw, Redakcya Prezegladu Tygodniowego. 437
                   + xvi pp. Translated by Szymon Dickstein and Józef
                   Nusbaum-Hilarowicz. D, LNH.

741.   1955   Warsaw, Academy of Sciences. xii + 526 pp. Trans-
                   lated by Szymon Dickstein and Józef Nusbaum-
                   Hilarowicz. Preface and edited by Jan Prüffer and
                   Henryk Szarski, Biblioteka Klasyków Biologii. L,
                   LNH.

742.   1959   Warsaw, Academy of Sciences. ix + 578 pp. Trans-
                   lated by Szymon Dickstein and Józef Nusbaum-
                   Hilarowicz. Preface and edited by Jan Prüffer and
                   Henryk Szarski. Prepared by J. Duszyńska, Z. Górska,
                   K. Kowalska and B. Matuszewski. Collected Works
                   Vol. 2. Biblioteka Klasyków Biologii. DLC.

PORTUGUESE

743.   [?192–]   Oporto, Livraria Chardron, de Lello y Irmão. xvi +
                   477 pp. Translated by Joaquim dá Mesquita Paúl.
                   Biblioteca Racionalista. LNH; 760(1).

744.   1939   Lisbon, Editorial Inquérito. 89 pp. Chapters 1 & 2 only

with title *A Seleccao artificial*. Translated and with notes by Lôbo Vilela. Cadernos Inquérito, Sér. F. Ciência No. 2. L.

745. 1961   Oporto, Lello. 505 pp. Translated by Joaquim dá Mesquita Paúl.

ROMANIAN

746. 1950   Vârset, Frătie si Unitate. 48 pp. Extracts only with biography by M. Prenant.

747. 1957   Bucharest, National Academy. lxxi + 398 pp. Translated by I. E. Fuhn. Clasicii Ştiinţei Universale Vol. 2. C, L, LNH.

RUSSIAN

748. 1864   St Petersburg, A. I. Glazunov. xiv + 399 pp. Translated by S. A. Rachinskiĭ. Censor's permission dated 23 Dec. 1863. T.   [437

749. 1865   St Petersburg, A. I. Glazunov, As No. 748. Second edition.   [?438

750. 1873   St Petersburg, A. I. Glazunov. xv + 380 pp. Third edition. Translated by S. A. Rachinskiĭ.

751. 1896   St Petersburg, A. Porokhovshchikov printed. 3 parts, 539 pp. Translated by M. Filippov. Collected Works. Supplement to *Nauchnoe Obozrenie*, Vol. 1.

752. 1896   St Petersburg, O. N. Popov. xii + 327 + 3 pp. Translated and introduction by K. Timiryazev. Collected Works Vol. 1, part 2.

753. 1896   St Petersburg, O. N. Popov. As No. 752. Second printing.

754. 1897   St Petersburg, A. Notovich. xxv + 337 pp. Abridged by Anna Trachevskaya. L.

755. 1907   Moscow, Yu. Lepkovskiĭ. 431 + 3 pp. Translated and edited by K. A. Timiryazev. Collected Works Vol. 1.

756. 1909   St Petersburg, V. I. Gubinskiĭ. 402 + ii pp. Second edition. Translated by M. Filippov.

757. 1910   St Petersburg, V. V. Bitner, *Vestnik znaniya*. 525 + 3 pp. Translated by A. A. Nikolaev. Edited by V. V. Bitner. Collected Works Vol. 4.

758. 1926   Moscow-Leningrad, State Edition. 466 pp. Translated by A. K. [sic] Timiryazev, M. A. Menzbir, P. A.

Petrovskiĭ and A. P. Pavlov. Supplementary article by
M. A. Menzbir. Collected Works Vol. 1, part 2.

759.   1929   Leningrad, P. P. Soĭkin. 62 pp. Selected passages from,
and from *The descent of man*. Translated and introduced
by M. N. Vinogradov. Klassiki mirovoi Nauki, supplement to *Vestnik znaniya*. = No. 1120.

760.   1935   Moscow-Leningrad, Sel'khozgiz. 630 pp. Translated
by K. A. Timiryazev. Introduction and corrections by
N. I. Bukharin. Biographical sketch by I. S. Kharmats.
Index by N. I. Vavilov. Klassiki Estestvoznaniya. LNH.

761.   1937   Moscow-Leningrad, Sel'khozgiz. 608 pp. Translated by
K. A. Timiryazev. Edited by N. I. Vavilov and V. L.
Komarov. Introduction by V. L. Komarov. Klassiki
Estestvoznaniya.

762.   1937   Moscow-Leningrad, State Edition. lxiv + 762 pp.
Translated by K. A. Timiryazev, M. A. Menzbir, A. P.
Pavlov and P. A. Petrovskiĭ. Introduction by K. A.
Timiryazev, Foreword by V. A. Komarov. Klassiki
Biologii i Meditsiny.

763.   1939   Moscow, Academy of Sciences U.S.S.R. pp. 253–678.
Translated by K. A. Timiryazev, M. A. Menzbir, A. P.
Pavlov and P. A. Petrovskiĭ. Corrected and revised by
A. D. Nekrasov and S. L. Sobol'. Collected Works Vol.
3.

764.   1950   Moscow, Academy of Sciences, U.S.S.R. As No. 763.

765.   1952   Moscow, State Edition of Agricultural Literature. 483
pp. Translated and introduction by K. A. Timiryazev.
LNH; 763(1).

SERBIAN

766.   1878   Belgrade, State Publishing House xxviii + 431 pp.
Translated by Milan M. Radovanovich. D.

767.   1948   Belgrade, Borivoje Nedic. xi + 460 pp. Translated by
Nedeljko Dirac. LNH.

SLOVENE

768.   1951   Ljubljana, Slovenski Knjižni Zavod. 462 pp. Translated
by Ružena Škerlj.

769.   1964   Ljubljana, Dražavna Založba Slovenije. As No. 768.
LNH.

770. 1877   Madrid & Paris, Biblioteca Perojo. vii + 573 pp.
                Translated by Enrique Godinez. Contains 2 letters from
                Darwin not printed elsewhere. D, L.   [440

771. [?1877]   Madrid, J. de Rojas. x + 589 pp. Second edition.
                Translated by Enrique Godinez. 766(1).

772. [c. 1902] Valencia, Editorial Prometeo. 3 vols. Translated by
                A. López White. Biblioteca Filosófica y Social.

773. 1903   Valencia, Francisco Sempere. 3 vols. Translated by A.
                López White.

774. [1908]   Valencia, Francisco Sempere. 3 vols. As No. 773.
                767(2).

775. 1909   Barcelona, Libreria de Feliú y Susanna. 199 pp. Extracts
                only. Translated by Aurelio Medina. Biblioteca Roja.

776. 1921   Madrid, Calpe. 3 vols. Translated by Antonio de
                Zulueta. Colección Universal 434–436, 457–460, 461–
                463.

777. 1928   Barcelona, Editorial Vértice. 196 pp. Extracts. As No.
                775.

778. 1930   Madrid, Espasa-Calpe. Vol. 1 only, of 3. As No. 776.

779. 1932   Madrid, Espasa-Calpe. 3 vols. As No. 776. Colección
                Universal 461–63. 768(1).

780. [c. 1940] Madrid, Ediciones Ibericas. 2 vols. Translated by M. J.
                Barroso-Bonzón. LNH.

781. 1950   Madrid, Bergua. 2 vols. Translated by M. J. Barroso-
                Bonzón.

782. 1950   Madrid, Ediciones Ibericas. As No. 780.

783. 1959   Mexico City, Universidad Nacional Autónoma de
                Mexico. 2 vols. Translated by Antonio de Zulueta.
                Revised and introduced by Juan Comas. 6159678(2).

784. 1961   Mexico City, Orijalbo. xxiii + 409 pp. Translated by
                José P. Marco. Second issue.

785. 1963   Madrid, EDAF. 517 pp. Translated by Anibal Froucé.

786. 1964   Mexico City, Diana. 503 pp. Translated by Santiago A.
                Ferrari. Eighth edition.

787. 1965   Madrid, EDAF. As No. 785.

788. 1966   Barcelona, Bruguera, 668 pp. Translated by José P.
                Marco. Edited by Angeles Cardona de Gibert. Intro-
                duction by D. Rafael de Buen Lozano. Libro Clásico.

789. [1966]   Madrid, Bergua. 2 vols. Translated by M. J. Barroso-
                Bonzón. Biblioteca de Bolsillo. No. 62. 765(1).

790.	1967	Barcelona, Bruguera. As No. 788.
791.	1969	Barcelona, Bruguera. As No. 790.
792.	1970	Barcelona, Zeus. Translated by Juan Godo.
792a.	1970	Madrid, EDAF. 533 pp. Translated by Anibal Froucé.
792b.	1972	Barcelona, Bruguera. As No. 791.

SWEDISH

793. 1869   Stockholm, Hiertas Förlags Expedition. xi + 420 pp. Translated by A. M. Snelling.   [441

794. 1909   Stockholm, Albert Bonnier. 263 pp. Translated by Nils Holmgren. Vetenskap och Bildning No. 1. 770(1).

795. 1919   Stockholm, Albert Bonnier. As No. 794.

TURKISH

796. 1970   Ankara, Sevinç Matbaasi. 469 pp. Translated by Öner Ünalan.

UKRAINIAN

797. 1936   Kharkov, State Medical Publishing House. 674 pp. Translated by V. V. Derzhavin. Edited and introduction by I. M. Molyakov.

798. 1949   Kiev-Kharkov, State Agricultural Publishing House. 443 pp. Edited by G. O. Kobzar. Introduction by K. A. Timiryazev. With *Autobiography* (No. 1547).

Query to Army Surgeons

This is certainly a printed Darwin document and it is the only one of which no copy in its original form is known to survive, although its text does. In the first edition of *The descent of man* (Vol. I, pp. 244–245) Darwin writes, in a footnote, 'In the spring of 1862 I obtained permission from the Director-General of the Medical department of the Army, to transmit to the surgeons of the various regiments on foreign service a blank table, with the following appended remarks, but I have received no returns'. He does not state there that the remarks were printed, but the table is referred to in a letter to Wallace in 1864 where he writes 'printed forms'. The query is extremely important in view of recent evidence on the adaptation of dark skinned races to their environment, although Darwin should perhaps have asked his question about native troops rather than about European. I have enquired carefully of Army libraries but have been unable to trace any surviving copy. The entry here must therefore be conjectural.

ENGLISH

799.   1862   [?London. Single sheet, blank except for appended re-
                marks of 269 words.] No copy known.

Fertilisation of Orchids

Life and letters (Vol. III, p. 274) quotes Asa Gray as saying that 'if the Orchid-book (with a few trifling omissions) had appeared before the "Origin" the author would have been canonised rather than anathemat-ised by the natural theologians', and notes that a review in the *Literary Churchman* found only one fault 'that Mr. Darwin's expression of admiration at the contrivances in orchids is too indirect a way of saying, "O Lord, how manifold are Thy works."'. Darwin himself wrote to John Murray on September 24th, 1861, 'I think this little volume will do good to the "Origin", as it will show that I have worked hard at details'. From a publisher's point of view however the book was not a success.

It was concerned with working out in detail the relationships between sexual structures of orchids and the insects which fertilise them, their evolution being attributed to natural selection. It is therefore the first of the volumes of supporting evidence. It was much praised by botanists, but sold only about 6,000 copies before the turn of the century. The first edition, published on May 15 1862, is, like the early editions of *The origin of species*, an octavo in twelves. It has an inserted folding leaf which bears 'Figure I', whilst those in the text are numbered II to XXXIV. I have not seen any figure for the number of copies printed, although it cannot have been more than 2,000 and was probably less. It was bound in plum cloth, vertically lined and with an orchid gilt on the front cover. It is the only Murray Darwin between 1859 and 1910 not bound in green. There are thirty-two pages of inserted advertisements, dated December 1861. It sold slowly, and there is a later case in a cloth of the same colour but without the vertical lines; this may have advertisements as late as January 1871.

In 1869, Darwin published a paper (No. 1748) which is an English version of some matter which was prepared for insertion in the first French translation of the book. This matter was incorporated in the second English edition of 1877. The text of this was considerably altered and the inserted Figure I is now incorporated. Its title is condensed by the omission of *On* and *British and Foreign* as well as the last phrase. It is an octavo in eights and the binding is in standard form. This was placed on stereos and appeared up to a seventh impression in 1904. The same stereos were used for an American edition, in which country the first edition did not appear. There has been no facsimile of the first edition and the only printing since 1904 has been a recent facsimile of an American issue of the second edition of 1895. Both editions were translated into French and German in Darwin's lifetime, the first French, of 1870, containing the additions mentioned above; it has appeared in three further languages since.

ENGLISH

800.	1862	London, John Murray. *On the various contrivances by which British and foreign orchids are fertilised by insects, and on the good effects of intercrossing.* 8vo in 12s, 195 mm, vi + 365 pp, one folding plate, 33 text woodcuts. Binding: plum cloth; variant *a.* vertically lined, inserted advertisements December 1861; variant *b.* no vertical lines, advertisements dated April 1868 or January or September 1871. Price 9s. CD, C, D, L; T, 1184(29). [208
801.	1877	London, John Murray. *The various contrivances by which orchids are fertilised by insects.* Second edition. 8vo in 8s, 190 mm, xvi + 300 pp., 38 text woodcuts. Half title: *On the fertilisation of orchids by insects, &c. &c.* Binding: standard green cloth. CD, C, L, LNH; T, 1279(14). [209
802.	1877	New York, D. Appleton. xvi + 300 pp. Second edition, revised. From stereos of No. 801. 1280(9). [442
803.	1882	London, John Murray. As No. 801, but third thousand, and half-title *The various contrivances by which orchids are fertilised by insects.* T, 1281(2) [210
804.	1884	New York, D. Appleton. As No. 802. T, 1282(5). [443
805.	1885	London, John Murray. As No. 803, still third thousand. T, ?1283(1). [211
806.	1885	London, John Murray. As No. 805, but fourth thousand. T, ?1283(1).
807.	1886	New York, D. Appleton. As No. 804. 1284(6). T, 1285(4). [213

808. 1888   London, John Murray. As No. 806 still fourth thou-
             sand. T, 1285(4).
809. 1889   New York, D. Appleton. As No. 807. T, 1286(4).
810. 1890   London, John Murray. As No. 808, but fifth thousand.
             T, 1287(1).   [214
811. 1892   New York, D. Appleton. As No. 809. 1288(3).
812. 1895   New York, D. Appleton. As No. 811. 1289(4).
813. 1898   New York, D. Appleton. As No. 812. 1290(3).
814. 1899   London, John Murray. As No. 810, but sixth impres-
             sion of the second edition. D; T, 1291(4).   [216
815. 1903   New York, D. Appleton. A No. 813. 1292(2).
816. 1904   London, John Murray. As No. 814, but 8vo in 4s, and
             seventh impression of the second edition. Binding: leaf
             green cloth. T, 1293(5).   [217
817. 1972   New York, Abrahams Magazine Service. xvi + 300
             pp. Facsimile of No. 812 (1895). DLC.

FRENCH

818. 1870   Paris, C. Reinwald. iii + 352 pp. Translated by L.
             Rérolle. See also No. 1748. D; 835(2).   [444
819. 1891   Paris, C. Reinwald. Second edition. As No. 818. 836(1).
                                                                     [445

GERMAN

820. 1862   Stuttgart, Schweizerbart. vi + 226 pp. Translated by
             H. G. Bronn. D, BS; 1251(1).   [446
821. 1887   Stuttgart, Schweizerbart. xi + 259 pp. Second edition.
             Translated by J. V. Carus. Collected Works Vol. 9, part
             2. L; T, 1296(1).   [447
822. 1899   Stuttgart, Schweizerbart. As No. 821. 1297(1).

ITALIAN

823. 1883   Turin, Unione. 207 pp. Translated by Giovanni Cane-
             strini and Lamberto Moschen. L.   [448

ROMANIAN

824. 1964   Bucharest, National Academy. viii + 489 pp. With
             Cross and self fertilisation = N. 1271 Clasicii Ştiinţei
             Universale No. 4. L, BS; T, 65–86257.

RUSSIAN

825.	1900	St Petersburg, O. N. Popov. vii + 136 pp. Translated by I. Petrovskiĭ. Collected Works Vol. 4, part 1.
826.	1901	St Petersburg, O. N. Popov. As No. 825.
827.	1908	Moscow, Ya. Lepkovskiĭ. 168 pp. Translated by I. Petrovskiĭ. Collected Works Vol. 4, part 1.
828.	1928	Moscow-Leningrad, State Edition. pp. 1–181. Translated by I. Petrovskiĭ. Edited by K. A. Timiryazev. Collected Works Vol. 4, part 1.
829.	1950	Moscow, Academy of Sciences U.S.S.R. pp. 69–254. Translated by I. Petrovskiĭ. Corrected and revised by E. W. Wulf. Introduction and notes by I. M. Molyakov. L.

Memoir of Professor Henslow

Henslow was Professor of Botany at Cambridge when Darwin was at Christ's and they were personal friends—'the man who walked with Henslow'. Later, he looked after the Beagle material when it reached England, and the Letters on geology (No. 1) were addressed to him. Henslow himself had been invited to join the Beagle before Darwin was, as had Leonard Jenyns, the writer of this biography. There is only the one edition which must have remained in print for some time because the blue cloth case is much later than the original purple. Darwin's recollections only are reprinted in Lady Barlow's Darwin and Henslow (1967, pp. 221–224) in full, together with his further notes on his old friend which were printed in his Autobiography. A considerable portion of them is also printed in Romanes' obituary notice (Charles Darwin, pp. 7–10, Macmillan, London 1882) which had previously appeared in Nature; they also occur in Life and letters (Vol. I, pp. 186–188).

ENGLISH

830.	1862	London, John Van Voorst. In Jenyns, Leonard later Blomefield Memoir of the Rev. John Stevens Henslow M.A., F.L.S., F.G.S., F.C.P.S., late Rector of Hitcham and Professor of Botany in the University of Cambridge. 8vo in 12s, 190 mm, ix + 278 pp, photographic portrait. Recollections by Darwin pp. 51–55. Binding: variant a. purple cloth, inserted advertisements dated

Dec. 1860; variant *b*. blue cloth. Price 7*s*. 6*d*. C, L; T, 470(7).

831.   (1967)   In No. 1598, pp. 221–224. Darwin's recollections only.

RUSSIAN

832.   1959   Moscow, Academy of Sciences U.S.S.R. pp. 162–165. Darwin's recollections only. Translated by S. K. Ait. Notes by S. L. Sobol'. Collected Works Vol. 9. L; DLC.

Climbing Plants

A detailed description of the three forms in which the first edition of this work are found is given in the *Journal of the Society for the Bibliography of natural History*, Vol. VI, p. [293]; they are summarized here in Nos. 833–835. All three are from the same setting of type, but the first makes up most of a double number of the *Journal and Proceedings of the Linnean Society*. Copies of it are found with the remaining pages (119–128) discarded, but it can always be recognized by the extraneous matter on page 118 and by the absence of a separate title leaf for Darwin's paper. The wrappers, if preserved, are green.

The other two are offprints, one commercial and one for the author. Both have tipped in title leaves, both are in buff wrappers, and in both the title, and the author and his honours, are the same. They differ in the note on the source of the original, in the imprint, and in one having the front wrapper printed from the same setting of type as the title page and the other having it plain. In the first the note reads [*From the* JOURNAL OF THE LINNEAN SOCIETY.]; the imprint is the same as that of the part, except that it has been reset and there is no comma after Roberts. In the other the note reads [*Being Nos.* 33 & 34 *of the* 9*th Volume of the* JOURNAL OF THE LINNEAN SOCIETY, *Section Botany*.]. The imprint is LONDON:/PRINTED BY TAYLOR AND FRANCIS,/ RED LION COURT, FLEET STREET./1865. The part of the *Journal* and the commercial offprint give no indication that Taylor and Francis were the printers.

The offprint was listed in the *English Catalogue*, Vol. II, under the name of Longmans, at a price of 4*s*. Copies that I have seen in libraries and in commerce have almost invariably been of the commercial form, and the facsimile (1969) is the same. A copy of the true author's offprint was sold at Sotheby's in 1972: it was inscribed 'From the Author' in Darwin's own hand, and had 'W. B. Tegetmeier 1865' on the plain front wrapper in the latter's hand. Tegetmeier (1816–1912), an expert on fancy birds, was an old friend and correspondent.

The second edition is usually described as the first edition in book form, which is a doubtful statement because the first edition was available commercially, as shown above, and, being of 118 pages, can hardly be considered as a pamphlet. It was however the first edition in hard covers and appeared, much enlarged, with Murray's imprint, in an arches style case, in 1875. According to *Life and letters*, it was published in September, but Murray's list of printings in later issues gives November. There were 1,500 copies, and there was a reprint of a further 500 in September 1876, probably the smallest issue of any Murray Darwin. The third thousand of 1882 has an appendix to the preface, dated that year, and a five line note of errata on the verso of the last leaf of the contents. These refer to author's errors, rather than to literals and they remain uncorrected through subsequent reprintings from stereos: this edition is therefore the final text. The reissue of 1888, also third thousand, is the first in a standard binding, but the fourth thousand of the same year and the fifth of 1891 revert to the arches style. It was reprinted as late as 1937, the last of all Murray Darwins, and in this form remained in print until 1965. The first edition did not appear in America, nor was it translated in Darwin's lifetime, but has a recent facsimile. The second appeared in French, German and Italian and in America from English stereos.

ENGLISH

833. 1865   London, Longman, Green, Longman, Roberts, & Green and Williams & Norgate, for the Linnean Society of London. On the movements and habits of climbing plants. *Journal of the Proceedings of the Linnean Society of London*, Vol. 9, nos 33 & 34, pp. 1–128, 13 text woodcuts. Darwin's paper pp. 1–118. Issued 12 June. Binding: green printed wrappers of the parts. This is the double part as issued to Fellows.   [219

834. 1865   London, Longman, Green, Longman, Roberts & Green and Williams & Norgate. *On the movements and habits of climbing plants*. 8vo, 220 mm, t.p. + 118 pp, 13 text woodcuts. '[From the JOURNAL OF THE LINNEAN SOCIETY.]' and '[Price Four Shillings.]' on the title page. Binding: green printed paper wrappers. This is Darwin's paper alone offered commercially. C, L; T, 1169(6).   [219a

835. 1865   London, Taylor and Francis printed. Content as No. 834. Binding: buff unprinted wrappers. This is the author's offprint. CD.

836. 1875   London, John Murray. *The movements and habits of climbing plants*. Second edition. 8vo, 190 mm, viii + 208 pp, 13 text woodcuts. Binding: green cloth, arches style. Price 6s. CD, C, D, L; T, 1125(13).   [220

837. 1876   London, John Murray. As No. 836, but second thousand. LNH; T, 1126(2).   [221

838. 1876   New York, D. Appleton. viii + 208 pp. Second edition revised. From stereos of No. 836. T, 1127(27).   [449

839. 1882   London, John Murray. As No. 837, but third thousand, and with appendix to preface dated 1882. L; T, 1128(3).   [222

840. 1883   New York, D. Appleton. As No. 838. 1129(2).

841. 1884   New York, D. Appleton. As No. 840. 1130(7).

842. 1885   London, John Murray. As No. 839, still third thousand. D; 1131(1).   [223

843. 1888   London, John Murray. As No. 842, still third thousand. L; T, 1132(2).   [224

844. 1888   London, John Murray. As No. 843, but fourth thousand. T, 1133(1).   [225

845. 1888   New York, D. Appleton. As No. 841. T, 1134(9).

846. 1891   London, John Murray. As No. 844, but fifth thousand. T, 1135(9).   [226

847. 1893   New York, D. Appleton. As No. 845.

848. 1896   London, John Murray. As No. 846, but seventh impression of the second edition. T.   [227

849. 1897   New York, D. Appleton. As No. 847. 1136(5).

850. 1901   New York, D. Appleton. As No. 849. 1137(3).

851. 1905   London, John Murray. ix + [1] + 208 pp. Binding: leaf green cloth. T.

852. 1906   London, John Murray. As No. 851. T, 1138(6).   [228

853. [   ]   London, John Murray. Pagination and binding as No. 851.

854. 1929   London, John Murray. As No. 853.   [229

855. 1937   London, John Murray. As No. 854. The last of all Murray Darwins. T.   [230

856. 1969   Brussels, Editions Culture et Civilisation. Facsimile of No. 834, but 217 mm and no price on title page.

857. 1972   New York, Abrahams Magazine Service. Facsimile of No. 847 (1893).

FRENCH

858.   1877   Paris, C. Reinwald. viii + 270 pp. Translated by
              Richard Gordon. D; T, 1124(2).   [450

859.   1890   Paris, C. Reinwald. As No. 858.   [451

GERMAN

860.   1876   Stuttgart, Schweizerbart. viii + 160 pp. Translated by
              J. V. Carus. Collected Works Vol. 9, part 1. D, L;
              801(2).   [452

861.   1899   Stuttgart, Schweizerbart. As No. 860. Second edition.
              Collected Works Vol. 9, part 1.

862.   [c. 1905] Stuttgart, Schweizerbart. As No. 861.

ITALIAN

863.   1878   Turin, Unione, 127 pp. Translated by Giovanni Cane-
              strini and P. A. Saccardo. D.   [453

ROMANIAN

864.   1970   Bucharest, National Academy. xxii + 446 pp. Trans-
              lated by Eugen Margulius. With *Movement in plants*
              = No. 1348. Clasicii Ştiinţei Universale Vol. 8. LSc.

RUSSIAN

865.   1900   St Petersburg, O. N. Popov. 100 pp. Translated by I.
              Petrovskiĭ. Edited by K. A. Timiryazev. Collected
              Works Vol. 4, part 1.

866.   1908   Moscow, Yu. Lepkovskiĭ. 114 pp. Translated by I.
              Petrovskiĭ. Collected Works Vol. 3.

867.   1928   Moscow-Leningrad, State Edition. pp. 183–303. Trans-
              lated by I. Petrovskiĭ. Edited by K. A. Timiryazev.
              Collected Works Vol. 4, part 1.

868.   1941   Moscow, Academy of Sciences U.S.S.R. pp. 35–142.
              Translated by I. Petrovskiĭ. Corrected, revised and
              introduction by N. G. Kholodniĭ. Notes by S. L.
              Sobol'. Collected Works Vol. 8. L, BS.

Memorial to the Chancellor of the Exchequer

ENGLISH

869.   1866   *Memorial to the Right. Hon. the Chancellor of the Exchequer.* [Benjamin Disraeli]. Dated May 14. Not seen.

870.   1873   In letter from P. L. Sclater entitled Transfer of the South Kensington Museum, containing 'Copy of a memorial presented to the Right Hon. the Chancellor of the Exchequer [Benjamin Disraeli]' dated May 14 1866, signed by Darwin and twenty-four others. *Nature, Lond.* Vol. 9, p. 41. Nov. 20. = No. 1766.

Queries about Expression

Darwin states on page 15 of *The expression of the emotions,* 1872, that he 'circulated, early in the year 1867, the following printed queries'. He adds that he had appended in manuscript a few additional remarks on some later copies, and prints sixteen queries with a final note relating to expected answers. In the course of the book, he repeatedly refers to answers which he had received from people who were in contact with non-European races, and, on pages 19–22, gives the names of twenty-nine who had replied.

Five copies of a single printed sheet are known, two and a corrected proof at Cambridge and two in America; they are dated from Down only with the year 1867. Another edition in leaflet form was also printed; this one in America at the instigation of Asa Gray. It can safely be dated on, or slightly before, March 26, 1867, but no copy is known to survive. It is not, therefore, possible to comment on its text except by inference.

Another version was published anonymously in *Notes and queries for China and Japan.* It is in a query dated July, 1867, and signed R. S.; Robert Swinhoe was a consular official and ornithologist stationed at Amoy at the time; the part is dated August 31st, 1867. Darwin is described as 'a friend in England'. This text contains seventeen queries instead of sixteen; the one not present in the leaflet is No. 16 'As a sign to keep silent, is a gentle hiss uttered?', the only query which is about vocalization rather than expression. Five questions, Nos 2, 5, 7, 10 and 13, are shorter, and there are minor differences of wording and arrangement. It therefore differs considerably from the English printed leaflet.

Finally, it was printed in the *Annual Report of the Smithsonian Institution of Washington,* for 1867 (1868, p. 324). This text is very close to that of *Notes and queries for China and Japan,* differing only in minor points and in the presence of americanisms. The printer's copy from which it was composed does not survive in the Institution. The late text in *The expression of the emotions* is certainly from a printed or manuscript copy of the English leaflet, from which it differs only in trivial points.

R. B. Freeman and P. J. Gautrey have examined these five versions in two papers (*Bull.Brit.Mus.nat.Hist.* (hist.Ser.), Vol. 4, pp. 205–219 and *J.Soc.Biblphy nat.Hist.*, Vol. 7, pp. 259–263). They also examined manuscript versions of the questions and associated letters; the English leaflet is reproduced in facsimile in the first paper. They conclude that Darwin was mistaken in saying in *The expression of the emotions* that the queries which he prints there were circulated early in 1867. They also conclude that the earlier ones, up to the autumn of 1867 at least, were in manuscript. It follows that the American edition, of which no copy is known, probably prints the text of a manuscript version, with some americanisms and a slight change in the address. This is followed by that printed in *Notes and queries for China and Japan*, which is also set from a manuscript version, and is the first edition in English, as opposed to American. The English pamphlet then becomes the third printing and that by the Smithsonian the fourth. They also suggest that the Smithsonian was printed from a copy of the American leaflet and that the americanisms can be attributed to Asa Gray, rather than to the editor of the Smithsonian *Report*. Their arguments can be disproved if a copy of the English leaflet, or an earlier printed version of it, which was certainly in print before March 1867, can be found. Darwin's statement of 'early in the year 1867' is at present impossible to reconcile with the known facts.

ENGLISH

871.	1867	?Boston or Cambridge, Mass. ?Single sheet. Printed for Asa Gray before 26 March. 50 copies. No copy known.
872.	1867	Hong Kong. in R[obert] S[winhoe]. Signs of emotion among the Chinese. *Notes and Queries on China and Japan* Vol. 1, p. 105. August 31. Anonymous.
873.	[1867]	[No place, publisher or printer, ?London]. [dropped title] *Queries about expression*. Single sheet, 208 × 130 mm. Printed on one side only. Late in the year. C; ICF, PPAmP [231
874.	1868	Washington, Smithsonian Institution. Queries about expression for anthropological enquiry. *Annual Report of the Board of Regents of the Smithsonian Institution*, Misc. Document No. 86, for 1867, p. [324].

875. 1872–   London, John Murray. In all editions, issues and trans-
              lations of *The expression of the emotions in man and
              animals*. pp. 15–16 in first edition. See Nos 1141 to 1215.
876. 1972   In Freeman, R. B. & Gautrey, P. J. Charles Darwin's
              Queries about expression. *Bull.Brit.Mus.nat.Hist.* (hist.
              Ser.) Vol. 4, pp. 205–219, 1 plate. Photocopy of No.
              873 with comparison with other versions. See also
              Jnl Soc.Biblphy nat.Hist. Vol. 7, pp. 259–63 (1975).

Variation under Domestication

This represents the only section of Darwin's big book on the origin of
species which was printed in his lifetime and corresponds to its first two
intended chapters. A second section, on natural selection, has been
transcribed from the manuscript notes by R. C. Stauffer and appeared in
1975 (No. 1583). The Russian title of No. 925, which is described
below, reads, in translation, 'On the origin of species. Section I.' etc., and
shows that as late as 1867 Darwin still intended to go ahead with the
whole. But, when the first English edition was ready, in 1868, he did
not use the full title.

A large part of it contains detailed facts about artificial selection and
discussion of them, but it also contains, in Chapter XXVII, his pro-
visional hypothesis of pangenesis; one which he thought was new, but
has a long back history. It is his longest work and, being so detailed, was
never a very successful one, selling only about five thousand copies in
his life time and eight before the end of the century.

The first edition in English, of 1868, was in two volumes demy
octavo, the only Murray Darwin to appear in this format, and it occurs
in two issues. 1,500 copies of the first were published on January 30th,
having been held up for the completion of the index. Murray had
sold 1,250 at his autumn sale in the previous year and *Life and letters*
(Vol. III, p. 99) states that the whole issue was sold out in a week.
This statement must mean that the booksellers had taken them up,
because there was no method of knowing whether the public had
actually bought them. The second, of 1,250 copies, was issued in
February. The title pages are identical and neither the cases nor the
inserted advertisements are certain means of distinguishing them. They
are most easily distinguished by their errata. In the first issue there are
five on page vi of Vol. I, and nine in seven lines on page viii of Vol. II.
In the second all these have been corrected, but a single new one is given
on page vi of Vol. I. The two issues have considerable textual differences, and Darwin himself refers, in *More letters* (Vol. I, pp. 320–321),

to one of these which occurs in a footnote on page 404 of the first volume of the second issue. It is a story of the progeny of a hairless dog in support of the, erroneous, idea of telegony.

The inserted advertisements cannot always, as is sometimes stated, be used to distinguish them. In Vol. I there are usually, but by no means always, 32 pages dated April 1867. In Vol. II there is one leaf of advertisements, in both issues, dated February 1868; this is not inserted, as usually stated, but is part of the book (214) and should therefore be present in all copies. Copies in publisher's cloth can usually be distinguished by the spine titling. The cases of both are in a characteristic green cloth, which is smooth, and the top and bottom rules on the spine are in a style not found elsewhere. In the first issue the imprint is in one line 'LONDON, JOHN MURRAY.'; whereas in the second it is in two 'LONDON/JOHN MURRAY.' Copies of the second issue do occur with one line imprints, without any indication that they have been transferred, but rarely. Pairs also exist, with contemporary inscriptions in both volumes, in which the first volume is of the second issue and the second of the first. I have never seen a pair the other way round. The price of both issues was £1. 8s. for the two volumes.

The text was extensively altered for the second edition of 1875, and the format was reduced to the usual crown octavo. The case is in arches style, with 32 pages of inserted advertisements dated January 1876 or later. This is the final text and later issues, to 1899, are from stereos. The case changes to standard form in the fifth thousand in 1885, but I have seen a set of this date, and another of 1888, in which Vol. I is in arches style and Vol. II is in standard, although in both the volumes had clearly been bought together. I have also seen a set of 1888 with both volumes in arches style.

The last Murray edition, which was reset and had the illustrations transferred to twenty-four plates, appeared in 1905 and it has not been issued here since. In America, the first edition, based on the first English, appeared from Orange Judd in 1868, but the second, from English stereos, was put out by Appleton. There has been a recent facsimile, based on the second issue of the first edition, from Brussels. The book was translated into French, German, Italian and Russian in Darwin's lifetime, and into a further four languages since. The first Russian edition, which is dated 1868 on the volume title page, is of particular interest. It is the only work, in his lifetime, of which any part appeared in foreign translation before it appeared in English. Correspondence at Cambridge shows that the translator was sent copies of corrected proofs as they were ready. It was published in seven parts of which four, perhaps to the end of Chapter XV, appeared in 1867; the next two appeared in 1868, and the last not until 1869, because he had been away in Russian Asia. The title is given in full, in English translation, under No. 925 and has been discussed above.

ENGLISH

877. 1868 London, John Murray. *The variation of animals and plants under domestication*. 8vo, 220 mm, 2 vols, viii + 411, viii + 486 [487–488] pp, 43 text woodcuts. 4 lines errata in Vol. 1, 7 lines in Vol. 2. Binding: green cloth, imprint in one line. January. Price £1. 8s. See No. 925 for a partly earlier edition. CD, C, D, L, LNH; T, 1254 part (25). [232

878. 1868 London, John Murray. [First edition, second issue.] As No. 877, but textual changes and 1 line erratum in Vol. 1, none in vol. 2. Binding: as No. 877, but imprint almost invariably in two lines. February. Inserted advertisements often February in Vol. 1, April in Vol. 2. T, 1254 part (25). [233

879. [1868] New York, Orange Judd & Co. 2 vols. Preface by Asa Gray. L; 1255(23). [455

880. 1875 London, John Murray. Second edition. Fourth thousand. 8vo, 190 mm, 2 vols. Binding: green cloth arches style. CD, C, L, LNH; T, 1256(11). [234

881. 1876 New York, D. Appleton. 2 vols. Second edition. From stereos of No. 880. 1257(14).

882. 1880 London, John Murray. As No. 880, and fourth thousand.

883. 1882 London, John Murray. As No. 882, but fifth thousand. Binding: standard green cloth, or arches style. [236

884. 1883 New York, D. Appleton. As No. 881. T.

885. 1884 New York, D. Appleton. As No. 884. 1258(4).

886. 1885 London, John Murray. As No. 883, and fifth thousand. L; T, 1259(1). [237

887. 1886 London, John Murray. As No. 886, and fifth thousand. [238

888. 1887 New York, D. Appleton. As No. 885. 1260(3). [239

889. 1888 London, John Murray. As No. 887, but sixth thousand. T. [240

890. 1890 London, John Murray. As No. 889, but seventh thousand. T. [241

891. 1890 New York, D. Appleton. As No. 888, but fourth thousand. 1262(8). [456

892. 1892   New York, D. Appleton. As No. 891.

893. 1893   London, John Murray. As No. 890, but eighth
               thousand. T, 1263(4).   [242

894. 1894   New York, D. Appleton. As No. 892.

895. 1896   New York, D. Appleton. As No. 894. 1265(24).

896. 1897   New York, D. Appleton. As No. 895. 1266(8).

897. 1898   New York, D. Appleton. As No. 896. 1267(1).

898. 1899   London, John Murray. As No. 893, but eighth im-
               pression of the second edition. D; T, 1268(4).   [243

899. 1899   New York, D. Appleton. As No. 897.

900. 1900   New York, D. Appleton. As No. 899. 1270(14).

901. [c. 1900] New York, D. Appleton. 2 vols. As No. 900, but
               Selected Works, Westminster Edition. 1,000 copies. T,
               787(4).

902. 1905   London, John Murray. 2 vols. No thousand given. Text
               reset, figures now on 24 plates. Edited by Francis
               Darwin. Binding: leaf green cloth. L; T, 1271(6).   [244

903. 1915   New York, D. Appleton. As No. 900. Popular Uni-
               form Edition.

904. 1920   New York, D. Appleton. As No. 900. 1272(4), 1273(1).

905. 1925   New York, D. Appleton. As No. 904. 1274(1).

906. 1928   New York, D. Appleton. As No. 905.

907. 1968   New York, Landmarks in Science. 2 vols. Microprint
               edition.

908. 1969   Brussels, Editions Culture et Civilisation. 2 vols.
               Facsimile of No. 878, 218 mm.

909. 1972   New York, Abrahams Magazine Service. 2 vols.
               Facsimile of No. 895 (1896).

DUTCH

910. [1889–1890] Arnhem-Nijmegen, E. & M. Cohen. 2 vols.
               Translated by H. Hartogh Heijs van Zouteveen. Intro-
               duction by H. Hartogh Heijs van Zouteveen and T. E.
               Winkler.

911. [c. 1892] Arnhem-Nijmegen, E. & M. Cohen. As No. 910, but
               Darwin's Biologische Meesterwerken Vols 2–3. LNH;
               1275(1).

FRENCH

912. 1868   Paris, C. Reinwald. 2 vols. Translated by J. J. Moulinié.
               Preface by Carl Vogt. D; T, 837(4).   [457

913.   1879–1880 Paris, C. Reinwald. 2 vols. Translated by É Barbier.
        Preface by Carl Vogt. BS; 838(3).   [458

GERMAN

914.   1868   Stuttgart, Schweizerbart. 2 vols. Translated by J. V.
                Carus. D; 1276(5).   [459
915.   1873   Stuttgart, Schweizerbart. 2 vols. Second edition. As
                No. 914. L, BS; T, 1277(3).   [460
916.   1878   Stuttgart, Schweizerbart. 2 vols. Third edition. As No.
                915. Collected Works Vols 3 & 4. D, L.   [461
917.   1906   Stuttgart, Schweizerbart. 2 vols. As No. 916. Fourth
                edition.
918.   1910   Stuttgart, Schweizerbart. 2 vols. Fourth edition. As No.
                917. Collected Works Vols 3 & 4.

HUNGARIAN

919.   1959   Budapest, National Academy. 2 vols. Translated by
                Mme J. Pusztai.

ITALIAN

920.   1876   Turin, Unione. 824 pp. Translated by Giovanni Cane-
                strini. 1278(1). Reissued in 1878, with paper covers so
                dated.   [467
921.   1914   Turin, Unione. As No. 920.

POLISH

922.   1888–1889 Warsaw, Redakcya Prezegladu Tygodniowego. 2
                vols. Translated by Józef Nusbaum.
923.   1959   Warsaw, Academy of Sciences. 2 vols. Translated by
                Kasimierz Brończyk. Edited by Marian Michniewicz
                and Henryk Szarski. Collected Works Vol. 3. Biblio-
                teka Kalsyków Biologii. DLC.

ROMANIAN

924.   1963   Bucharest, Academy of Sciences. 772 pp. Translated by
                E. Margulius. Clasicii Ştiinţei Universale No. 3. C, L,
                LNH; 63-48743(1).

RUSSIAN

925.   1867–1868 St Petersburg, F. S. Sushchinskiĭ. parts. Parts 1–4
       1867, parts 5–6 1868, part 7 1869. Translated title *On
       the origin of species. Section 1. The variation of animals and
       plants under domestication. The domestication of animals
       and the cultivation of plants.* Translated by V. O. Kova-
       levskiĭ. Edited by I. M. Sechenov, the botanical parts
       by A. Gerd. Parts 1–4 at least represent the first publica-
       tion of this work in any language, preceding No. 877.

926.   1868 [= 1867–1869] St Petersburg, F. S. Sushchinskiĭ. 2 vols.
       Issue of No. 925 in book form. D, L.   [463

927.   1896   St Petersburg, A. Porokhovshchikov printed. 233 +
       xxiv pp. *Variation* only. Translated by M. Filippov.
       Collected Works. Supplement to *Nauchnoe Obozrenie*
       Vol. 6. See also Nos 928 & 929.

928.   1898   St Petersburg, A. Porokhovshchikov. Printed 232 pp.
       Pangenesis only. Translated by M. Filippov. Collected
       Works. Supplement to *Nauchnoe Obozrenie* Vol. 6. See
       also Nos 927 & 929.

929.   1898   St Petersburg, A. Porokhovshchikov printed. 83 pp.
       The laws of variation only. Translation edited by M.
       Filippov. Collected Works. Supplement to *Nauchnoe
       Obozrenie* Vol. 6. See also Nos 927 & 928.

930.   1899   St Petersburg, O. N. Popov. vii + 572 pp. Translated
       by V. O. Kovalevskiĭ. Adapted by M. A. Menzbir and
       K. A. Timiryazev. Collected Works Vol. 3.

931.   1908–1909 Moscow, Yu. Lepkovskiĭ. iii + 622 + lviii pp.
       Translated and edited by P. P. Sushkin and F. Krashenin-
       nikov. Collected Works Vols 7–8.

932.   1928   Moscow-Leningrad, State Edition. Translated by V. O.
       Kovalevskiĭ. Corrected by M. A. Menzbir. Collected
       Works Vol. 3.

933.   1941   Moscow-Leningrad, Sel'khozgiz. 619 pp. Translated
       by P. P. Sushkin and F. N. Krasheninnikov. Edited by
       K. A. Timiryazev. Newly revised by F. N. Krashenin-
       nikov and S. N. Bogolyubskiĭ. Klassiki Estestvozna-
       niya.

934.   1951   Moscow, Academy of Sciences. 881 pp. Translated by
       E. N. Pavlovskiĭ. Introduction by N. I. Nuzhdin.
       Annotated by S. N. Bogolyubskiĭ, V. O. Vitt and
       others. Collected Works Vol. 4. L.

Discourse to the Plinian Society

The Plinian Society was a student natural history society in the University of Edinburgh, founded by Professor Robert Jameson in 1823. Darwin was elected a member on November 28, 1826. Its minute book, in the University Library, shows that he attended eighteen out of nineteen possible meetings and took part in discussions. He addressed the Society once, on March 27, 1827, on two observations on sea-shore animals.—1. That the ova of *Flustra* possess organs of motion, 2. that the small black globular body hitherto mistaken for the young of *Fucus loreus* is in reality the ovum of *Pontobdella muricata*.

He had been in the habit of examining shore animals, particularly in the company of Robert Edmond Grant, and the discourse was the result of this work. Grant published papers on both these animals, that on the polyzoan in the *Edinburgh new Philosophical Journal*, Vol. 3, pp. 107–118, 337–342, 1827, and that on the leech in the *Edinburgh Journal of Science*, Vol. 7, pp. 161–162, 1827, in which he acknowledges Darwin. The ova of *Flustra* are not in fact eggs but pilidium larvae, and those of *Pontobdella* are cocoons full of eggs. The second observation was not new; Sir John Dalyell had illustrated the life cycle in a fine water colour dated July 1823 which is reproduced, as Plate 1, in the second volume of *The powers of the Creator displayed in the creation*, (3 vols, 1851–58).

The Society did not print its communications, but it is noticed by Sir Walter Elliot in a presidential address of 1870. Darwin's own annotated copy of this notice is at Cambridge. It is mentioned in his *Autobiography*, and can be found, with two photographs of holograph from Darwin's notebook, in a paper by J. H. Ashworth (Nos 1570 & 1749). Nos 1573 and 1764 also refer to it.

ENGLISH

935.   1870   In Elliot, *Sir* Walter Opening address by the President. *Trans.bot.Soc.Edinb.*, Vol. 11, pp. 1–42, for 1870–74. Footnote p. 17. In *Proc.* for Nov., 1870.

The Descent of Man

Darwin wrote, in the preface to the second edition, of 'the fiery ordeal through which this book has passed'. He had avoided the logical outcome of the general theory of evolution, bringing man into the scheme, for twelve years, and in fact it had, by that time, been so much accepted that the clamour of the opposition was not strident. He had also been preceded in 1862 by Huxley's *Man's place in nature*. The book, in its first edition, contains two parts, the descent of man itself, and selection in relation to sex. The word 'evolution' occurs, for the first time in any of Darwin's works, on page 2 of the first volume of the first edition, that is to say before its appearance in the sixth edition of *The origin of species* in the following year. The last chapter is about sexual selection in relation to man, and it ends with the famous peroration about man's lowly origin, the wording of which differs slightly in the first edition from that which is usually quoted. In a letter dated March 28, 1871 (*Emma Darwin*, Vol. II, pp. 202–203) Darwin mentions the help that his daughter Henrietta Emma had given him in reading the manuscript and correcting the style, and calls her 'my very dear coadjutor and fellow-labourer'.

The first edition is in two volumes and occurs in two issues which can not be distinguished by their title pages, inserted advertisements or bindings. They have, however, important textual differences. The first issue can be recognized by the errata on the verso of the title leaf of Volume II, seventeen errata for Volume I and eight for Volume II. The verso of the title leaf of Volume II of the second issue has a list of nine other works by Darwin and no errata. The verso of the half title leaf of Volume II of the first issue bears the printer's note, but it is blank in the second. The first issue has a note on a tipped in leaf (pp. [ix–x]) in Volume II which refers to 'a serious and unfortunate error' which affects pages 297–299 in Volume I, and pages 161 and 237 in Volume II. In the second issue this leaf is absent and the relevant pages have been entirely reset. The easiest way to distinguish the two issues of Volume I alone is to look at the first word on page 297. It is 'transmitted' in the first issue and 'When' in the second. Both issues have sixteen pages of inserted advertisements for Murray's popular works in Volume I, and sixteen pages of Murray's standard works in Volume II, all dated January 1871. The first issue, of 2,500 copies, was published on February 24, and the second, of 2,000 copies, in March. Both cost £1. 4s. and were in standard bindings. The end-papers of the first issue are invariably, in my experience, dark green almost black; whilst those of the second may be the same, or dark brown.

The above descriptions refer to ordinary trade copies. Darwin's own copy of Volume I of the first issue, now at Cambridge, differs in three points and is, in my experience, unique. Firstly, it is dated 1870 on the title page; secondly the wording on the title page differs slightly from that of the trade edition; and thirdly the spine gilding of the case differs. These points are summarized under No. 936. It is known that Wallace received his complimentary copy late in 1870, and other complimentaries may have gone out at the same time, so that other copies like Darwin's own may exist. The presentation copy to William Boyd Dawkins, however, is dated February 17. In the first American edition, which is not printed from English stereos, Volume I is based on the first issue text and Volume II on the second. Volume II gives sixteen errata for Volume I, the compositor having noticed 'dragon-flys' (p. 344) as being wrong, and none for Volume II. The passage about the serious error is retained, except for that part which refers to pages 161 and 237 of Volume II. I have seen a copy of Volume I which is dated February 25, so that it is probable that the two volumes were not issued together. There is a second American issue of Volume I which follows the text of the English second.

There were two further issues of the two volume English edition, in April and in December of 1871, the seventh and eighth thousands. Small changes were made in the texts of each, and Darwin remarks, in the preface to the second edition, 'during the successive reprints of the first edition of this work . . . I was able to introduce several important corrections'.

The second edition of 1874, the tenth thousand, is in one volume in three parts, instead of the two of the first, sexual selection in relation to man being separated off as the third part. It is extensively revised and contains a note on the brains of man and apes by T. H. Huxley at pp. 199–206, and a five line errata slip. This and the subsequent four printings are octavos in twelves, whilst that of 1882 becomes an octavo in eights; all are in standard bindings. The eleventh thousand of 1875 has the errata corrected as well as small textual changes. The twelfth thousand of 1877 has added at the end, pp. 620–624, a supplemental note which is reprinted from *Nature* of November 2 1876, p. 18. This is the final definitive text, and subsequent one volume issues until the turn of the century are from stereos of it.

In 1888, there was an entirely new printing in two volumes, the Library Edition, uniform with the similar edition of *The origin of species* printed in the same year. This had two later issues, and the same stereos, repaginated, were then used for the one volume issues of the Edwardian period. Although not nearly so much in demand as *The origin of species*, the work has appeared in a number of library series, especially in America, and has been almost continuously in print, either in full or abridged; it has also appeared in combination volumes with *The origin of species*. There is a Brussels facsimile of the seventh thousand in 1969, and a New York one of the second edition in 1974, but no facsimile of the first issue of the first edition has yet appeared. The Limited Editions

Club of New York issued a handsome quarto in 1971, which, like their *Origin of species*, was produced by the Griffin Press, Adelaide: unfortunately it omits the parts on selection in relation to sex and is therefore useless as a text.

It was translated into Danish, Dutch, French, German, Italian, Polish, Russian and Swedish in Darwin's lifetime and into ten further languages since. These include two in Yiddish, one from America and one from Poland, the only Darwins in this language.

ENGLISH

936. 1870, 1871 London, John Murray. *The descent of man, and selection in relation to sex.* 8vo, 2 vols, Vol. 1 190 mm, Vol. 2 185 mm, 76 text woodcuts. 25 errata on verso of title leaf to Vol. 2. Title page of Vol. 1 reads WITH/ILLUSTRATION./IN TWO VOLUMES.—VOL. I. Binding: Vol. 1 as Vol. 2 but gilt rules below and above the ornamental rules on spine; Vol. 2 standard green cloth. Price £1. 4s. CD. Note: known only from Darwin's own copy. Vol. 2 is identical with Vol. 2 of No. 937.

937. 1871 London, John Murray. All as No. 936, except date of Vol. 1, title page of Vol. 1 reads IN TWO VOLUMES.—VOL. I/WITH ILLUSTRATIONS. Page heights may be 190 or 185 mm. Binding: both volumes standard green cloth, with 195 or 190 board height. [February]. CD, C, D, L, LNH; T, 457 part (28).
[245

938. 1871 London, John Murray. All as No. 937 and page heights 190 or 185 mm, but textual changes, and works by the same author on verso of title leaf of Vol. 2. Binding: as No. 937 including two board heights. [March.] CD; T, 457 part (28).
[246

939. 1871 London, John Murray. All as No. 938, but seventh thousand and text changes. [April.] T.
[247

940. 1871 London, John Murray. All as No. 939, but eighth thousand and text changes. [December.]
[248

941. 1871 New York, D. Appleton. 2 vols. Vol. 1 based on No. 937, Vol. 2 on No. 938. T, 460 part (20).
[464 part

942. 1871 New York, D. Appleton. 2 vols. Both based on No. 938. T, 460 part (20).
[464 part

943. 1872 New York, D. Appleton. As No. 942. 461(11).
[465

944.   1874   London, John Murray. Second edition, tenth thousand.
              8vo in 12s, 185 mm, xvi + 688 pp. Note by T. H.
              Huxley pp. 199–206. Five line errata slip. Binding: as
              No. 940. CD, C, L; T, 463(5).   [249

945.   1875   London, John Murray. As No. 944, but eleventh
              thousand, errata corrected and text changes. D; T,
              475(2).   [250

946.   1875   New York, D. Appleton. xvi + 688 pp. From stereos
              of No. 944. 474(7).   [470

947.   1876   New York, D. Appleton. As No. 946. 476(2).

948.   1877   London, John Murray. 8vo in 12s. xvi + 693 pp.
              Twelfth thousand, revised and augmented. Contains
              No. 1773. Binding: as No. 945. T, 477(1).   [251

949.   1877   New York, D. Appleton. 2 vols. ?As No. 947. 478(1).

950.   1878   New York, D. Appleton. As No. 947. 479(1).

951.   1879   London, John Murray. As No. 948, but thirteenth
              thousand. T, 482(1).   [252

952.   1879   New York, D. Appleton. As No. 950. 481(3).

953.   1881   London, John Murray. As No. 951, but fourteenth
              thousand. T, 482(1).   [253

954.   1881   New York, D. Appleton. As No. 952. T.

955.   1882   London, John Murray. As No. 953, but 8vo in 8s and
              fifteenth thousand. CD; T, 483(6).   [254

956.   1882   New York, D. Appleton. As No. 954. 484(5).

957.   1883   London, John Murray. As No. 955, but seventeenth
              thousand L, LNH; T, 485(2).   [255

958.   1883   New York, D. Appleton. As No. 956. 486(5).

959.   1885   London, John Murray. As No. 957, but nineteenth
              thousand. T, 487(3).   [256

960.   1885–1886 New York, Humboldt Publishing Co. 4 parts.
              Humboldt Library of Science Nos 74–77. 488(5). Un-
              dated issues occur.

961.   1886   New York, D. Appleton. As No. 958, called new
              edition. 489(3).

962.   1886   New York, John B. Alden. With *Origin of species*, 2
              vols in one. The principal works of Charles Darwin.
              Spine title Darwin's Select Works. = No. 419. 612(2),
              772(4).

963.   1887   London, John Murray. As No. 959, but twenty-first
              thousand. T.   [257

964.   1888   London, John Murray. As No. 963 and twenty-first
              thousand. T.   [258

965. 1888   London, John Murray. 2 vols. Twenty-second thous-
            and. First issue of Library Edition. Binding: grey-green
            cloth, Uniform with Nos 422 & 1452. L; T, 490(7).
                                                              [259

966. 1888   London, John Murray. As No. 964, but twenty-third
            thousand. T.   [260

967. 1888   New York, D. Appleton. As No. 961. 491(7).

968. 1889   London, John Murray. As No. 966, but twenty-fifth
            thousand. T, 492(3).   [261

969. 1889   New York, D. Appleton. As No. 967. 493(1).

970. 1890   London, John Murray. As No. 968, but twenty-
            seventh thousand. T, 494 part (2).   [262

971. 1890   London, John Murray. As No. 970, but twenty-ninth
            thousand. T, 494 part (2).   [263

972. 1890   London, John Murray. As No. 971, but no thousand
            given and called new edition. 494 part (2).   [264

973. 1890   New York, A. L. Burt. vii + 797 pp. The Home
            Library. 495(2).

974. 1891   London, John Murray. 2 vols. Second issue of Library
            Edition. Twenty-third thousand [sic]. As No. 965. D;
            T, 496(6).   [265

975. 1892   New York, D. Appleton. As No. 969. 497(3).

976. 1894   London, John Murray. As No. 972, but thirty-first
            thousand. T.   [267

977. 1895   New York, D. Appleton. As No. 975. 498(1).

978. [1895] New York, Thomas Y. Crowell. 705 pp. Standard
            Library.

979. 1896   London, John Murray. As No. 976, but thirty-third
            thousand. L; T, 499(2).   [268

980. [?1896] New York, American Publishers Corporation. 705 pp.
            Century edition.

981. 1896   New York, D. Appleton. As No. 977. 500(21).

982. 1897   New York, D. Appleton. As No. 981. 501(5).

983. 1898   London, John Murray. 2 vols. Third issue of Library
            Edition. As No. 974, but no thousand given. T.   [269

984. 1898   New York, D. Appleton. As No. 982. 503(3).

985. 1899   London, John Murray. As No. 979, but thirty-fifth
            thousand. T.   [270

986. 1899   London, E. Lloyd. Chapter 21 only in *The International
            Library of Famous Literature*. Vol. XIII, pp. 5931–5945.
            Edited by Richard Garnett, Leon Vallée, A. Brandt and
            D. G. Mitchell, L; T.

987. 1899   New York, D. Appleton. As No. 984. 505(8).
988. [?189–]   New York, A. L. Burt. As No. 973, but Library the of
                  World's Best Books. 465(26).
989. [?189–]   New York, Caldwell. xii + 672 pp. Library of Famous
                  Books by Famous Authors. 466(2), 502(1).
990. [?189–]   New York, Caldwell. 705 pp. Berkeley Library. 469(3).
991. [?189–]   New York, Caldwell. 705 pp. As No. 990, but Athen-
                  aeum Library.
992. [?189–]   New York, Hurst & Co. 705 pp. New edition. T,
                  471(6). Later printings, Companion Books.
993. [?189–]   New York, Lovell, Coryell & Co. 705 pp. 472(1).
994. [?189–]   Philadelphia, McKay. 705 pp.
995. [?189–]   New York & London, Merrill & Baker. vii + 797 pp.
                  T.
996. [?189–]   Chicago & New York, Rand, McNally & Co. xii +
                  672 pp. Some printings Alpha Library. 462(8).
997. [?189–]   Chicago, Thompson & Thomas. 705 pp. 468(1).
998. [?189–]   Chicago, Henneberry. xii + 672 pp.
999. 1900   New York, P. F. Collier. 705 pp. Library of Universal
                  Literature, Science. Vol. 3. T, 508(2).
1000. [c. 1900]   New York, D. Appleton. xvi + 688 pp. Selected
                  Works, Westminster Edition. 1000 copies. 464(5).
1001. 1901   London, John Murray. xix + 1031 pp. No thousand
                  given. From repaginated stereos of No. 983. Binding:
                  leaf green cloth. C, L; T, 511(6).   [271
1002. 1901   New York, D. Appleton. As No. 987. 512(4).
1003. 1901   New York, P. F. Collier. 2 vols. Library of Universal
                  Literature, Part I, Science Vols 2 & 3.
1004. 1902   New York, P. F. Collier. 2 vols. As No. 1003. 513(13).
1005. 1904   New York, J. A. Hill. 2 vols. Second edition. Introduc-
                  tion called 'The last link' by Ernst Haeckel. The New
                  Science Library Vols 6 & 7. Edition de luxe. 514(7).
1006. 1906   London, John Murray. As No. 1001. T, 515(4).   [272
1007. 1906   New York, D. Appleton. As No. 1002.
1008. 1909   London, John Murray. As No. 1006. L; T.   [273
1009. 1909   New York, D. Appleton. As No. 1007. 516(15).
1010. [?190–]   New York, Thomas Y. Crowell. 538 pp. 509(1),
                  ?467(2).
1011. [?190–]   New York, Thomas Y. Crowell. x + 698 pp. Astor
                  Prose Series. 510(1).
1012. [?190–]   New York, A. L. Foule. xvi + 688 pp. International
                  Science Library. T, 470(3).

1013. [?190–] New York & London, Merrill & Baker. xii + 672 pp. World's Famous Books. 473(6).

1014. [?190–] Philadelphia, J. Wanamaker. xii + 672 pp. Columbia Library. 507(2).

1015. [?190–] Akron, Ohio, The Werner Company. xvi + 688 pp. International Science Library.

1016. [?190–] Akron, Ohio, The Werner Company. xvi + 688 pp. As No. 1015. Second edition. 506(4).

1017. 1912 New York, P. F. Collier. 2 vols. As No. 1004. 513(13).

1018. 1913 London, John Murray. As No. 1008. With list of editions giving prices on verso of half-title leaf. See No. 1019. T, 520 part (3).   [274

1019. 1913 London, John Murray. As No. 1018, but half-title leaf a cancel, with list of editions altered and not giving prices. T, 520 part (3).   [275

1020. 1913 New York, D. Appleton. As No. 1009. 521(2).

1021. 1915 New York, D. Appleton. As No. 1020. Some copies Popular Uniform Edition.

1022. 1917 New York, D. Appleton. As No. 1021. 522(1).

1023. (1919) New York, Burt & Co. As No. 988. 523(1).

1024. [?191–] New York, Merrill & Baker. As No. 1013. 518(3).

1025. [?191–] Chicago, Rand, McNally & Co. As No. 996. 517(1).

1026. 1920 New York, D. Appleton. As No. 1021. Not Popular Uniform Edition.

1027. 1922 London, John Murray. As No. 1018. T.   [276

1028. 1922 New York, D. Appleton. As No. 1026.

1029. 1925 New York, D. Appleton. As No. 1028. 524(2).

1030. 1926 New York, Vanguard Press. vii + 129 pp. Abridged with title *The substance of the descent of man*. Summarized by Newell R. Tripp. 525(7).

1031. 1927 New York, D. Appleton. As No. 1029. 526(4).

1032. 1927 New York, Vanguard Press. As No. 1030. Second printing.

1033. 1930 London, Watts. xi + 244. Part 1 and last chapter of Part 3 only. Preface by Leonard Darwin. Thinker's Library No. 12. L; T, 528(2).   [277

1034. 1930 New York, D. Appleton. As No. 1031. 527(2).

1035. 1936 London, Watts. As No. 1033. Thinker's Library No. 12. T.   [278

1036. [1936] New York, Modern Library. xvi + 1000 pp. With *The origin of species. Descent of man* pp. 387–924, 941–1000. = No. 554. Modern Library Giants. T, 708(38).

1037. 1936   Harmondsworth, Penguin Books. xvi + 1000 pp.
               U.S.A. printed = No. 1036 with new title leaf. = No.
               555. L; T.   [279

1038. 1945   London, Watts. As No. 1035. Thinker's Library No.
               12. T.   [280

1039. 1952   Chicago, William Benten, Encyclopaedia Britannica
               Inc. xiii + 659 pp. With *The origin of species. Descent of
               man* pp. 253–600, 611–659. Great Books of the Western
               World No. 49. = No. 576. T, 776 part (9).

1040. [1955] Chicago, Encyclopaedia Britannica Inc. As No. 1039.
               Great Books of the Western World No. 49. = No. 577.
               DLC, 776 part (9).

1041. [?1962] New York, Modern Library. As No. 1036. With *The
               origin of species.* = No. 595. C; 67–56018(2).

1042. 1969   Brussels, Editions Cultures et Civilisation. 2 vols. Fac-
               simile of No. 939, but 218 mm.

1043. 1971   [New York], Limited Editions Club, Griffin Press
               Adelaide printed. 4to, xvii + 362 pp. Preface and note
               on p. [184] by Ashley Montagu. Omits part of Ch. 8
               and all of Chs 9–16. 1500 copies. Not in commerce.
               Binding: quarter morocco and wood veneer. DLC, T.

1044. 1971   New York, Heritage Press. Commercial edition of No.
               1043.

1045. 1972   New York, Abrahams Magazine Service. xvi + 688 pp.
               Facsimile of No. 981 (1896).

1046. 1974   Detroit, Gale Research, Facsimile of No. 944.

BULGARIAN

1047. 1927   Vidin, Ya. Bozhniov. 518 pp. Translated by P. Balev.
               531(1).

CZECH

1048. 1906   Chicago, Workers' College. 278 pp. Translated by
               Josef Jiří Kral. 533(1).

1049. 1970   Prague, Academy of Sciences. Translated by Josef Wolf
               and Zara Wolfová.

DANISH

1050. 1874–1875 Copenhagen, Gyldendal. 2 vols. Translated by J. P.
               Jacobsen. L; 535(2).   [471

1051. 1909 Copenhagen, Gyldendal. iv + 336 pp. Second edition. Translated by J. P. Jacobsen. Revised by Frits Heide. Works Vol. 2. Uniform with Nos 644 & 1512. Some copies 2 vols in one. LNH; T, 778(1).

1052. 1967 Copenhagen, Christian Ejlers. 264 pp. Translated by J. P. Jacobsen. Revised by Ove Frydenberg, Uniform with No. 647. LNH.

DUTCH

1053. 1871–1872 Delft, Ijkema & Van Gijn. 2 vols. Translated by H. Hartogh Heijs van Zouteveen. D.

1054. 1882 Haarlem, J. J. Van Brederode. 2 vols. Translated by H. Hartogh Heijs van Zouteveen. 537(1).

1055. 1884–1885 Arnhem-Nijmegen, E. & M. Cohen, 2 vols. Translated by H. Hartogh Heijs van Zouteveen. 538(1).

1056. 1889–1890 Arnhem-Nijmegen, E. & M. Cohen. 2 vols. Translated by H. Hartogh Heijs van Zouteveen and T. C. Winkler. Collected Works Vols 4 & 5. Includes some small papers from serials.

1057. [?1909] Arnhem-Nijmegen, E. & M. Cohen. As No. 1056. Collected Works Vols 4 & 5. LNH.

FRENCH

1058. 1872 Paris, C. Reinwald. 2 vols. Translated by J. J. Moulinié. Preface by Carl Vogt. BS; T, 540(2). [473

1059. 1873–1874 Paris, C. Reinwald. 2 vols. Second edition. Translated by J. J. Moulinié. Corrected by É. Barbier. Preface by Carl Vogt. 541(3). [474

1060. 1875 Paris, C. Reinwald. As No. 1059. Second edition. 542(1).

1061. 1881 Paris, C. Reinwald. xxvii + 721 pp. Third edition. Translated by É. Barbier. Preface by Carl Vogt. D; T, 543(1). [475

1062. 1891 Paris, C. Reinwald. As No. 1061.

1063. 1907 Paris, Schleicher Fréres. xv + 660 pp. 28 plates. Translated by É. Barbier.

1064. [   ] Paris, Schleicher Fréres. As No. 1063. Probably several undated issues.

GERMAN

1065. 1871[–1872] Stuttgart, Schweizerbart. 2 vols. Second edition.

Translated by J. V. Carus. L, BS; T, 545(4). Some sets dated 1871, 1872.   [476

1066. 1875   Stuttgart, Schweizerbart. 2 vols. Third edition. Translated by J. V. Carus. Collected Works Vols 5 & 6. L; 546(2).   [477

1067. 1881   Stuttgart, Schweizerbart, 2 vols. Collected Works Vols 3 & 4. L.   [478

1068. 1883   Stuttgart, Schweizerbart. xii + 659 pp. Fourth edition. Translated by J. V. Carus. L.Sc; 547(2).   [479

1069. 1890   Stuttgart, Schweizerbart. 2 vols. Fifth edition. Translated by J. V. Carus. Collected Works Vols 5 & 6. DLC.

1070. 1893   Halle am Saale, O. Hendel. viii + 878 pp. Translated by Georg Gärtner. Bibliothek der Gesamtlitteratur des In- und Auslandes. Nos 667–681; L; 549(3).

1071. [1895] Leipzig, Ph. Reclam jun. 2 vols. Translated by David Haek. Universal-Bibliothek Nos 3216–3225. 548(3).

1072. 1899   Stuttgart, Schweizerbart. x + 772 pp. Fifth edition. Translated by J. V. Carus. 550(1).

1073. 1902   Stuttgart, Schweizerbart. 2 vols. As No. 1069. Collected Works Vols 5 & 6.

1074. 1902   Leipzig, Bibliograph Institut. 2 vols. Translated by Paul Seliger. Meyers Volksbücher Nos 1311–1328.

1075. [1908–1909] Leipzig, A. Kröner. 2 vols. Translated by Heinrich Schmidt. Volks-Ausgabe. 551(2), 552(4).

1076. 1913   Leipzig, Bibliograph. Institut. 2 vols. As No. 1074. Meyers Volksbücher Nos 1668–1685.

1077. 1919   Stuttgart, Schweizerbart. As No. 1072, but sixth edition.

1078. (1921) Leipzig, Ph. Reclam jun. 2 vols. Translated and edited by Carl W. Neumann. Universal-Bibliothek Nos 3216–3220a, b, c.

1079. 1923   Leipzig, A. Kröner. xii + 327 pp. *Descent* only. Translated by Heinrich Schmidt. Taschenausgabe Vol. 28. 553(2).

1080. [1925] Berlin, D. Hendel. viii + 878 pp. As No. 1070. Hendel-Bücher Nos 667–681.

1081. 1932   Leipzig, Kröner. xxvi + 347 pp. Translated by Heinrich Schmidt. Taschenausgabe Vol. 28.

1082. [1952] Leipzig, Reclam. 3 vols in one. 651 pp. Translated by Carl W. Neumann. Notes by Georg Uschmann.

1083. 1966   Stuttgart, Kröner. Translated by Heinrich Schmidt. As No. 1081.

HUNGARIAN

1084. 1884   Budapest, Academy of Sciences. 2 vols. Translated by
               Török Aurel and Entz Géza. Compared with the
               original and with a biography by Margó Tivador.
               Scientific Publications Nos XXIII–XXIV. 555(1), 18–
               14045.   [480

1085. 1910   Budapest, Az Athenaeum. 2 vols. Translated by Entz
               Géza, Fülöp Zsigmond and Madssar József. 556(1).

1086. 1923   Budapest, Az Athenaeum. 2 vols. As No. 1085. 557(1).

1087. 1961   Budapest, Gondolat. 895 pp. Translated by Katalin
               Katona.

1087a. 1971   Bucharest, Kriterion. 207 pp. Extracts only with ex-
               tracts from *Origin of species* = No. 705a.

ITALIAN

1088. 1871   Turin, Unione. 671 pp. Translated by Michele Lessona.
               D; 559(1).   [481

1089. 1888   Turin, Unione, As No. 1088. 560(2).   [482

1090. 1913   Milan, Bruciati. 605 pp. New Edition. Translated by
               M. Lessona.

1091. 1914   Milan, Bruciati. As No. 1090.

1092. 1920   Turin, Unione. Fourth issue. As No. 1089.

1093. 1925   Milan, Toffaloni. 484 pp. Translated by M. Lessona.
               Biblioteca di Coltura Moderni. 561(1).

1094. 1926   Sesto San Giovanni, Barian. 492 pp. Translated by M.
               Lessona.

1095. 1933   Sesto San Giovanni, Barian. 563 pp. Translated by M.
               Lessona.

1096. [1945]   Milan, Editoriale Italiana. 480 pp. Translated by M.
               Lessona. 562(1).

1097. 1949   Milan, Universale Economica. Translated by Franco
               Paparo.

1098. 1966   Rome, Editoriale Riuniti. Translated by Franco Paparo.

1099. 1966–1967 Rome, Avanzini e Torraca. Translated by Mario
               Migliucci and Paola Fiorentini. I Classici per Tutti.

1099a 1972   Milan, Longanesi. 1205 pp. Il meglio in antropologia
               with *Expression of the emotions* = No. 1202a.

JAPANESE

1100. (1949)   Tokyo, Kaizōsha. 2 vols. Translated by Shūzō Ishida.
               ?Collected Works.

POLISH

1101.   1874   Kraków, 'Kraju'. 246 pp. All published. Translated by
                 Ludwik Masłowski. D. |483

1102.   1929   Translated by M. Ilecki.

1103.   1959–1960 Warsaw, Academy of Sciences. 2 vols. Translated
                 by Stanisław Panek and Krystyna Zaćwilichowska.
                 Edited by Eugenia Stołyhwo and Stanisław Hiller. Col-
                 lected Works Vols 4 & 5. Biblioteka Klasyków
                 Biologii. DLC (Vol. 1 only). Vol. 4 is a translation of
                 Part 1 only, i.e. *The descent of man*, of the first English
                 edition 1871, No. 937. Vol. 5 is a translation of the
                 second English edition 1874, No. 944.

PORTUGUESE

1104.   [1910–1912] Oporto, Magalhæs y Moniz. 262 pp. Translated
                 and abridged by Joao Corrêa d'Oliveira. Biblioteca do
                 Educação Intellectual. ViU.

1105.   [19—]   São Paulo, Cultura Moderna. 236 pp. Edited by A.
                 Roitman. Las Grandes Obras. 564(1).

ROMANIAN

1106.   1967   Bucharest, National Academy. xvi + 553 pp. Trans-
                 lated by Eugen Margulius. Compared with the Russian
                 translation by Nicolae Botnauric, the German by Ion
                 T. Tarnavschi, the French by Vasile D. Mârza. Intro-
                 duction by Vasile D. Mârza. Clasici Ştiinţei Universale
                 No. 6. D, LSc; T, DLC.

RUSSIAN

1107.   1871   St Petersburg, V. Demakov for *Znanie*. xv + 439 pp.
                 Abridged.

1108.   1871–1872 St Petersburg, A. Morigerovskiĭ printed. 3 parts.
                 Translation edited by G. E. Blagosvetlov.

1109.   1871–1872 St Petersburg, Cherkasov. 2 vols. Translated and
                 edited by I. M. Sechanov. D.

1110.   1873   St Petersburg, Cherkasov. As No. 1109 but second
                 revised edition.

1111.   1873–1874 St Petersburg, *Delo*. 2 vols. Second edition. Trans-
                 lated and edited by G. E. Blagosvetlov.

1112.   1896   St Petersburg, Ya. I. Liberman. 320 pp. Translated by
                M. Filippov. Collected Works. Supplement to *Nauchnoe
                Obozrenie* Vol. 2. 567(1).

1113.   1896   St Petersburg, O. N. Popov. xii + 424 + iii pp. Trans-
                lated by I. M. Sechenov. Collected Works Vol. 2,
                part 1.

1114.   1899   St Petersburg, O. N. Popov. As No. 1113, but second
                edition.

1115.   1903   St Petersburg, V. I. Gubinskiĭ. As No. 1114.

1116.   1908   St Petersburg, V. I. Gubinskiĭ. As No. 1115, but third
                edition.

1117.   1908   Moscow, Yu. Lepkovskiĭ. viii + 492 pp. Translated by
                Yu. Lepkovskiĭ. Collected Works Vols 5 & 6.

1118.   1909   St Petersburg, V. V. Bitner, *Vestnik znaniya*. 3 vols.
                730 pp. Translated by A. A. Nikolaev. Edited by V. V.
                Bitner. Collected Works Vols 1–3.

1119.   1927   Moscow-Leningrad, State Edition. 623 pp. Translated
                by I. M. Sechenov. Introduction by M. A. Menzbir.
                Collected Works Vol. 2, part 1.

1120.   1929   Leningrad, P. P. Soĭkin. 62 pp. Selected passages, and
                from *The origin of species*. Translated and introduced by
                M. N. Vinogradov. Klassiki morovoi nauki, supple-
                ment to *Vestnik znaniya*. = No. 759.

1121.   1953   Moscow, Academy of Sciences U.S.S.R. 656 pp.
                Translated by I. M. Sechenov. Corrected and revised
                by A. D. Nekrasov & I. M. Polyakov. Introduction
                and notes by Ya. Ya. Roginskiĭ & A. D. Nekrasov.
                Collected Works Vols 4 & 5. L; DLC.

SLOVENE

1122.   1950   Novi Sad, Matica Srpska. 446 pp. Translated by
                Nedeljko Dirac.

SPANISH

1123.   [?19—] Barcelona, Centro Editorial Presa. 170 pp. ?Extracts.
                569(1).

1124.   [1902] Valencia, J. Sempere. 213 pp. Translated by A. López
                White. Biblioteca Filosófica y Social.

1125.   [192–] Barcelona, Atlante. Biblioteca Libros Rojos.

1126.   [192–] Barcelona, Maucci. Los Grandes Pensadores.

1127. 1933   Madrid, Libreria Bergua. 2 vols.

1128. [1939]   Santiago de Chile, Zig-zag. 552 pp. Biblioteca de Cultura. 570(2).

1129. [1943]   Buenos Aires, Albatros. 797 pp. Los Grandes Eruditos. 571(1).

1130. 1963   Madrid, EDAF. 517 pp.

1131. 1964   Mexico City, Diana. xi + 797 pp. Seventh edition.

1132. 1966   Madrid, Ibéricas. 2 vols. Translated by M. J. Barroso-Bonzón.

1133. 1967   Madrid, EDAF. As No. 1130, but third edition.

1134. 1967   Mexico City, Editora Nacional. 213 pp. Translated by A. Lopez White.

1135. 1970   Madrid, EDAF. As No. 1133, but fourth edition.

SWEDISH

1136. 1872   Stockholm, Albert Bonnier. 2 vols. in one. Translated by Rudolf Sunderström. D; T, 573(2).

TURKISH

1137. 1968   Ankara, Başnur Matbaasi. Translated by Yavuz Erkoçak, from a German edition

YIDDISH

1138. 1921   New York, Meisel. 3 vols. Translated by Y. A. Merison. Essay on Darwinism by J. A. Thomson. 575(1) Vol. I only.

1139. 1926   New York, Meisel. As No. 1138. Volume titles dated 1923. L.

1140. 1936   Warsaw. 157 pp. Translated by M. Holzblatt. ?Extracts.

The Expression of the Emotions

This is an important member of the evolutionary set, and it was written, in part at least, as a confutation of the idea that the facial muscles of expression in man were a special endowment. Darwin had no personal research experience in the subject, but he had read widely and enquired of his scientific colleagues. He had also circulated, in 1867, his printed leaflet *Queries about expression* (Nos 871–876) to acquaintances who were in touch with primitive peoples. The replies to the *Queries* were drawn on heavily for the substance of the book, and a version of the *Queries* themselves is printed in it (pp. 15–16).

It is stated that Murray published 7,000 copies of the first edition on November 26, 1872, and that 5,267 were taken up at his autumn sale. However, there are two issues of the first edition and at least two states of the plates, with a third state in some copies of the tenth thousand of 1873. In the first issue, there are four leaves of preliminaries, the first being a blank before the title leaf, and the only signature is *b* on the fourth leaf. The last two signatures are 2B² and 2C³, being three leaves of index and two leaves of integral advertisements; only 2B1 and 2C1 are signed. In the second issue there are three leaves of preliminaries, the blank being absent and the third leaf being signed *b*. The last two signatures are 2B¹ and 2C⁴, with 2B1, 2C1 and 2C2 signed.

So far as I can see, there are no textual differences except for a misprint 'htat' in the first line of page 208 in the second issue. There are however four small points on the first page of the integral advertisements. In the first issue, the wavy rule below 'RECENT WORKS' runs from the right of the second E to the left of the O; there is a comma after 'Portrait' in the first entry; the second line of the first entry is not aligned to the right with the line above it; and in the second entry there is a comma after 'illustrations'. In the second issue, the wavy rule has been shifted about half a letter to the right; there is a full point after 'Portrait'; the second line is aligned to the right; and there is a full point after 'Illustrations'. The last three points bring the first two advertisements up to the house practice used for the rest. The issue dated 1873 always has the same make up as the second issue of 1872 except that the integral advertisements (2C3–4) have been discarded in some copies.

In all three issues, the dropped title on page [1] reads 'On the expression . . .'. All were in standard cases, and cost 12s. The third issue may contain inserted advertisements dated as late as January 1883, showing that it remained in print after Darwin's death.

The 1872 issues have seven heliotype plates of which the first, second and sixth are folding. All seven exist in two states, one with the plates numbered in Arabic, the other numbered in Roman. In both, Arabic numerals are used to designate the individual photographs, but these differ both in structure and position in the two sets. All the plates bear the word 'Heliotype' except that it has been cut away from Plate V by the binder in some short copies with the Roman plates. The list of illustrations on page vi gives the plates with Roman numerals and on page 25 Darwin writes 'These plates are referred to by Roman numerals' as indeed they are throughout the text. It seems probable that the Arabic set was the earlier. The run was 7000 copies which is perhaps

144   THE WORKS OF CHARLES DARWIN

long for gelatine plates; they may have been replaced when wearing out or when the error was noticed. The two states seem to occur at random in the two issues of the text, and Darwin's own copy, at Cambridge, has the Roman, but I have never seen a mixed set.

A third state is found only in the three plates which are folding in the first two. The photographs have been rearranged and none of them fold. This state does not occur in the issues of 1872, but in that of 1873 these plates are folding in some copies and not folding in others; in both states they are numbered in Roman, and when folding are identical with those of the Roman plates of 1872.

A second edition appeared in 1890, and, in his preface to it, Francis Darwin writes that his father had accumulated notes on the subject which he had been unable to use because the first edition was not exhausted in his lifetime. He incorporates these notes as well as adding his own footnotes in brackets. This represents the final text, and the printings of 1901 and 1905, though reset, are not altered. Two recent American editions have contained introductions by such distinguished behaviourists as Margaret Mead and Konrad Lorenz, and there is a Brussels facsimile of 1969. It was translated into Dutch, French, German, Italian, Polish and Russian in Darwin's life time and into four further languages since. The second Dutch edition of 1890 incorporates Darwin's additions and corrections, but is not a translation of Francis Darwin's edition of the same year.

ENGLISH

1141. 1872   London, John Murray. *The expression of the emotions in man and animals.* 8vo, 183 mm, vi + 374 pp, 7 heliotype plates (3 folding), numbered in Arabic. Last signatures 2B² 2C³ with 2B1 and 2C1 signed. See also No. 1142. Binding: standard green cloth but more shiny than others. Price 12s. D, L; T, 881 (35), not distinguished from No. 1142   [281 part

1142. 1872   London, John Murray. 8vo, 189 mm. All as No. 1141 but last signatures 2B¹ 2C⁴ with 2B1, 2C1 and 2C2 signed. Plates numbered in Arabic or Roman. Binding: as No. 1141. Holdings not distinguished from No. 1141 except CD; T.   [281 part

1143. 1873[= 1872] New York, D. Appleton. iv + 374 pp. From stereos of No. 1141, but letter signatures replaced by numbers and 8vo in 12s. Issued December 1872. T, 883(24).   [484

1144.	1873	London, John Murray. As No. 1142, but tenth thousand and 2C3–4 discarded in some copies. 3 plates folding in some copies only. C, D, L, LNH; T, 882(4). [282
1145.	1888	New York, D. Appleton. As No. 1143. 884(3).
1146.	1890	London, John Murray. 8vo, viii + 394 pp. Second edition. Edited by Francis Darwin. Binding: standard green cloth. CD, C, L; T, 885(2). [283
1147.	1890	London, John Murray. As No. 1146, but twelfth thousand. [284
1148.	1890	New York, D. Appleton. 374 pp. As No. 1145. 886(4).
1149.	1892	London, John Murray. As No. 1147, but eleventh thousand [sic]. T, 887(6). [285
1150.	1892	New York, D. Appleton. As No. 1148. 888(2).
1151.	1896	New York, D. Appleton. vi + 372 pp. 889(20). [485
1152.	1897	New York, D. Appleton. As No. 1151. 890(12).
1153.	1898	New York, D. Appleton. As No. 1152. 891(8).
1154.	1899	New York, D. Appleton. As No. 1153. 892(15). [486
1155.	[c. 1900]	New York, D. Appleton. As No. 1154, but Westminster Edition, limited to 1000 copies.
1156.	1901	London, John Murray. As No. 1149, but twelfth thousand. Binding: standard green cloth, not leaf green. T, 893(2) [286
1157.	1904	London, John Murray. As No. 1156, but no thousand given. Binding: leaf green cloth. C; 894(5). [287
1158.	1905	New York, D. Appleton. As No. 1154. 895(2).
1159.	1910	New York, D. Appleton. As No. 1158. 896(6).
1160.	1913	New York, D. Appleton. As No. 1159. 897(1).
1161.	1915	New York, D. Appleton. As No. 1160. Popular Uniform Edition.
1162.	1915	New York, D. Appleton for the Brunswick Subscription Company. As No. 1160, but The World's Greatest Scientists.
1163.	1916	New York, D. Appleton. As No. 1160. 898(4).
1164.	1920	New York, D. Appleton. As No. 1163. 899(5).
1165.	1921	London, John Murray. As No. 1157. 900(3).
1166.	1924	New York, D. Appleton. As No. 1164. 901(4).
1167.	1929	New York, D. Appleton. As No. 1166. 902(6).
1168.	1934	London, Watts. ix + 179 pp. Revised and abridged by C. M. Beadnell. Thinker's Library No. 47. L; T, 903(5). [288
1169.	1943	London, Watts. As No. 1168. Thinker's Library No. 47.
1170.	1948	London, Watts. As No. 1169. Thinker's Library No.

47. L; 904(2).   [289

1171.   (1955)   New York, Philosophical Library. xi + 372 pp. Preface
                 by Margaret Mead. 905(30).

1172.   (1965)   Chicago, University of Chicago Press. xiii + 372 pp.
                 Introduction by Konrad Lorenz. Text from No. 1143.
                 Phoenix Books Pss 526. C, L; T, 65–17286(14).

1173.   1967   Chicago, University of Chicago Press. As No. 1172,
                 but second impression.

1174.   1969   Westport, Conn., Greenwood Press. xi + 372 pp.
                 Preface by Margaret Mead. Reprint of No. 1171.

1175.   1969   Brussels, Editions Culture et Civilisation. vi + 374 pp.
                 Facsimile of No. 1141, but 218.

1176.   1969   Chicago, University of Chicago Press. As No. 1173,
                 but third impression.

1177.   1970   Chicago, University of Chicago Press. As No. 1176,
                 but fourth impression.

1178.   1972   New York, Abrahams Magazine Service. 374 pp.
                 Facsimile of No. 1151 (1896).

1179.   1973   Chicago, University of Chicago Press. As No. 1177,
                 and fourth impression.

1180.   1975   Chicago, University of Chicago Press. As No. 1179,
                 but fifth impression.

CZECK

1181.   1964   Prague, NČSAV. Translated by Josef Král and Václav
                 Příhoda.

DUTCH

1182.   1873   The Hague, Joh. Ijkema. ix + 435 pp. Translated by
                 H. Hartogh Heijs van Zouteveen. D.   [487

1183.   [1890]   Arnhem-Nijmegen, E. & M. Cohen. v + 462 pp. New
                 edition. Translated by H. Hartogh Heijs van Zouteveen.
                 Contains the same revisions as No. 1146, but is not a
                 translation of it. Also contains a supplement Moleschott, J.
                 Charles Darwin Herdacht, written in 1882. Collected
                 Works Vol. 6. LNH.

FRENCH

1184.   1874   Paris, C. Reinwald. vi + 404 pp. Translated by Samuel
                 Pozzi and René Benoist. D; T, 879(2).   [488

1185. 1877   Paris, C. Reinwald. As No. 1184, but second edition.
               LSc; 880(3).   [489

1186. 1890   Paris, C. Reinwald. x + 400 pp. Second edition.   [490

GERMAN

1187. 1872   Stuttgart, Schwiezerbart. viii + 384 pp. Translated by
               J. V. Carus. BS; T, 789(4), 790(4).

1188. 1874   Stuttgart, Schweizerbart. As No. 1187, but second
               edition. BS.   [491

1189. 1877   Stuttgart, Schweizerbart. viii + 344 pp. Third edition.
               Collected Works Vol. 7, D, L, BS.   [492

1190. 1881   Stuttgart, Schweizerbart. As No. 1189. Collected
               Works Vol. 5. L.   [493

1191. 1884   Stuttgart, Schweizerbart. As No. 1190. Collected
               Works Vol. 7. 792(3).   [494

1192. [188–] Halle am Saale, O. Hendel. viii + 368 pp. Translated
               by Theodor Bergfeldt. 791(1).

1193. 1892   Stuttgart, Schweizerbart. As No. 1191.   [495

1194. 1896   Haale am Saale, O. Hendel. viii + 368 pp. Translated
               by Georg Gärtner. ?As No. 1192. Bibliothek der
               Gasamtlitteratur des In- und Auslandes Nos 963–971.

1195. 1901   Stuttgart, Schweizerbart. vi + 330 pp. Translated by
               J. V. Carus. Collected Works Vol. 7.

1196. 1910   Stuttgart, Schwiezerbart. As No. 1195. Collected
               Works Vol. 7.

1197. [1964] Düsseldorff, Rau. 292 pp. Translated by Theodor
               Bergfeldt. Notes by Ulrich Beer. T, 67–31881.

1198. 1966   Tübingen, Katzmann. 292 pp. Translated by Ulrich
               Beer. Introduction by Theodor Bergfeldt.

HUNGARIAN

1199. 1963   Budapest, Gondolat Kiadó. 895 pp. Translated by János
               Pusztai.

ITALIAN

1200. 1878   Turin, Unione. 284 pp. Translated by Giovanni
               Canestrini and F. Bassani.

1201. 1892   Turin, Unione. As No. 1200. 878(1).   [496

1202. 1914   Turin, Unione. As No. 1201. Seventh printing.

1202a. 1972   Milan, Longanesi. 1205 pp. Il meglio in antropologia.
               With *Descent of man.* = No. 1099a.

POLISH

1203. 1873   Warsaw, Józefa Sikorski. 321 + xi pp. Translated by
               Conrad Dobrski. D.

1204. 1959   Warsaw, Academy of Sciences. vii + 288 pp. Trans-
               lated by Zofia Majlert and Krystyna Zaćwilichowska.
               Edited by R. J. Wojtusiak. Collected Works Vol. 6.
               Biblioteka Klasyków Biologii. DLC.

ROMANIAN

1205. 1967   [Bucharest], National Academy. xi + 242 pp. Trans-
               lated by Eugen Margulius. Introduction by Vasile D.
               Mârza. With Essay on instinct = No. 1448. Clasici
               Ştiinţei Universale No. 7. D, LSc; T.

RUSSIAN

1206. 1872   St Petersburg, F. S. Suchinskiĭ printed. v + 335 pp.
               Translation edited by V. O. Kovalevskiĭ.

1207. 1896   St Petersburg. ii + 184 pp. Translation edited by V. O.
               Kovalevskiĭ. Collected Works Vol. 2, part 2.

1208. 1896   St Petersburg, A. Porokhovshchikov printed. 221 + 3
               pp. Translated by M. Filippov. Collected Works. Sup-
               plement to Nauchnoe Obozrenie Vol. 4.

1209. 1899   St Petersburg, O. N. Popov, As No. 1207. Second
               edition. Collected Works Vol. 2, part 2.

1210. 1908   St Petersburg, Ya. Lepkovskiĭ. vi + 211 + ii pp. Trans-
               lated by F. N. Krasheninnikov. Collected Works Vol.
               3, part 1.

1211. 1912   St Petersburg, V. V. Bitner, Vestnik znaniya. 274 pp.
               Translated by A. A. Nikolaev. Collected Works Vol. 5,
               part 1.

1212. 1927   Moscow–Leningrad, State Edition. Translated by V. O.
               Kovalevskiĭ. Collected Works Vol. 2, part 2.

1213. 1953   Moscow, Academy of Sciences U.S.S.R. pp. 681–920.
               Translated by E. N. Pavlovskiĭ. Introduction and notes
               by S. G. Gellerstein. Collected Works Vol. 4. L.

SPANISH

1214. [c. 1902] Valencia, F. Sempere. 2 vols. Translated by Eusebio
               Heras. Biblioteca Filosófica y Social.

1215. [192–] Barcelona, Atlante. 2 vols. Los Pequeñõs Grandes
               Libros, Vols 21–22.

Boyd Dawkins Testimonials

This is the third and last of the printed pamphlets known to me which
contains a testimonial letter from Darwin. A general note on these is
given under the first, that for Edward William Brayley in 1845 (No.
324). William Boyd Dawkins had been appointed to the Chair of
Geology at Owens College in 1872, but did not get the Woodwardian
Chair at Cambridge and remained at Manchester for the rest of his long
working life.

ENGLISH

1216. [1873] Cambridge, University Press printed. *Testimonials in
               favour of W. Boyd Dawkins, M.A., F.R.S., F.G.S. a
               candidate for the Woodwardian Professorship of Geology.*
               [in the University of Cambridge]. 12mo, 218 mm [cut],
               10 pp. Darwin's letter p. 2. No binding. C; T (xerox).

Insectivorous Plants

These meticulous studies form a minor contribution to the evolutionary
series by the study of the adaptations of such plants to impoverished
conditions. Darwin was helped by various physiologists and chemists in
the experimental work, particularly by Professor Edward Frankland of
the Royal College of Chemistry. His sons helped with the illustrations,
George doing those for *Drosera* and *Dionaea* and Francis those for
Aldrovanda and *Utricularia*. He himself was no draughtsman, but text
figures 7 and 8 were cut from his drawings.

The book was published on July 2, 1875, in a standard binding
without inserted advertisements. It is stated that 3,000 were printed of
which 2,700 were sold to the trade at once. This cannot be strictly true
because both the second and third thousands of the same year stated their
thousands on the title pages. The second has an errata slip of six lines,
and in the third these six have been corrected, but another six have been
found and again occur on a slip. The same slip is present in the fourth
thousand of 1876. It was not printed again in Darwin's lifetime, but a
second edition, edited by Francis appeared dated 1888. According to
Murray's list this was issued in January 1889. It contains some small
corrections taken from Darwin's marked copy of the first edition, as

well as textual additions and footnotes by his son which are all contained in brackets.

The American editions are from stereos of the first English. It has not been reprinted in England since 1908, but there is a Brussels facsimile of the first edition in 1969 as well as a New York one of an American printing of 1896. It was translated into French, German, Italian and Russian in Darwin's lifetime, and into Romanian since.

ENGLISH

1217.	1875	London, John Murray. *Insectivorous plants*. 8vo in 12s, 190 mm, x + 462 pp. 30 text woodcuts. Binding: standard green cloth. Price 14s. CD, L; T, 983 part (22). June. [290
1218.	1875	London, John Murray. As No. 1217, but second thousand and with errata slip. July. C, L; T, 983 part (22). [291
1219.	1875	London, John Murray. As No. 1218, but third thousand and new errata slip. D, L; T, 983 part (22). [292
1220.	1875	New York, D. Appleton. x + 462 pp. From stereos of No. 1217. T, 984(25). [497
1221.	1876	London, John Murray. As No. 1219 and with same errata slip, but fourth thousand. L; T, 985(3). [293
1222.	1883	New York, D. Appleton. As No. 1220. 986(4). [498
1223.	1884	New York, D. Appleton. As No. 1222. 987(4).
1224.	1886	New York, D. Appleton. As No. 1223. 988(3).
1225.	1888	London, John Murray. 8vo, xiv + 337 pp. Second edition. Revised by Francis Darwin. Binding: as No. 1217. CD, C; T, 989(6). [294
1226.	1889	New York, D. Appleton. As No. 1224. 991(4).
1227.	1893	London, John Murray. As No. 1225, but sixth thousand. T, 992(9). [295
1228.	1896	New York, D. Appleton. As No. 1226. 993(20). [499
1229.	1897	New York, D. Appleton. As No. 1228. 994(15). [500
1230.	1899	New York, D. Appleton. As No. 1229.
1231.	1900	New York, D. Appleton. xvi + 376 pp. 995(17). [501
1232.	[c. 1900]	New York, D. Appleton. xiv + 376 pp. Selected Works. Westminster Edition. 1000 copies. T, 990(2).
1233.	1908	London, John Murray. As No. 1227, but no thousand given. Binding: leaf green cloth. T, 997(4). [296
1234.	1915	New York, D. Appleton. As No. 1231. Some copies Popular Uniform Edition. 998(2).

1235. 1969   Brussels, Editions Culture et Civilisation. Facsimile of
              No. 1217, but 218 mm.

1236. 1972   New York, Abrahams Magazine Service. x + 462 pp.
              Facsimile of No. 1228 (1896).

FRENCH

1237. 1877   Paris, C. Reinwald. xxiii + 540 pp. Translated by Éd.
              Barbier. Introduction and notes by Charles Martin. D;
              T, 1199(3).   [502

GERMAN

1238. 1876   Stuttgart, Schweizerbart. viii + 412 pp. Translated by
              J. V. Carus. Collected Works Vol. 8. D, L, BS; T,
              982(2).   [503
1239. 1881   Stuttgart, Schweizerbart. As No. 1238. Collected
              Works Vol. 8. L.
1240. 1889   Stuttgart, Schweizerbart. As No. 1239. Second edition.
              Collected Works Vol. 8.
1241. 1899   Stuttgart, Schweizerbart, As No. 1240. Collected
              Works Vol. 8.

ITALIAN

1242. 1878   Turin, Unione. 312 pp. Translated by Giovanni Cane-
              strini and P. A. Saccardo. D, L.   [504

ROMANIAN

1243. 1965   [Bucharest], National Academy. xxii + 497 pp. Trans-
              lated by Eugen Margulius. Introduction by Vasile
              Mârza & Ion Tarnavschi. With *Forms of flowers* = No.
              1301. Clasicii Ştiinţei Universale No. 5. L, BS; T, 67-
              89264.

RUSSIAN

1244. 1876   Moscow, V. P. Plemyannikov. 3 parts. 168 + 393 pp.
              Apparently translations of the first three English issues.
1245. 1900   St Petersburg, O. N. Popov. 250 + ii pp. Translated
              by Z. and F. Krasheninnikov. Edited by K. A. Timiry-
              azev. Collected Works Vol. 4.

1246. 1908   Moscow, Yu. Lepkovskiĭ. iv + 263 pp. Translated by
               Z. and F. Krasheninnikov. Collected Works Vol. 4.
1247. 1929   Moscow-Leningrad, State Edition. 294 pp. Translated
               by Z. and F. Krasheninnikov. Collected Works Vol. 4,
               part 2.
1248. 1938   Moscow, Academy of Sciences U.S.S.R. pp. 253–586,
               635–644. Translated by F. N. and Z. G. Krashenin-
               nikov. Corrected and revised by N. G. Kholodniĭ.
               Collected Works Vol. 7. L; DLC.

Cross and Self Fertilisation

This survey of the nature of the mechanisms favouring cross fertilisation
and the advantages to be gained by it was considered by Darwin to
'form a complement to that on the "Fertilisation of Orchids"'. It was
too technical and too detailed to command a wide sale. The first edition,
which has an errata slip of three lines facing page viii, was published on
November 10, 1876, and 1,500 copies were sold before the end of the
year. It was issued in a standard binding, without inserted advertisements, at a price of 12s. In both this and the second edition the spine
titles spell fertilisation with a 'z', whilst the title pages spell it with an 's'.

The second edition of 1878 is not greatly altered, indeed first and last
words on each page remain the same up to page 370, where the addition
of a large footnote necessitates the resetting of all the rest of the book.
The final printing of 1915 describes itself, on the verso of the title leaf,
as 'Second edition', whilst it calls the true second edition a reprint. It is
however no more than a reprint from stereos, although remarkable for
being the last, by fifteen years, to appear in the standard case.

The American printings are from English stereos. There is a New
York facsimile of an American printing of 1895, but other than that the
work has never reappeared in English. It was translated into French,
German and Italian in Darwin's lifetime, and into three further languages since his death.

ENGLISH

1249. 1876   London, John Murray. *The effects of cross and self
               fertilisation in the vegetable kingdom.* 8vo, 190 mm, viii +
               482 pp., 1 diagram, 109 tables, 3 line errata slip. Bind-
               ing: standard green cloth. Price 12s. CD, C, D, L; T,
               859(23).   [297

| 1250. | 1877 | New York, D. Appleton. viii + 482 pp. From stereos of No. 1249, but errata corrected and with a new errata slip of 6 lines. T, 860(19). [505 |

1250. 1877 New York, D. Appleton. viii + 482 pp. From stereos of No. 1249, but errata corrected and with a new errata slip of 6 lines. T, 860(19).   [505

1251. 1878 London, John Murray. viii + 487 pp. Second edition. Binding: as No. 1249. D, L; T, 861(5).   [298

1252. 1883 New York, D. Appleton. As No. 1250. 862(3).

1253. 1885 New York, D. Appleton. As No. 1252. 863(4).

1254. 1888 London, John Murray. As No. 1251. T, 864(4).   [299

1255. 1889 New York, D. Appleton. As No. 1253. D; 865(2).

1256. 1891 London, John Murray. As No. 1254, but called third edition.   [300

1257. 1892 New York, D. Appleton. As No. 1255. 866(6).   [506

1258. 1895 New York, D. Appleton. As No. 1257. 867(6).

1259. 1898 New York, D. Appleton. As No. 1258. 868(5).

1260. 1900 London, John Murray. As No. 1256, but fifth impression. Binding: as No. 256, not leaf green. T, 869(7).

                                                                    [301

1261. 1902 New York, D. Appleton. As No. 1259. 870(4).

1262. 1915 London, John Murray. As No. 1260, but no impression given. Title leaf a cancel. Binding: as No. 1260, not leaf green. T.   [302

1263. 1916 London, John Murray. As No. 1262. Binding: not seen.

1264. 1972 New York, Abrahams Magazine Service. 482 pp. Facsimile of No. 1258 (1895).

FRENCH

1265. 1877 Paris, C. Reinwald. xv + 496 pp. Translated and annotated by Édouard Heckel. D; T, 840(4).

GERMAN

1266. 1877 Stuttgart, Schweizerbart. viii + 459 pp. Translated by J. V. Carus. Collected Works Vol. 10. D, L; T, 1314(3).

                                                                    [508

1267. 1899 Stuttgart, Schweizerbart. As No. 1266. Second edition.

1268. 1910 Stuttgart, Schweizerbart. As No. 1267.

ITALIAN

1269. 1878 Turin, Unione. 346 pp. Translated by Giovanni Canestrini and P. A. Saccardo. 871(1).   [509

POLISH

1270. 1964   Warsaw, Academy of Sciences. vii + 407 pp. Trans-
               lated by Halina Bielawska, A. Kurlandzka, W. Prazmo,
               A. Putrament and Z. Turecka. Edited by Aniela
               Makarewicz. Collected Works Vol. 7. Biblioteka
               Klasyków Biologii. DLC.

ROMANIAN

1271. 1964   [Bucharest], National Academy. viii + 489 pp. With
               Fertilisation of orchids = No. 824. Clasicii Ştiinţei
               Universale No. 4. L, BS; T, 65–86257.

RUSSIAN

1272. 1938   In Yarovizatsiya Nos 1–2 (16–17), pp. 13–74. Chapters
               7 & 12 only, translated by V. Yu. Grosman.
1273. 1939   Moscow-Leningrad, Sel'khozgiz. 339 pp. Translated
               by V. A. Rybin and L. N. Kohanovskiĭ. Introduced
               and edited by V. L. Komarov.
1274. 1950   Moscow, Academy of Sciences U.S.S.R. pp. 255–626.
               Translated by V. A. Rybin. and L. N. Kohanovskiĭ.
               Introduction and notes by I. M. Polyakov. Collected
               Works Vol. 6. L.

Royal Commission on Subjecting Live Animals to Experiments

Darwin gave his verbal evidence to the Royal Commission on the
afternoon of November 8, 1875, Viscount Cardwell, the Chairman,
coming to the door to receive him. He states that he had not personally
carried out any physiological experiments, but had been a signatory to
a memorandum sponsored by the British Association for the Advancement of Science. Emma Darwin, in a letter to her son Leonard, written
on that day, describes his evidence as 'a sort of confession of faith about
the claims of physiology and the duty of humanity'.

His verbal evidence is contained verbatim in the main blue book and
briefly in the digest. The report itself was reprinted in 1906, but without
the evidence.

ENGLISH

1275. 1876   London, Her Majesty's Stationery Office. *Report of the
               Royal Commission on the practice of subjecting live animals
               to experiments for scientific purposes; with the minutes of*

evidence and appendix. Fol., xxiii + 388 pp. *Viscount* Cardwell *Chairman*, Nathaniel Baker *Secretary*. Darwin's evidence p. 234, paras 4662–4672. Command 1397. Binding: blue printed wrappers of the series. Price 4s. 4d. C, L.

1276. 1876   London, Her Majesty's Stationery Office. *Digest of evidence taken before the Royal Commission on the practice of subjecting live animals to experiments for scientific purposes: with an alphabetical list of witnesses*. Fol., iv + 42 pp. Digest of Darwin's evidence p. 34. Command 1397.I. Price 6d. C, L.

Different Forms of Flowers

Much of the content of this had previously been published in the *Journal of the Linnean Society of London* and elsewhere. Had Darwin not chosen such genetically complex examples, he might have approached more nearly to an understanding of the laws of particulate inheritance. Like *Cross and self fertilisation*, it was too technical a work to command a large sale, and only about 2,000 copies were sold in Darwin's lifetime, and perhaps 4,000 before the end of the century.

The first edition, of 1,250 copies, was issued on July 9, 1877, in a standard case, at a cost of 10s. 6d. It has thirty-two pages of inserted advertisements which are dated January or March. The second, again of 1,250 copies, appeared in July 1880 with a new preface which surveys the recent literature, and in which Darwin states that 'the text has been left as it originally appeared excepting that a few errors have been corrected'. This is then the definitive text, but in the third thousand of 1884 Francis Darwin added another preface which again brings the literature up to date.

American editions were from English stereos, and the book was not reprinted after 1903 until a Brussels facsimile appeared in 1969. It was translated only into French and German in Darwin's lifetime, and into four further languages since his death.

ENGLISH

1277. 1877   London, John Murray. *The different forms of flowers on plants of the same species*. 8vo, 190 mm, viii + 352 pp, 15 text woodcuts, 38 tables. Binding: standard green cloth. Inserted advertisements Jan. or Mar. 1877. Price 10s. 6d. CD, C, D, L; T, 843(15).   [303

1278. 1877   New York, D. Appleton. viii + 352 pp. From stereos of
               No. 1277. 845(18).   [510

1279. 1878   London, John Murray. 8vo, xvi + 352 pp. Second
               edition. Binding: as No. 1277. T, DLC.

1280. 1880   London, John Murray. As No. 1279. CD; 846(3). [304

1281. 1884   London, John Murray. xxiv + 352 pp. Third thousand.
               Preface by Francis Darwin. D, L; T, 847(2).   [305

1282. 1886   New York, D. Appleton. As No. 1278. 849(5).

1283. 1888   London, John Murray. As No. 1281, still third thous-
               and. T, 850(2).   [306

1284. 1889   London, John Murray. As No. 1283. 851(3).

1285. 1889   New York, D. Appleton. As No. 1282. 852(1).

1286. 1892   London, John Murray. As No. 1284, but fourth
               thousand. L; T, 853(8).   [307

1287. 1893   New York, D. Appleton. As No. 1285. 854(4).

1288. 1896   New York, D. Appleton. As No. 1287. 855(31).

                                                                [511

1289. 1897   New York, D. Appleton. As No. 1288.

1290. 1899   New York, D. Appleton. xxiv + 351 pp. From stereos
               of No. 1281. 856(1).

1291. [c. 1900] New York, D. Appleton. xxiv + 351 pp. As No.
               1290. Selected Works, Westminster Edition. 1,000
               copies. T, 848(3).

1292. 1903   New York, D. Appleton. As No. 1290. 857(8).

1293. 1915   New York, D. Appleton. As No. 1292. Popular Uni-
               form Edition.

1294. 1969   Brussels, Editions Culture et Civilisation. viii + 352 pp.
               Facsimile of No. 1277, but 218 mm.

1295. 1972   New York, Abrahams Magazine Service. viii + 352 pp.
               Facsimile of No. 1288 (1896).

FRENCH

1296. 1878   Paris, C. Reinwald. xxxvi + 361 pp. Translated by
               Édouard Heckel. With an analytical preface by Amédée
               Guillaume August Coutance. D, L; T, 839(1).   [512

GERMAN

1297. 1877   Stuttgart, Schweizerbart. viii + 304 pp. Translated by
               J. V. Carus. Collected Works Vol. 9, part 3. L; 1295(1).
                                                                [513

1298. 1899   Stuttgart, Schweizerbart. As No. 1297. Second edition.
              Collected Works Vol. 9, part 3.

ITALIAN

1299. 1884   Turin, Unione. 239 pp. Translated by Giovanni
              Canestrini and Lamberto Moschen.

JAPANESE

1300. 1949   Tokyo, Kaizōsha. Collected Works Vol. 14.

ROMANIAN

1301. 1965   [Bucharest], National Academy. xxii + 497 pp. Trans-
              lated by Eugen Margulius. Introduction by Vasile
              Mârza and Ion Tarnavschi. With *Insectivorous plants* =
              No. 1243. Clasicii Ştiinţei Universale No. 5. L, LSc; T,
              67–89264.

RUSSIAN

1302. 1948   Moscow, Academy of Sciences U.S.S.R. pp. 31–251.
              Translated by A. P. Il'inskiĭ and E. D. D'yakov.
              Introduction by A. P. Il'inskiĭ. Collected Works Vol. 7.
              L.

Down Friendly Club

Life and letters (Vol. I, pp. 142–143) explains that Darwin had helped to
found the village Friendly Club and had acted as its treasurer for thirty
years, but does not mention this leaflet. The Club had its annual meeting
at Down House, usually on Whit Monday. After the Friendly Societies
Act of 1875 (38 & 39 Vict. Ch. 60), and an amending Act of 1876 (39 &
40 Vict. Ch. 22), under which the Downe Club would have been
placed in Class 5 'Local Village and Country Societies', there seems to
have been dissatisfaction; some members wanted to disband and share
out the proceeds. The leaflet was distributed to members, in February
1877, to dissuade them, successfully, from this course. Emma Darwin
(Vol. II, p. 237) wrote to Francis on Whit Tuesday, February 3rd, 1879,
that the band was expected that day. Only the copy in the Darwin
archive at Cambridge is known. The facsimile copies carry the quotation from *Life and letters* on the verso of the text leaf.

ENGLISH

1303. 1877   No place, no printer. *To members of the Down Friendly
               Club*. Single sheet, 267 × 210 mm. Dated February 19.
               CD.

1304. 1973   [London, University College London printed.] [4] pp.
               210 × 197 mm. Reduced facsimile of No. 1303. Text
               p. [1]. Note by R. B. Freeman & P. J. Gautrey p. [2]
               Pp. [3–4 blank]. On card. 50 copies. C, L; T.

Biographical Sketch of an Infant

Although originally published in a serial, this paper demands a place
here because it has since appeared in books and as a pamphlet. It was
written up from observations in his diary on his first-born son William
Erasmus, from 1839–1841. The previous number of *Mind* (p. 252) had
contained a translation of a paper on the same subject by Hippolyte
Taine which first appeared in *Revue philosophique* for 1876. Darwin sent
it to the editor, George Croom Robertson, with some hesitation—'If
you do not think fit, as is very likely, will you please return it to me'.
He notes that he had used some of his observations in *The expression of
the emotions*. C. Ounsted, in a recent reprint (No. 1308), says that he
'conquered, as the reader will see, most of developmental psychology
in a single sweep'.

It was translated in the same year into French, German and Russian,
and, in 1914, appeared as a pamphlet in Armenian.

ENGLISH

1305. 1877   A biographical sketch of an infant. *Mind*, Vol. 2, pp.
               285–294. July. = No. 1779.

1306. [1956] In No. 1613.

1307. 1957   In No. 1614.

1308. 1971   In *Developmental Medicine and Child Neurology*, Vol. 13,
               No. 5, Suppl. No. 24, 8 pp. Preface by C. Ounsted,

1309. 1974   In Gruber, Howard E. *Darwin on man*. pp. 464–474. See
               No. 1582.

ARMENIAN

1310. 1914   Shusha. 26 pp. Translated from Russian No. 1316 by
               Ovak Stepanyats.

FRENCH

1311.   1877   In *Rev. Sci.* Vol. 13, pp. 25–29.

GERMAN

1312.   1877   In *Kosmos.* Vol. I, pp. 367–376.
1313.   1885–1886 In No. 1602. L; T.

RUSSIAN

1314.   1877   Moscow, University of Moscow. 14 pp. Translated by
                   V. [= V. N. Benzengr]. Reprinted from *Moscow medical
                   Journal.*
1315.   1881   St Petersburg, M. A. Hahn printed. 24 pp.
1316.   1900   St Petersburg, V. M. Nadutkin. 41 pp. Second edition.
                   Also contains the paper by H. Taine from *Mind*, Vol.
                   2, pp. 252–259.
1317.   1953   Moscow, Academy of Sciences U.S.S.R. pp. 932–940.
                   Translated by S. H. Hellerstein. Collected Works Vol.
                   5. L.

Flowers and Their Unbidden Guests

This English translation of Kerner's book contains a brief prefatory
letter by Darwin in praise of it.

ENGLISH

1318.   1878   London, C. Kegan Paul. in Kerner [von Marilaun],
                   Anton *Flowers and their unbidden guests. With a prefatory
                   letter by Charles Darwin . . . the translation revised and
                   edited by W. Ogle* etc. 8vo, 198 mm, xvi + 164 pp,
                   3 plates. Darwin' letter pp. v–vi. Translation of *Die
                   Schützmittel der Blüthen gegen unberufene Gaste*, Inns-
                   bruck 1876. The original is without Darwin's letter.
                   Binding: green or brown cloth. Inserted advertise-
                   ments dated '78', '79' or '7.81'. Price 9s. CD, C, L; T,
                   775(7).   [308

Erasmus Darwin

Ernst Krause's short scientific biography of Darwin's grandfather had
originally appeared in the German periodical *Kosmos* in February 1879,
a *Gratulationsheft* for his seventieth birthday. This translation was pub-

lished in November, and in it Krause altered the text to refer, indirectly, to Samuel Butler's *Evolution old and new* which had appeared in May. The alterations are not specifically noticed in the book, and Butler took strong exception to them, an exception which resulted in a sordid and one-sided quarrel in which Darwin remained silent.

Darwin's own biographical contribution, which was based on family papers, is longer than the original article, and, in recognition that it contains his work, the binding is standard green cloth. Festing Jones, in his *Samuel Butler, a memoir* (Vol. I, p. 320, 1919) states that the translation was instigated by Charles Darwin and his brother Erasmus. The price was 7s. 6d. and the *Autobiography* notes that, by May 1881, only 800 or 900 copies had been sold.

The so-called second edition of 1887, which was edited by Francis Darwin, consists of sheets of the first, or from stereos, except that page [1] has been reset with the dropped title altered from 'Preliminary notice' to 'Erasmus Darwin'. The title changes to give Darwin more credit for the work, and the preliminaries are altered to include a note, on page v, which states that Krause had altered his text in the first edition from that of the original German; there are also seven errata on page [xii]. There is a freak copy at the University of Toronto which has a title page and preface of the first edition, bound with the additional matter and text of the second. It is a school prize, bound in full calf, and cannot be a made-up copy.

An American edition, from English stereos, appeared in 1880, but there were no later reprints of the work except for a facsimile of the first edition in 1971. Darwin's notice alone appeared in German in 1880, and has since been translated into Russian.

ENGLISH

1319. 1879   London, John Murray. In Krause, Ernst *Erasmus Darwin. Translated from the German by W. S. Dallas, with a preliminary notice by Charles Darwin.* 8vo, 185 mm, iv + 216 pp, portrait, 2 full page text woodcuts. Darwin's notice pp. 1–127. Krause's biography alone first published in *Kosmos* Vol. 3, February 1879. Binding: standard green cloth. Price 7s. 6d. C, L; T, 140(16).
[309

1320. 1880   New York, D. Appleton. 8vo in 12s, iv + 216 pp. From stereos of No. 1319, but without signatures and no caption to portrait. 141(19).

1321. 1887   London, John Murray. *The Life of Erasmus Darwin* . . .

being an introduction to an essay on his scientific work. Second edition. 8vo, 190 mm, xi + 216 pp. Darwin's notice pp. 1–217. Text as No. 1319, with preliminaries altered. Binding: as No. 1233. C, L; 147(4).   [310

1322. (1971) Westmead, Farnborough, Hants, Gregg International, Meisenheim, Glan, West Germany printed. Facsimile of No. 1319. T.

GERMAN

1323.   1880   Leipzig, E. Günther. vi + 236 pp. Darwin's notice pp. 1–72. Darwinstische Schriften No. 6. L; 142(3).

[515

RUSSIAN

1324.   1959   Moscow, Academy of Sciences U.S.S.R. pp. 251–306. Darwin's notice only. Translated by V. N. Sukachev. Introduction by S. L. Sobol'. Collected Works Vol. 9. L.

The Power of Movement in Plants

This was an extension of the work on climbing plants to show that the same mechanisms hold good for flowering plants in general. It was another specialist book and seems to have sold fewer copies than any other, and was not reprinted in England after the year of Darwin's death until modern facsimiles appeared of the first thousand in 1966 and the second in 1969.

The first edition was published on November 6, 1880, and it is recorded that 1,500 copies were sold at Murray's autumn sale. It was in a standard binding and cost 15s. There are thirty-two pages of inserted advertisements dated May 1878; to have them more than two years earlier than the date of the book is unusual, but this is normal and they are present in Darwin's own copy, at Cambridge. In this issue there are two lines of errata on page x which are corrected in the second thousand of the same year. In this second thousand, the advertisements may be the same as those in the first, but are more often dated November 1880. In the third thousand of 1882, the last Murray printing, the preface is slightly altered. In all three, the spine title differs from the form on the title page, reading 'The movements of plants'.

It appeared in French, German and Russian by 1882, and in Italian and Romanian later.

ENGLISH

1325.   1880   London, John Murray. *The power of movement in plants.*
               8vo, 188 mm, x + 592 pp, 196 text woodcuts. Assisted
               by Francis Darwin. Binding: standard green cloth.
               Price 15s. CD, C, D, L; T, 1203(20).   [311

1326.   1880   London, John Murray. As No. 1325, but second thous-
               and. T.   [312

1327.   1881   New York, D. Appleton. x + 592 pp. From stereos of
               No. 1325. 1204(20).   [516

1328.   1882   London, John Murray. As No. 1326, but third thous-
               and. T. 1205(1).   [313

1329.   1883   New York, D. Appleton, As No. 1327. 1206(5).

1330.   1885   New York, D. Appleton. As No. 1329. 1207(3).

1331.   1888   New York, D. Appleton. As No. 1330. 1208(8).

1332.   1892   New York, D. Appleton. As No. 1331. 1209(4).

1333.   1896   New York, D. Appleton. As No. 1332. 1210(8).

1334.   1897   New York, D. Appleton. As No. 1333. 1211(13).

1335.   1898   New York, D. Appleton. As No. 1334. 1212(4).

1336.   1900   New York, D. Appleton. As No. 1335.

1337.   [c. 1900] New York, D. Appleton. As No. 1336, but West-
               minster Edition, limited to 1000 copies.

1338.   1915   New York, D. Appleton. As No. 1336, but Popular
               Uniform Edition.

1339.   1966   New York, Da Capo Press. xviii + 592 pp. Introduc-
               tion by Barbara Gillespie Pickard. Facsimile of No.
               1325. T, 65–23402.

1340.   1969   Brussels, Editions Culture et Civilisation. x + 592 pp.
               Second thousand. Facsimile of No. 1326, but 218 mm.

1341.   1972   New York, Abrahams Magazine Service. x + 592 pp.
               Facsimile of No. 1333 (1896).

FRENCH

1342.   1882   Paris, C. Reinwald. xxvi + 599 pp. Translated and with
               notes and a preface by Édouard Heckel. D; T, 909(3).
                                                                [517

GERMAN

1343.   1881   Stuttgart, Schweizerbart. ix + 506 pp. Translated by
               J. V. Carus. Collected Works Vol. 13. L, BS; T,
               802(1).   [518

1344. 1899 Stuttgart, Schweizerbart. As No. 1343. Second edition. Collected Works Vol. 13.

1345. 1910 Stuttgart, Schweizerbart. As No. 1344. Second edition. Collected Works Vol. 13.

1346. 1919 Stuttgart, Schweizerbart. As No. 1345. Second edition.

ITALIAN

1347. 1884 Turin, Unione. 406 pp. Translated by Giovanni and Riccardo Canestrini. D. [519

ROMANIAN

1348. 1970 [Bucharest], National Academy. xxii + 446 pp. Translated by Eugen Margulius. With *Climbing plants.* = No. 864. Clasicii Ştiinţei Universale No. 8. LSc; T.

RUSSIAN

1349. 1882 Kiev, F. A. Johanson, University Press. vii + 443 pp. Translated by G. Miloradovich and A. Kobelyatskiĭ.

1350. 1941 Moscow, Academy of Sciences U.S.S.R. pp. 153–517. Translated by N. A. Lyubinskiĭ. Edited and introduction by N. G. Kholodniĭ. Notes by S. L. Sobol' and N. G. Kholodniĭ. Collected Works Vol. 8. L, LSc; DLC.

Prehistoric Europe

1351. 1881[= 1880] London, Edward Stanford. In Geikie, James *Prehistoric Europe. A geological sketch.* 8vo, 229 mm, xviii + 592 pp, 2 tinted plates (one folding), 11 text woodcuts. Extracts from 2 letters by Darwin pp. 141–142. Issued late in 1880. Binding: blue cloth. Price £1. 5s. C, L; T, 698(22). [314

Letter on Vivisection

This letter by Darwin was written to Professor Frithiof Holmgren, Professor of Physiology at Uppsala, on April 14, 1881, and it appeared in *The Times* on the 18th and later in *Nature* and the *British Medical Journal.*

In the same year, it appeared in a pamphlet which also contains two other letters, one of them to Darwin, by George R. Jesse, the Honorary Secretary of the Society for the total Abolition and utter Suppression of Vivisection. I have not been able to see a copy of the first edition, but its existence is inferred from the second.

ENGLISH

1352.   1881   [Letter to Frithiof Holmgren on vivisection.] *The Times*,
                London. April 18. Letter dated April 14. = No. 1792
                (part).

1353.   1881   Mr Darwin on vivisection. *Nature*, London, Vol. 23,
                p. 583. April 21. Reprint of No. 1352. = No. 1792
                (part).

1354.   1881   Mr Darwin on vivisection. *British Medical Journal*,
                London. Vol. 1, p. 660. Reprint of No. 1353. = No.
                1792 (part).

1355.   1881   [First edition of No. 1356.] Not seen.   [315

1356.   1881   London, William Pickering. In Jesse, George *compiler
                Correspondence with Charles Darwin . . . on experiment-
                ing upon living animals.* Second title *History of the founda-
                tion and operations of the Society Abolition Vivisection* [sic].
                8vo, 210 mm, 12 pp. Second edition. First letter a
                reprint of No. 1352. L; 552(1).   [316

Vegetable Mould and Worms

This last book is outside the main stream of Darwin's work, and reverts to his earlier geological interests. He had indeed published papers on mould in 1838 and in 1840 (Nos 1648 & 1655). The famous 'worm-stone' is still to be seen at Down House. The book was remarkably successful, selling 6,000 copies within a year, and 13,000 before the end of the century. To begin with it sold far faster than *The origin of species* had.

The first edition went to press on May 1, 1881, and was published on October 10. The issue was said to have been of 2,000 copies, but this cannot be entirely correct because copies of the second thousand have this printed on the title page. However these two are otherwise identical. The binding was standard with the word 'Earthworms' in the spine title, although this does not occur on the title page. The price was 9s. The third, fourth and fifth thousands were printed before the end of 1881, and each states its thousand on its title page. The third has a two item errata slip inserted before page [1], but the second erratum is itself wrong, attempting to correct 1° 49′ to 2° 45′, whereas the text reads 2° 4′. 1° 49′ is however the figure given in the first two issues. In the fourth thousand these two errata have been corrected; in the fifth there are textual changes which do not affect the collation.

Darwin comments that he corrected the sixth thousand of 1882, but the seventh, of which some copies are dated 1882 and others 1883, has a footnote at the end of the introduction, signed F[rancis] D[arwin], which refers, in four lines, to some work of P. E. Müller's which his father had been told about but had not seen. In the eleventh thousand, of 1888, this note is enlarged to nine lines by a reference to a further paper of Müller's which was published in 1884. In this issue Francis Darwin's initials are omitted, but the date of the first edition, October 10, 1881, is added. A collection of texts, although the changes are small, seems to call for first, third, fourth, fifth, sixth, seventh and eleventh thousands. Later printings were from stereos of 1888 until 1904 when the text was reset and the figures transferred to plates.

The work appeared in America in 1882, some copies being in the U.S.A. form of the International Scientific Series, although no work wholly by Darwin was published in the English series put out by King and later by Kegan Paul. After a long gap, since an American printing of 1915, an important edition, with an introduction by *Sir* Albert Howard, appeared in 1945 and has been reprinted three times since. A Brussels facsimile of the second thousand appeared in 1969. Translations into French, German, Italian and Russian appeared before the end of 1882, but Armenian in 1896 seems to have been the only language added since.

ENGLISH

1357. 1881   London, John Murray, *The formation of vegetable mould, through the action of worms, with observations on their habits.* 8vo, 183 mm, vii + 326 pp, 15 text woodcuts. Binding: standard green cloth. Price 9s. CD, C, D, L; T, 918(17).   [317

1358. 1881   London, John Murray. As No. 1357, but second thousand. T.   [318

1359. 1881   London, John Murray. As No. 1358, but third thousand and with errata slip. T.   [319

1360. 1881   London, John Murray. As No. 1359, but fourth thousand and with errata corrected. C; T.   [320

1361. 1881   London, John Murray. As No. 1360, but fifth thousand (corrected), and with textual changes. L; T.   [321

1362. 1882   London, John Murray. As No. 1361, but sixth thousand
               (corrected), and with textual changes, CD, L; T, 919(2).
                                                                    [322

1363. 1882   New York, D. Appleton. vii + 326 pp. From stereos of
               No. 1357. Some copies International Scientific Series
               Vol. XXXVII. 921(14).   [520

1364. 1882   London, John Murray. vii + 328 pp. Seventh thousand.
               Corrected by Francis Darwin. 920(3).

1365. 1883   London, John Murray. As No. 1364 and seventh
               thousand. L; T.   [323

1366. 1883   London, John Murray. As No. 1365, but eighth thous-
               and. T, 922(1).   [324

1367. 1883   London, John Murray. As No. 1366, but ninth thous-
               and. CD; T, 923(1).   [325

1368. 1883   New York, D. Appleton. As No. 1363 and some copies
               International Scientific Series. T.

1369. 1885   New York, D. Appleton. As No. 1368. 925(2).

1370. 1886   New York, D. Appleton. As No. 1369. 926(1).   [521

1371. 1887   New York, Humboldt Publishing Co. 95 pp. Extracts
               only. Library of Popular Science Vol. 9, No. 92. Later
               undated issues. T, 927(6).

1372. 1888   London, John Murray. As No. 1367, but tenth thous-
               and. T, 928(3).   [326

1373. 1888   London, John Murray. As No. 1372, but eleventh
               thousand. Altered footnote on p. 7. T, 929(3).   [327

1374. 1888   New York, D. Appleton. As No. 1370. 930(5).

1375. 1889   New York, Humboldt Publishing Co. As No. 1371.
               931(2).

1376. 1890   New York, D. Appleton. As No. 1374. 932(7).   [522

1377. 1892   London, John Murray. As No. 1373, but twelfth
               thousand. T, 933(2).   [328

1378. 1892   New York, D. Appleton. As No. 1376. 934(3).

1379. 1895   New York, D. Appleton. As No. 1378. 935(2).

1380. 1896   New York, D. Appleton. As No. 1379. 936(16).

1381. 1897   London, John Murray. As No. 1377, but thirteenth
               thousand. Price 6s. See No. 1382. T, 937(7).   [329

1382. 1897   London, John Murray. Price 2s. 6d. Not seen. Advert-
               ised by publisher.   [330

1383. 1897   New York, D. Appleton. As No. 1380. 938(15).

1384. 1898   New York, D. Appleton. As No. 1383. 939(11).

1385. 1899   New York, D. Appleton. As No. 1384. 940(1).

1386. 1900   New York, D. Appleton. As No. 1385. 941(3).

1387. [c. 1900] New York, D. Appleton. As No. 1297. Selected Works, Westminster Edition. 1,000 copies. 917(1).

1388. 1902 New York, D. Appleton. As No. 1386. 942(2).

1389. 1904 London, John Murray. viii + 296 pp. Thirteenth thousand [sic], 10 plates. The text figures of earlier issues transferred to plates, Binding: leaf green cloth; late cases have spine titling in black, not gilt. C; T, 943(10).   [331

1390. 1907 New York, D. Appleton. As No. 1388. 944(2).

1391. 1911 New York, D. Appleton. As No. 1390. 945(3).

1392. 1915 New York, D. Appleton. As No. 1391. Popular Uniform Edition. 946(2).

1393. [1944] Emaus, Pa., Organic Gardening. 64 pp. Extracts only. 947(2).

1394. (1945) London, Faber & Faber. 153 pp. Title *Darwin on humus and the earthworm. The formation of vegetable mould* etc. Introduction by *Sir* Albert Howard. C, L; T, 828(5), 948(6).   [332

1395. (1945) London, Faber & Faber. As No. 1394, but second impression.

1396. (1948) London, Faber & Faber. As No. 1395, but third impression.

1397. [1949] Emaus, Pa., Organic Gardening. As No. 1393. Organic Gardening Library No. 25. 949(2).

1398. (1966) London, Faber & Faber. As No. 1396, but fourth impression. 66–9240/CD, 67–92887.

1399. 1967 New York, Humanities Press. U.S.A. edition of No. 1398.

1400. 1969 Brussels, Editions Culture et Civilisation. vii + 326 pp. Second thousand. Facsimile of No. 1358, but 218 mm.

1401. 1972 New York, Abrahams Magazine Service. vii + 326 pp. Facsimile of No. 1380 (1896).

ARMENIAN

1402. 1896 Tiflis, Armyanskoe Izdatel'skoe Obshchestvo. 47 pp. Extracts only. Translated from the Russian by Levi Melik-Adamyan,

FRENCH

1403. 1882 Paris, C. Reinwald. xxviii + 264 pp. Translated by M. Lévêque. Preface by Edmond Perrier. BS; T, 1229(2).   [523

GERMAN

1404. 1882   Stuttgart, Schweizerbart. vii + 184 pp. Translated by
               J. V. Carus. Collected Works Vol. 14, part 1. D, L; T,
               803(3).
1405. 1884   Stuttgart, Schweizerbart. As No. 1404.   [524
1406. 1899   Stuttgart, Schweizerbart. As No. 1405. Second edition.
               Collected Works Vol. 14, part 1.

ITALIAN

1407. 1882   Unione, Turin. 140 pp. Translated by M. Lessona.

RUSSIAN

1408. 1882   Moscow, S. P. Arkhipov. vii + 204 pp. Translated by
               M. Lindeman.
1409. 1882   Moscow, A. P. Vasil'ev. iv + 186 pp. Translated by
               M. A. Menzbir.
1410. 1899   St Petersburg, O. N. Popov. 100 pp. Translated by
               M. A. Menzbir. Collected Works Vol. 4, part 1.
1411. 1912   St Petersburg, *Vestnik Znaniya*, V. V. Bitner. Trans-
               lated by A. A. Nikolaev. Edited by V. V. Bitner.
               Collected Works Vol. 5, part 2.
1412. 1929   Moscow-Leningrad, State Edition, pp. 295–469. Trans-
               lated by M. A. Menzbir. Collected Works Vol. 4,
               part 2.
1413. 1936   Moscow, Academy of Sciences U.S.S.R. pp. 113–238.
               Translated by M. A. Menzbir. Introduction and edited
               by V. V. Stanchinskiĭ. Collected Works Vol. 2. L;
               DLC.

Studies in the Theory of Descent

1414. 1882   London, Sampson Low. In Weismann, August *Studies
               in the theory of descent. With notes and additions by the
               author . . . with a prefatory notice by Charles Darwin.*
               8vo, 218 mm, 2 vols, xxv + 400, 401–729 pp, 8 colour
               plates. Translated and edited by Raphael Meldola.
               Darwin's notice pp. v–vi. Text is a translation, with
               additions by the author, of *Studien zur Descendenz-
               Theorie.* Leipzig 1875–1876. Binding: green cloth.
               Price £2. C, L; T, DLC.   [333

RUSSIAN

1415.   1939   Moscow, Academy of Sciences U.S.S.R. p. 755. Dar-
                 win's notice only. Translated and with notes by S. L.
                 Sobol'. Collected Works Vol. 3. L; DLC.

Animal Intelligence

Romanes sent this to the press before Darwin's death, and the preface
contains a note to that effect. The book is largely made up of long
quotations from the work of others, including *The origin of species* and
The descent of man; but it also contains a number of extracts from
Darwin's notes on behaviour, especially of the social insects, which he
had lent to Romanes. These had not appeared elsewhere until Stauffer's
transcription of the second part of the 'big book' on the origin of species
in 1975 (No. 1583). They are discussed below under Romanes' *Essay on
instinct*, 1883.

The nine so-called editions are mere reprintings from stereos with
new title leaves, a bad habit of the International Scientific Series.

ENGLISH

1416.   1882   London, Kegan Paul Trench and Co. In Romanes,
                 George J. *Animal intelligence*. 8vo, 185 mm, xiv + 520
                 pp, 6 text woodcuts. Extracts from Darwin's notes
                 throughout. International Scientific Series Vol. XLI.
                 Binding: red cloth of the series. Price 5s. C, L; T. [334
1417.   1882   London, Kegan Paul Trench and Co. As No. 1416, but
                 second edition.   [335
1418.   1883   London, Kegan Paul Trench and Co. As No. 1417, but
                 third edition. L; T.   [336
1419.   1883   New York, D. Appleton. xiv + 520 pp. As No. 1416
                 and from stereos. International Scientific Series No.
                 XLIV. DLC.   [526
1420.   1886   London, Kegan Paul Trench and Co. As No. 1418, but
                 fourth edition. DLC.   [337
1421.   1889   London, Kegan Paul Trench and Co. As No. 1420, but
                 fifth edition.   [338
1422.   1892   London, Kegan Paul Trench and Co. As No. 1421 and
                 fifth edition.
1423.   1892   New York, D. Appleton. As No. 1419. International
                 Scientific Series Vol. XLIV.

1424.   1896   London, Kegan Paul Trench and Co. As No. 1422, but
                sixth edition. T. |339

1425.   1898   London, Kegan Paul Trench and Co. As No. 1424, but
                seventh edition. T.   [340

1426.   1904   London, Kegan Paul Trench and Co. As No. 1425, but
                eighth edition.   [341

1427.   1910   London, Kegan Paul Trench and Co. As No. 1426, but
                ninth edition. L.   [342

1428.   1970   New York, Gregg International. Facsimile of No. 1416.

FRENCH

1429.   1887   Paris, F. Alcan. 2 vols. Preface by Édmond Perrier.
                Bibliotheque Scientifique Internationale Vols LVIII &
                LIX.   [527

1430.   1889   Paris, F. Alcan. 2 vols. As No. 1429, but second edition.
                Bibliotheque Scientifique Internationale Vols LVIII &
                LIX.

1431.   1898   Paris, F. Alcan. 2 vols. As No. 1430, but third edition.
                Bibliotheque Scientifique Internationale Vols LVIII &
                LIX.

Fertilisation of Flowers

1432.   1883   London, Macmillan. In Müller, Hermann *The fertilisa-
                tion of flowers* . . . *with a preface by Charles Darwin.* 8vo,
                223 mm, x + 669 pp, 186 text woodcuts. Translated
                by D'Arcy W. Thompson. Darwin's preface pp. vii–x.
                Text is translation of *Die Befruchtüng* der *Blumen durch
                Insekten.* Leipzig 1873. Binding: green cloth. Price
                £1. 1s. C, L; T, 862(26).   [343

RUSSIAN

1433.   1950   Moscow, Academy of Sciences U.S.S.R. pp. 652–654.
                Darwin's preface only. Translated by V. A. Rybin.
                Notes by I. M. Polyakov. Collected Works Vol. 6. L;
                DLC.

Essay on Instinct

This forms an appendix to Romanes' *Mental evolution in animals,* 1883.
It was read at a meeting of the Linnean Society of London on December

6, 1883 (see No. 1804), but it was not published in the *Journal*, although
a page proof copy, for pages 347–378, of Volume 17, No. 102, due to be
issued for February 29, 1884, survives at Christ's College Cambridge.
The paper was doubtless withdrawn because its content had already
appeared in the book late in the previous year.

The manuscript forms part of Chapter X of the second part of
Darwin's 'big book' on the origin of species. Stauffer, in No. 1583
(1975, pp. 463–466) shows that folios 50–116, except 80–97, were printed
complete, as well as a few other passages woven into the text. He also
gives a new transcript of the whole and discusses its history, quoting
from Ethel Duncan Romanes' life of her late husband (1896).

ENGLISH

1434. 1883   London, Kegan Paul Trench and Co. In Romanes,
George John *Mental evolution in animals. With a posthu-
mous essay on instinct by Charles Darwin.* 8vo, 218 mm,
411 pp, 2 charts (one folding), 3 text woodcuts.
Darwin's essay pp. [355]–384 and index pp. 405–411.
See also No. 1804. Binding: maroon cloth. Price 12s.
C, L; T.   [344

1435. 1884   New York, D. Appleton. 411 pp. As No. 1434 and
from stereos. DLC.   [528

1436. 1885   London, Kegan Paul Trench and Co. As No. 1434. T.
                                                       [345

1437. 1895   New York, D. Appleton. As No. 1435.

1438. 1900   New York, D. Appleton. As No. 1437. 1201(4).

1439. 1970   New York, Abrahams Magazine Service. 411 pp.
Facsimile of No. 1343 (1884).

1440. (1975) London, Cambridge University Press. In No. 1583,
pp. 466–527. Complete transcript of Chapter X of
original mss.

FRENCH

1441 1884   Paris, C. Reinwald. xviii + 412 pp. Translated by H. C.
de Varigny.   [529

1442. 1891   Paris, F. Alcan. As No. 1441.

GERMAN

1443. 1885   Leipzig, E. Günther. vi + 456 pp. Translated by E.
Krause. L; 999(2).   [530

1444. 1886   Leipzig, E. Günther. In No. 1602, pp. 9–51. Darwin's
               essay only.   [531
1445. 1887   Leipzig, E. Günther. As No. 1443. Darwinistische
               Schriften, neue billige Ausgabe II, Vol. 5.   [532
1446. 1888   Leipzig, E. Günther. As No. 1445. LNH.

ITALIAN

1447. 1907   Turin, Fratelli Bocca. xv + 423 pp. Translated by
               Giovanni Scoccianti. Biblioteca di Scienze Moderna
               No. 31.

ROMANIAN

1448. 1967   [Bucharest], National Academy. xi + 242 pp. Trans-
               lated by Eugen Margulius. Introduction by Vasile D.
               Mârza. Clasicii Ştiinţei Universale No. 7. D, LSc.; T.

RUSSIAN

1449. 1894   *Journal of scientific Review*, St Petersburg. 39 pp.
               Darwin's essay only. Translated by M. Filippov.
1450. 1896   *Journal of scientific Review*, St Petersburg. 35 pp. Second
               edition. Darwin's essay only. Translated by M. Filippov.
1451. 1939   Moscow, Academy of Sciences U.S.S.R. pp. 713–724.
               Darwin's essay only. Translated and with notes by S. L.
               Sobol'. Collected Works Vol. 3. L; DLC.

Life and Letters and Autobiography

This heading is used to contain the original edition of *Life and letters*,
which is the first and basic life of Darwin, as well as its American and
foreign language equivalents. The work contains the first published
version of Darwin's autobiography, which was edited to avoid giving
offence to his widow, and therefore the heading also includes the
printings of the full text which first appeared in English in 1958,
although it had appeared in Russian translation, independently transcribed from the manuscript, in the previous year. It also includes the
one volume abridgement which first appeared in 1892.

The original edition went through five printings, totalling seven
thousand copies, in little more than a year, each one being slightly
corrected, and also appeared, in two instead of three volumes, in
America with frequent reprints. The abridged edition is not to be

considered merely as a short, and cheap version since it does contain matter not present in the original. The 1902 printing of it has a brief addition to the preface and a new portrait. Some recent editions of the autobiography also contain the autobiographical fragment which is proper to *More letters*.

The whole of *Life and letters* has appeared in French, German and Norwegian, the last the only Darwin in that language. The autobiography alone, or abridgements, have appeared in a further seventeen.

ENGLISH

1452. 1887 London, John Murray. Darwin, Francis *editor The life and letters of Charles Darwin, including an autobiographical chapter.* 8vo, 220 mm, 3 vols, ix + 395, [iv] + 393, iv + 418 pp., 6 errata in Vol. II p. [iv], 3 errata in Vol. III p. iv, 3 portraits, 3 plates, one facsimile of holograph. Binding: grey-green cloth as Nos 422 & 965. Price £1. 16s. C, L; T, 1087(17).   [346

1453. 1887 London, John Murray. As No. 1452, but fifth thousand revised and errata corrected. 1090(2).

1454. 1887 London, John Murray. As No. 1453, but second edition, with small corrections. 1088(4).   [347

1455. 1887 London, John Murray. As No. 1454, but third edition. Vol. I with 2 errata for Vol. II and 14 for Vol. III. Vol. III with 14 errata on slip. 1089(3).   [348

1456. 1887 New York, D. Appleton. 2 vols. T, 1091(15).

1457. 1888 London, John Murray. As No. 1455, but seventh thousand, revised. T, 1092(13).   [349

1458. 1888 New York, D. Appleton. 2 vols. As No. 1456. 1093(22).
                                                                    [534

1459. 1889 New York, D. Appleton. 2 vols. As No. 1458. 1094(1).

1460. 1891 New York, D. Appleton. 2 vols. As No. 1459. 1095(6).
                                                                    [535

1461. 1892 London, John Murray. [Abridged edition.] Darwin, Francis *editor Charles Darwin: his life told in an autobiographical chapter, and in a selected series of his published letters.* 8vo, 190 mm, vi + 348 pp., portrait, facsimile of holograph. Contains some matter not in No. 1452 etc. Binding: grey-green cloth. Price 7s. 6d. C, L; T, 811(4).   [350

1462. 1892 New York, D. Appleton. [Abridged edition.] vi + 352 pp. Text as No. 1461. 812(5).   [536

1463. 1893   New York, D. Appleton. 2 vols. As No. 1460. 1096(1).

1464. 1893   New York, D. Appleton. [Abridged edition.] As No. 1462. 813(15).

1465. 1896   New York, D. Appleton. 2 vols. As No. 1463. 1097(20).
                                                                    [537

1466. 1897   New York, D. Appleton. 2 vols. As No. 1465. 1098(6).

1467. 1898   New York, D. Appleton. 2 vols. As No. 1466. 1099(8).

1468. 1899   New York, D. Appleton, 2 vols. As No. 1467. 1100(5).

1469. [c. 1900] New York, D. Appleton. 2 vols. As No. 1468, but Westminster Edition, limited to 1000 copies.

1470. 1901   New York, D. Appleton. 2 vols. As No. 1468. 1101(5).

1471. 1902   London, John Murray. [Abridged edition.] New edition. As No. 1461, but with additions to preface. Binding: leaf green cloth, L; T, 814(5).   [351

1472. 1902   London, John Murray. [Abridged edition.] As No. 1471, but fourth thousand in this form.   [352

1473. 1902   London, John Murray. [Abridged edition.] As No. 1472, but sixth thousand in this form, and with 'Note to the second edition', referring to the replacement of the portrait by Julia Margaret Cameron with one by Elliot and Fry. Binding: variant *a.* as No. 1472; variant *b.* green buckram, paper label. T.   [353

1474. 1902   New York, D. Appleton. As No. 1470. DLC.

1475. 1904   New York, D. Appleton. As No. 1474. 1102(4).

1476. 1905   New York, D. Appleton. As No. 1475.

1477. 1908   London, John Murray. [Abridged edition.] As No. 1473. T, 815(2).   [354

1478. [1908] [Boston], Directors of the Old South Work. *The education of Darwin. The first section of Darwin's autobiography, written in 1876.* 20 pp. Old South Leaflets Vol. 8, No. 194. L; 858(10).

1479. 1909   Cambridge, University Press. in Seward, A. C. *editor Darwin and modern science. Essays in commemoration of the centenary of the birth of Charles Darwin and of the fiftieth anniversary of the publication of The origin of species.* 8vo, 235 mm, xvii + 595 pp, 2 portraits, 3 plates. Introductory letter from *Sir* Joseph Dalton Hooker. Dates of publication of Charles Darwin's books and of the principal events of his life pp. [xiii]–xvii, i.e. extracts from Autobiography and letters. Binding: green buckram bevelled boards. C, L; T, 504(24).

1480. 1909   New York, G. P. Putnam's Sons, Cambridge, Uni-

versity Press. All as No. 1479, but U.S.A. imprint
added. 507(4).

1481. 1909   Cambridge, University Press. In *Order of the proceedings
at the Darwin celebrations held at Cambridge June 22–June
24, 1909. With a sketch of Darwin's life.* 4to, 260 mm,
23 pp, 6 portraits, 5 plates, one map. Printed for the
University. A sketch of Darwin's life pp. 13–23, i.e.
extracts from Autobiography and letters. Binding:
brown paper printed boards, white parchment, some
copies buckram, spine. C; T.

1482. 1911   New York, D. Appleton. 2 vols. As No. 1476. 1103(9).

1483. 1919   New York, D. Appleton. 2 vols. As No. 1482. 1104(3).

1484. 1925   New York, D. Appleton. 2 vols. As No. 1483. 1105(4).

1485. 1929   London, Watts. Autobiography only with title *Autobiography of Charles Darwin.* iv + 54 pp. With notes by
Francis Darwin. Thinker's Library No. 7. L; T, 796(4).
[355

1486. 1929   New York, D. Appleton. Autobiography only. vi +
64 pp. Introduction by Robert C. Whitford. 797(2).

1487. 1931   London, Watts. As No. 1485, but second impression.
Thinker's Library No. 7. T.   [356

1488. 1937   London, Watts. As No. 1487, but third impression.
Thinker's Library No. 7. 798(2).

1489. 1942   London, Watts, As No. 1488, but fourth impression.
Thinker's Library No. 7.

1490. 1944   London, Watts. As No. 1489, but fifth impression.
Thinker's Library No. 7.

1491. 1945   London, Watts. As No. 1490. Thinker's Library No. 7.

1492. 1949   London, Watts. As No. 1491. Thinker's Library No. 7.

1493. [1950] New York, Schumann. Autobiography only, with title
Charles Darwin's autobiography. 266 pp. Introduced by
George Gaylord Simpson. The Life of Science Library
Vol. 17. 799(28).

1494. 1958   New York, Dover Publications. vi + 365 pp. Facsimile
of No. 1462 [Abridged edition.] DLC.

1495. 1958   New York, Peter Smith. As No. 1494.

1496. 1958   London, Constable. As No. 1493 and from same sheets,
but with paste-on cancel on title page. T.   [358

1497. (1958) London, Collins. *The autobiography of Charles Darwin
1809–1882. With the original omissions restored.* 8vo, 213
mm, 253 pp, 4 portraits. Edited and with appendix and
notes by his grand-daughter Nora Barlow. April.

Binding: green cloth. Price 16s. C, L; DLC, T. See also No. 1540 which is an earlier transcription of the same manuscript.   [371

1498. (1958) London, Collins. As No. 1497, but second impression. May.   [372

1499. (1958) London, Collins. As No. 1498, but third impression. November. C.

1500. 1958 New York, Harcourt Brace. 253 pp. U.S.A. edition of No. 1497. DLC.

1501. 1959 New York, Basic Books. 2 vols. Foreword by George Gaylord Simpson. Facsimile of No. 1458. DLC.

1502. 1959 New York, Harcourt Brace. As No. 1500. DLC.

1503. 1960 New York, Basic Books. As No. 1501. Second printing.

1504. 1961 New York, Collier. 254 pp. Introduction by George Gaylord Simpson. Men of Science Library AS94. 64–39266(1).

1505. 1962 Melbourne, Canberra, Sydney, F. W. Cheshire. Extracts from autobiography only, pp. 71–86 in Dow, Hume *editor Science speaks*. xiii + 165 pp. T.

1506. 1969 New York, Norton. Autobiography only. 253 pp. As No. 1500.

1507. 1969 New York, Johnson Reprint. 3 vols. Facsimile of No. 1481. Sources of Science No. 102.

1508. 1974 London, Oxford University Press. Autobiography pp. 8–88, fragment of 1838 pp. 3–7 in de Beer, *Sir* Gavin [the late] *editor Charles Darwin, Thomas Henry Huxley. Autobiographies*. Introduction by the editor. (Text of autobiography checked against the manuscript by James Kinsley). Oxford English Memoirs and Travels Series.

ENGLISH, BRAILLE

1509. 1962 London, National Institute for the Blind. Autobiography only. 3 vols. Standard English Braille, Grade 2. From No. 1497. LB.

ARMENIAN

1510. 1959 Erevan, Armenian Academy. 139 pp. Autobiography only. Translated from the Russian by K. Kumkumadzhyan. Edited by N. Malatyan and S. Atoyan.

BULGARIAN

1511. 1959 Sophia, Nov.Prosveta. 246 pp. Autobiography only. Translated by G. Ivanova et al.

DANISH

1512. 1909 Copenhagen, Gyldendal. 60 pp. Autobiography only. Translated by Frits Heide. With *Origin of species* = No. 644. Uniform with No. 1051. LNH; T.

1513. 1943 Copenhagen, Hasselbalch. 62 pp. Autobiography only. Kultur-Bibliothek Vol. 22.

FRENCH

1514. 1888 Paris, C. Reinwald. 2 vols. Translated by H. C. de Varigny. T.   [538

GERMAN

1515. 1887–1888 Stuttgart, Schweizerbart. 3 vols. Translated by J. V. Carus. Collected Works Vol. 14, part 2, Vols 15 & 16. T, 1083(1).   [539

1516. 1893 Stuttgart, Schweizerbart. iv + 386 pp. [Abridged version.] Translated by J. V. Carus. T.   [540

1517. 1910 Stuttgart, Schweizerbart. 3 vols. Second edition. As No. 1515. Collected Works Vol. 14, part 2, Vols 15 & 16.

1518. 1910 Stuttgart, Schweizerbart. As No. 1516. [Abridged version].

1519. (1959) Leipzig, Urania-Verlag. 199 pp. Autobiography only. Translated by Rolf Reurich. Edited by S. L. Sobol'. From the Russian translation of the original manuscript, No. 1540. DLC.

HEBREW

1520. 1948–1949 Tel-Aviv, Massadah. 120 pp. Autobiography only. Translated by A. Lev. 1195(1).

HUNGARIAN

1521. 1955 Budapest, Academy of Sciences. Autobiography only. Translated by Béla Szasz. With *Origin of species*. = No. 705. LNH.

178   THE WORKS OF CHARLES DARWIN

ITALIAN

1522. 1919   Milan, Istituto Editoriale Italiano. 183 pp. Auto-
               biography only. Raccoltadi Breviari Intellettuali No.
               158. 794(1).
1523. 1950   Milan, Cooperativa Libro Popolare. 83 pp. Auto-
               biography only. Translated by Luca Pavolini.
1524. 1962   Turin, G. Einaudi. xix + 224 pp. Autobiography only.
               Translated from No. 1497, Nora Barlow edition, by
               Luciana Fratini. Preface by Guiseppe Montalenti.

JAPANESE

1524a. 1972   Tokyo, Chikuma shobô. 264 pp. Nora Barlow version
               of Autobiography only. Translated by Yasugi Ryûichi
               & Egami Fuyoko.

KOREAN

1525. 1965   Seoul, Yangseogag. 309 pp. Autobiography only.
               Translated by Myeong-Hwa Hwang.

LATVIAN

1526. 1935   Riga, State Publishing House. Autobiography only.
               Translated by P. Galenicks. With Origin of species. =
               No. 737.

LITHUANIAN

1527. 1959   Vilnjus, State Publishing House. Autobiography only.
               With Origin of species. = No. 738 q.v. for translators.

NORWEGIAN

1528. 1889   Fagerstrand pr. Høvig, Bibliothek for de Tusen Hjem.
               3 vols. Vol. 1 translated by Peder Ulleland, vols 2 & 3
               by M. Søraas. Scientific parts edited by Olav Johan-
               Olsen. L; T, 1112(1).

POLISH

1529. 1891   Translated by Józef Nusbaum. ?Autobiography only.
1530. 1950   Translated by Jan Wilczyński. ?Extracts only.

1531. 1960   Warsaw, Academy of Sciences. xiii + 418 pp. [Abridged edition.] Translated by A. Iwanowska, A. Krasicka, J. Połtowicz and S. Skowron, under the guidance of A. Makarewicz, W. Michajłow and A. K. Petrusewicz. Edited by A. Straszewicz and Z. Wójcik. Collected Works Vol. 8. Biblioteka Klasyków Biologii. DLC.

ROMANIAN

1532. 1962   [Bucharest], National Academy. 250 pp. Autobiography only. Translated from English [i.e. No. 1497, Nora Barlow Edition] by Viorica V. Dobrovici; from Russian [i.e. No. 1540, S. L. Sobol' edition] by G. D. Dorogan. Collated by V. Dobrovici and V. Mârza. C, L; T.

RUSSIAN

1533. 1896   St Petersburg, A. Porokhovshchikov. 59 pp. Autobiography only. Translated by M. Filippov. Collected Works. Supplement to *Nauchnoe Obozrenie* Vol. 3.

1534. 1896   St Petersburg, O. N. Popov. 35 pp. Autobiography only. Translated by K. A. Timiryazev. Collected Works Vol. 1, part 1.

1535. 1898   St Petersburg, O. N. Popov. As No. 1534, but second edition.

1536. 1907   Moscow, Yu. Lepkovskiĭ. 44 pp. Autobiography only. Translated by K. A. Timiryazev. Collected Works Vol. 1.

1537. 1909   St Petersburg, V. V. Bitner, *Vestnik Znaniya*. pp. 6–66. Autobiography only. Translated by A. A. Nikolaev. Edited by V. V. Bitner. Collected Works Vol. 1, part 1.

1538. 1925   Moscow-Leningrad, State Edition. 42 pp. Autobiography only. Translated by K. A. Timiryazev. Collected Works Vol. 1, part 1.

1539. 1950   Moscow, Inostrannoĭ Lit.Rȳ. 390 pp. Translated by N. I. Feĭginson. Edited by A. E. Garisinovich. L; DLC.

1540. 1957   Moscow, Academy of Sciences U.S.S.R. *Recollections of the development of my mind and character (autobiography) 1876–1881.* 8vo, 220 mm, 251 pp, 12 plates on 8 leaves, 20 photographs in text. Translated from the manuscript by S. L. Sobol'. The autobiography is pp. [37]–153. The English title is on p. 38. This edition, which has the original omissions restored, precedes No. 1497 which is the first in English. C, D; T.

1541. 1958   Moscow, Academy of Sciences U.S.S.R. pp. 87–89, 132–134, 166–242. Autobiography and other extracts. Translated by V. N. Sukachev. Edited by S. L. Sobol'. Collected Works Vol. 9. D, L.

SERBIAN

1542. 1937   Belgrade, D. Gregorila. 184 pp. Autobiography only. Translated by Milan S. Nedić. Introduction by D. Miloyevic. L; 1118(1).

SLOVENE

1543. 1959   Ljubljana, Cankarǰeva Založba. Autobiography only. Translated by Ružena Skerlj. With an essay by Marcel Prenant.

SPANISH

1544. 1902   Madrid, B. Rodriquez Serra. 188 pp. Autobiography only. Translated by Ciro Bayo. Colección de Autobiografías Celebres No . 2.

1545. 1946   Buenos Aires, Editorial Elevación. 271 pp. Selections from the abridged, Francis Darwin, edition No. 1461. Translated by Argentina Carreras. Foreword by Alberta Palcos. En la Intimidad de los Grandes Hombres. 1116(1).

SWEDISH

1546. 1959   Stockholm, Natur och Kultur. 239 pp. Translated by Gösta Aberg.

UKRAINIAN

1547. 1949   Kiev-Kharkov, State Agricultural Publishing House. Autobiography only. Edited by G. O. Kobzar. With *Origin of species.* = No. 798.

More Letters

This collection contains almost entirely new matter although some extracts and a few whole letters are also found in *Life and letters*. It also contains a brief autobiographical piece (pp. 1–5) which is sometimes found in modern editions and translations of his main autobiography.

There is only the one original printing, but Murray sold some sets of sheets to Watts, and it occurs in the original blue of Murray's case as well as in the brown of Watts'. There is no indication on the title page of this change and I have even seen a copy in Watts' case with Murray's dust wrappers. There is a New York reprint from stereos in the same year as the first English and a facsimile in 1972, but it does not seem to have been translated except for a recent Russian version of the auto-biographical fragment and a description of Down House.

ENGLISH

1548. 1903   London, John Murray. Darwin, Francis & Seward, A. C. *editors. More letters of Charles Darwin. A record of his work in a series of hitherto unpublished letters.* 8vo, 215 mm, 2 vols, xxiv + 494, viii + 508 pp, 15 portraits. 12 line errata slip in Vol. 2. Binding: variant *a*. blue cloth, John Murray at foot of spine; variant *b*. brown cloth, Watts & Co. at foot of spine [? a remainder]. Price £1. 12s. C, L; T, 1122(22).   [359–60

1549. 1903   New York, D. Appleton. 2 vols. From stereos of No. 1548. 1123(25).

1550   1972   New York, Johnson Reprint. 2 vols. Facsimile of No. 1548. Sources of Science No. 137.

RUSSIAN

1551. 1959   Moscow, Academy of Sciences, U.S.S.R. [An auto-biographical fragment] from Vol. 1, pp. 1–5, at pp. 151–155. [Account of Down] from Vol. 1, pp. 35–36, at pp. 156–159. The former translated by S. K. Ait and S. L. Sobol'; the latter by S. L. Sobol'. Collected Works, Vol. 9. D, L; DLC.

Emma Darwin

Although a biography of Emma, this contains a large number of letters from Charles and is an important source of information about his day to day and family life. Edited by their fourth child, Henrietta Emma, it was first printed for private circulation amongst family and friends; the records of the Cambridge University Press show that there were 250 sets. The published edition is closely similar to the first, but the second volume starts in 1838, with their engagement, instead of in 1840.

ENGLISH

1552. 1904   Cambridge, University Press printed. Litchfield, H. E. *editor. Emma Darwin, wife of Charles Darwin. A century of family letters.* 8vo, 213 mm, 2 vols, 15 portraits, 4 plates. Privately printed, 250 copies. Not in commerce. Binding: blue buckram. C, L; T, 786(2).   [361

1553. 1915   London, John Murray. Litchfield, Henrietta E. *editor. Emma Darwin, A century of family letters, 1792–1896.* 8vo, 216 mm, i–ix, i–iv, xi–xxxi + 289, xxv + 326 pp, 15 portraits, 4 plates. First published edition, with text altered from that on No. 1552. The second pagination in Vol. I is a postscript of Erasmus Darwin, eldest son of Horace, killed at Ypres April 24 1915, by Bernard Darwin. Binding: blue cloth. Price £1. 1s. C, L; T, 784(20).   [362

1554. 1915   New York, D. Appleton. 2 vols. As No. 1553 and from stereos. 785(7).

Sketches of 1842 and 1844

When Francis Darwin put together *Life and letters* he did not know that the sketch of his father's evolutionary ideas, which was written in 1842, had survived. The pencil manuscript was discovered in 1896, after the death of his mother, in a cupboard under the stairs at Down House. Its dating is discussed in the preface to the first printing in 1908, and in that of 1958. The first, dated June 23, 1909, was not published but was printed for presentation to delegates to the Cambridge festivities in commemoration of the centenary of Darwin's birth and the fiftieth anniversary of the publication of *The origin of species*. I have seen a copy of it with the table plan, musical background and menu loosely inserted. Leaf *a*4 has a printed presentation note on the recto; this has been removed in some copies which were perhaps available outside the presentation issue.

Later in the same year it was reprinted and published together with the sketch of 1844, and in this printing most of the introduction, repaginated, and the whole of the sketch of 1842 are from the standing type of the first issue; the rest is new. Both sketches were reprinted for the International Congress of Zoology in 1958, and issued free to those who had subscribed as well as being available for purchase. The original printing and that of 1958 have recently appeared in facsimile.

ENGLISH

1555. 1909   Cambridge, University Press. Darwin, Francis *editor*. *The foundations of The origin of species, a sketch written in 1842.* 8vo, 220 mm, xxii + 53 pp, one portrait, one facsimile of holograph. Printed, not published, for presentation only. June. Binding: grey-buff paper boards, white parchment spine. C; T, 951(8).   [363

1556. 1909   Cambridge, University Press. Darwin, Francis *editor*. *The foundations of The origin of species. Two essays written in 1842 and 1844.* 8vo, 220 mm, xxix + 263 pp, one portrait, one facsimile of holograph. Sketch of 1842 pp. 1–53 and from same setting of type as No. 1555. Sketch of 1844 pp. 57–255. June. Binding: olive-green buckram bevelled boards. Price 17s. 6d. C, L; T, 952(25).

[364

1557. 1958   Cambridge, University Press. *Evolution by natural selection.* 8vo, 218 mm, viii + 288 pp. Sketch of 1842 pp. 39–88. Sketch of 1884 pp. 89–254. Also contains No. 360. With a foreword by *Sir* Gavin de Beer. Published for the XVth International Congress of Zoology, London, and for the Linnean Society of London. C, L; T, DLC.   [365

1558. 1963   New York, Viking Press. Essay of 1844 only. In No. 1618.

1559. 1969   New York, Kraus Reprint. Facsimile of No. 1555.

1560. 1971   New York, Johnson Reprint. Facsimile of No. 1557.

GERMAN

1561. 1911   Leipzig und Berlin, B. C. Teubner. viii + 325 pp. Translated by Maria Semon, from No. 1555. 954(2).

ITALIAN

1562. 1960   Turin, P. Baringhieri. 125 pp. Sketch of 1842 only.

Translated by B. Chiarelli. Also contains No. 369.
Enciclopedia di Autori Classici, diretta G. Colli.

1563.   1974   Rome, Newton Compton. in *Charles Darwin, introduzione all'evoluzionismo.* 302 pp. Introduction by Giuseppe Montalenti. Also includes No. 369.

RUSSIAN

1564.   1932   Moscow, in *Podznamenem marksizma*, Nos 5–6, pp. 87–114. Sketch of 1842 only. Translated by A. D. & L. I. Nekrasov. Foreword by A. D. Nekrasov.

1565.   1939   Moscow, Academy of Sciences, U.S.S.R. pp. 79–230. Translated by A. D. Nekrasov. Annotated and supplemented by A. D. Nekrasov and S. L. Sobol'. Collected Works Vol. 3.

Transcripts of Manuscripts

Under this general heading are placed all the, mostly recent, transcripts from unpublished manuscripts. Only two of them were left by Darwin in something like final form; the rest were either never intended for publication or were notes to be written up.

Nos 1580 and 1581 represent a reconstruction of a manuscript in English, whose present whereabouts is unknown, by translating back from a version printed in German. It was sent, with a sketch map, to Hermann Müller of Lippstadt, and there is a letter, in English, from Müller at Cambridge, dated May 5, acknowledging its receipt—'I have read with the greatest interest your curious observations "on the routes of the males of Bombus". The fact was quite unknown to me, and I will do my best for making observations'. This title for the manuscript is presumably that given by Darwin, and it differs from those given in either English version. The paper was translated into German by E. Krause and first published in 1885 (No. 1584). A précis of it, with the map, has recently appeared, translated from the English version, in a Russian children's book.

The second of these manuscripts which is in something approaching finished form is *Natural selection* (No. 1583). The monumental task of transcribing and editing this important work has recently been completed by Professor Robert C. Stauffer. It represents Chapters III to X and part of XI of Darwin's 'big book', which never appeared in the form which he had intended. The first part, being Chapters I and II of the manuscript which does not survive, appeared as *Variation under domestication* in 1868. Parts of Chapter X, on instinct, appeared in Romanes' *Mental evolution in animals* (No. 1434) in 1883, and extracts from the same chapter had also appeared in his *Animal intelligence* (No. 1416) in the previous year. Stauffer points out that a few extracts from Chapter IV, on variation under nature, appeared in Wallace's *Darwinism*, 1889, at pp. 46, 69 and 79–80. They occur on the same pages in the second edition of 1890. Some bits on hybridism from Chapter IX were used by Huxley in his paper 'On species and races and their origin' (*Proc.Roy.Instn*, Vol. 3, pp. 195–200, 1860). Darwin himself quarried from the manuscript for other books and papers.

ENGLISH

1566. 1933 Cambridge, University Press. Barlow, Nora *editor*. *Charles Darwin's diary of the voyage of H.M.S. Beagle*. 8vo, 230 mm, xxx + 451 pp, portrait, 2 plates, 2 folding maps. Binding: green cloth. Price £1. 1s. C, L; 817(19).   [368

1567. 1933 New York, The Macmillan Co. xxx + 451 pp. As No. 1566 and from the same sheets. 818(10).

1568. 1934 Cambridge, University Press. As No. 1566. D; T, 819(11).   [369

1569. 1964 New York, Kraus Reprint. Facsimile of No. 1567.

1570. 1935 In Ashworth, J. H. Charles Darwin as a student at Edinburgh, 1825–27. *Proceedings of the Royal Society of Edinburgh*, Vol. LV, pp. 97–113, 3 plates. Photographs of p. 3 & p. 7 of Darwin's notebook for March 28, 1827.

1571. 1945 London, Pilot Press. Barlow, Nora *editor*. *Charles Darwin and the voyage of the Beagle*. 8vo, 215 mm, 279 pp., one portrait, 14 plates on 7 leaves, one folding map. With an introduction by the editor. Binding: blue cloth. Price 15s. C, L; T, 809(8).   [370

1572. 1946 New York, Philosophical Library. 279 pp. As No. 1571. Photolitho reprint. 810(18).

1573. 1959 In de Beer, *Sir* Gavin *editor*. Darwin's journal. *Bulletin of the British Museum (Natural History). Historical Series*. Vol. 2, pp. 1–21. See No. 1588 for an earlier transcription.   [374

1574. 1960–1967 In de Beer, *Sir* Gavin, Rowlands, M. J. and Skramovsky, [*Mrs*] B. M. *editors*. Darwin' notebooks on transmutation of species. *Bulletin of the British Museum*

(*Natural History*). *Historical Series*.

Part I. First notebook [B] (July 1837–February 1838). Vol. 2, No. 2, pp. 23–73, January 1960. Edited by de Beer.

Part II. Second notebook [C] (February to July 1838). Vol. 2, No. 3, pp. 75–118, May 1960. Edited by de Beer.

Part III. Third notebook [D] (July 15 to October 2nd 1838). Vol. 2, No. 4, pp. 119–150, July 1960. Edited by de Beer.

Part IV. Fourth notebook [E] (October 1838–10 July 1839). Vol. 2, No. 5, pp. 151–183, September 1960. Edited by de Beer.

[Part V.] Addenda and corrigenda. Vol. 2, No. 6, pp. 185–200. October 1961. Edited by de Beer and Rowlands.

Part VI. Pages excised by Darwin. Vol. 3, No. 5, pp. 129–176. 21 March 1967. Edited by de Beer, Rowlands and Skramovsky.   [376

1575.   1960   In Barrett, Paul H. *editor* A transcription of Darwin's first notebook on 'Transmutation of species'. *Bulletin of the Museum of Comparative Zoology, Harvard* Vol. 122, pp. [245]–296, for 1959–1960. April 1960. An independant transcription of the first [B] notebook. Considerable extracts from the four notebooks [B–E] were published by Barrett in *The Centennial Review* Vol. 3, pp. 391–406, 1959. Extracts of B–E by Barrett are also given in No. 1582, pp. 439–463.

1576.   1962   Coral islands. *Atoll Research Bulletin* No. 88, 20 pp, 1 map, 2 leaves facsimilies. Introduction, map and remarks by D. R. Stoddart. The map is redrawn from the general chart in No. 10, Vol. II Appendix with the Low Archipelago from the same added.

1577.   1963   In Barlow, Nora *editor*. Darwin's ornithological notes. [Cambridge University Handlist (1960) No. 29 (ii)]. *Bulletin of the British Museum (Natural History)*. *Historical Series* Vol. 2, No. 7, pp. 201–278. With introduction, notes and appendix by the editor. Brackets in title are editorial. A brief but important passage on p. 262 had previously appeared, with slightly different text, in *Nature*, Lond. Vol. 136, p. 391, 1935.   [377

1578.   1963   In Olby, R. C. *editor*. Charles Darwin's manuscript of pangenesis. *British Journal of the History of Science* Vol. I, pp. 251–263, facsimile of fol. I of holograph.

1579. 1966 London, Constable. Olby, Robert C. *Origins of mendelism.* 8vo, 218 mm, 204 pp, 8 plates, text figs. Fols 55–60 only are printed at pp. 173–175. C, L; T, DLC.

1580. 1965 London, Dawsons of Pall Mall. In Freeman, R. B. *The works of Charles Darwin. An annotated bibliographical handlist.* [first edition]. 8vo, 223 mm, x + 81 pp, 5 plates. Translation of paper in No. 1602 at pp. 70–73, 1 plate, title 'On the flight paths of male humble bees'. C, L; T, DLC. [378

1581. 1968 In Freeman, R. B. *editor.* Charles Darwin on the routes of male humble bees. *Bulletin of the British Museum (Natural History). Historical Series* Vol. 3, pp. 177–189, one plate. Contains a [second] edition of No. 1580, with transcript of Darwin's original field notes.

1582. 1974 London, Wildwood House. In Gruber, Howard E. *Darwin on man. A psychological study of scientific creativity; together with Darwin's early and unpublished notebooks.* 8vo, 231 mm, xxv [xxvi–xxviii] + 495–[496] pp, portrait, text figs. M notebook pp. 266–328; N notebook pp. 329–351; Old and useless notes pp. 382–413; Essay on theology and natural selection pp. 414–422; Questions for Mr. Wynne pp. 423–425 = No. 265; Extracts from Beagle diary pp. 430–438, from No. 1566; Extracts from B–C–D–E transmutation notebooks pp. 439–463, from No. 1575; A biographical sketch of an infant pp. 464–474 = No. 1305. Transcribed and annotated by Paul H. Barrett, commentary by Howard E. Gruber. Foreword by Jean Piaget.

1583. 1975 London, Cambridge University Press. In Stauffer, R. C. *editor. Charles Darwin's Natural Selection; being the second part of his big species book written from 1856 to 1858.* 8vo, 227 mm, xii + 692 pp, 1 folding chart. Transcript pp. 25–566, miscellaneous fragments pp. 567–575.

GERMAN

1584. 1885 Leipzig, E. Günther. Über die Wege der Hummel-Männchen, in No. 1602, Vol. 2, pp. 84–88, one map. First edition of No. 1580. L; T, 975(8).

RUSSIAN

1585.   1935   Moscow, Academy of Sciences, U.S.S.R. pp. 423–564.
                 Diary only. Translated by D. L. Weiss. Edited by S. L.
                 Sobol'. Collected Works Vol. 1. Translation of No.
                 1560.

1586.   1949   Moscow, Academy of Sciences, U.S.S.R. 287 pp.
                 Translated by E. D. Manevich. Edited and with a
                 foreword by S. L. Sobol'. Translation of No. 1571.

1587.   1959   Moscow, Academy of Sciences, U.S.S.R. pp. 7–70.
                 Translated by E. D. Manevich. Edited by S. L. Sobol'.
                 Extracts from the notebooks in No. 1571. Collected
                 Works Vol. 9. D, L; DLC.

1588.   1957   Moscow, Academy of Sciences, U.S.S.R. Journal
                 (personal diary) 1838–1881. pp. [155]–192 in No. 1540.
                 Translated and edited by S. L. Sobol'. The English title
                 given here is on p. [156]. This edition precedes No.
                 1573.

1589.   1959   Moscow, Academy of Sciences U.S.S.R. pp. 128–150.
                 Reprint of No. 1588. Collected Works Vol. 9.

1590.   1939   Moscow, Academy of Sciences, U.S.S.R. pp. 734–738.
                 Translation by A. D. Nekrasov of No. 1584. Notes by
                 S. L. Sobol'. Collected Works Vol. 3.

1591.   1971   Moscow, Children's Literature Press. In Khalifman,
                 Iosif Aronovich [*Trumpeters sound the muster.*] 8vo, 158
                 pp, 32 plate pages, text figs. Précis, with map, pp. 119–
                 121 from No. 1581. T.

Collections of Letters

Only works containing important or large series of letters are included
here. De Beer (in No. 1595) gives about thirty further references to
publications which contain one or a few letters, but his list is far from
complete. The three basic biographical works, which contain many
letters, have been treated separately above (Nos 1452, 1548 & 1552). An
authoritative list must await the publication of the projected *Collected
letters*.

ENGLISH

1592.   1916   London, Cassell. In Marchant, *Sir* James *Alfred Russel
                 Wallace letters and reminiscences.* 8vo, 230 mm, 2 vols,
                 7 portraits, 3 plates, one facsimile of holograph.

Darwin–Wallace correspondence Vol. 1, pp. 127–320. Binding: blue cloth. Price £1. 5s. C, L; T, DLC. 8 letters printed in full in 'Some letters from Charles Darwin to Alfred Russel Wallace', *Christ's Coll. Mag.*, Vol. 23, pp. 214–31, 1909.

1593.   1916   New York, Harper & Brothers. As No. 1592, but viii + 507 pp, one portrait, one facsimile of holograph. Darwin–Wallace correspondence pp. 105–262. T.

1594.   1945   London, Pilot Press. Barlow, [*Lady*] Nora *editor*. *Charles Darwin and the voyage of the Beagle.* 8vo, 215 mm, 279 pp, 15 pls, 2 maps. Binding: blue cloth. Price 15s. = No. 1571. 38 letters, many not published elsewhere or incompletely.

1595.   1959   de Beer, *Sir* Gavin *editor*. Some unpublished letters of Charles Darwin. *Notes and Records of the Royal Society of London*, Vol. 14, pp. 12–66. 42 miscellaneous letters, including ten to Syms Covington which had been published in *The Sydney Mail*, August 9, 1884.

1596.   1960   de Beer, *Sir* Gavin *editor*. Further unpublished letters of Charles Darwin. *Annals of Science*, Vol. 14, pp, 81–115, for 1958. 64 miscellaneous letters.

1597.   1961   Stecher, Robert M. *editor* The Darwin-Innes letters. The correspondence of an evolutionist with his vicar, 1848–1884. *Annals of Science*, Vol. 17, pp. [201]–258.

1598.   (1967)   London, Bentham-Moxon Trust, John Murray. Barlow, [Lady] Nora *editor*. *Darwin and Henslow. The growth of an idea. Letters 1831–1860.* 8vo, 215 mm, xii + 251 pp, 4 portraits, 4 plates, 2 maps on one folding leaf, text figure. Price £1. 15s. Also contains Darwin's recollections of Henslow from No. 830, at pp. 221–224. Binding: green cloth. C, L; T, 67–106629.

1599.   1967   Berkeley & Los Angeles, University of California Press. U.S.A. edition of No. 1598, from stereos.

1600.   1969   Stecher, Robert M. *editor*. The Darwin-Bates letters. Correspondence between two nineteenth-century travellers and naturalists. *Annals of Science*, Vol. 25; part I, pp. 1–47; part II, pp. 95–125.

Collections of Short Papers

GERMAN

1601.   1878   Stuttgart, Schweizerbart. vi + 104 pp. Translated by

J. V. Carus. Collected Works Vol. 12, part 2. Contains
geological papers from serials. L; 451(9).

1602. 1885–1886 Leipzig, E. Günther. *Gesammelte kleinere Schriften
von Charles Darwin. Ein Supplement zu seinen grösseren
Werken.* 8vo, 195 mm, 2 vols, 3 portraits, one plate, one
facsimile of holograph. Translated by E. Krause. Contains Nos 366, pp. 3–8, 1444, pp. 9–51, 1584, pp. 84–88,
the last being first edition in any language. Darwinistische Schriften Nr. 17. Binding: fawn paper wrappers.
Price DM 10. L; T, 975(8)   [533

Selections

This is an unsatisfactory section. Every book about the history of the
theory of evolution contains quotations from Darwin's works, as do
many books about evolution in general, books about nineteenth century
thought and review articles about his work. It would be both impossible
and ridiculous to attempt to include them all. Included, therefore, are
only those whose authors set out to extract what they consider to be
relevant to their potential readers. These potted versions are pedagogical,
condescending and often arrogant. Darwin's more important texts are
available in every worthwhile general library throughout the world,
and should be read, not spoonfed.

The entries are also bibliographically unsatisfactory because such
books are not usually bought by scholarly libraries, and therefore,
though listed in national bibliographies, are not available for study. I am
sure that there are many omissions, particularly amongst the translations.

ENGLISH

1603. 1884 New York, D. Appleton. *Darwinism stated by Darwin
himself. Characteristic passages from the writings of Charles
Darwin.* 8vo, 198 mm, xv + 351 pp. Selected and
arranged by Nathan Sheppard. Binding: brown cloth.
Price in England: 7s. 6d. L; T, 830(16)   [541

1604. 1886 New York, D. Appleton. *Darwinism stated by Darwin
himself.* As No. 1603. 831(4).

1605. 1890 New York, D. Appleton. *Darwinism stated by Darwin
himself.* As No. 1604. 832(2).

1606. [1902] New York & London, Street & Smith. *Selections from
'The origin of species', 'The descent of man', 'The expression*

of the emotions in man and animals', 'Animals and plants', 'Insectivorous plants' and 'The formation of vegetable mould'. 8vo, xiii + 213 pp. Little Classics. 1230(3).

1607. 1939   London, Cassell. *The living thoughts of Darwin.* 8vo, 146 pp, one portrait. Presented by Julian Huxley, assisted by James Fisher. Living Thoughts Library No. 2. L; 1107(3).   [379

1608. 1939   New York, Longmans Green & Co. *The living thoughts of Darwin.* 151 pp. U.S.A. edition of No. 1607. Presented by Julian Huxley, assisted by James Fisher. 1108(25).

1609. 1939   Philadelphia, David McKay Co. *The living thoughts of Darwin.* 151 pp. As No. 1608. 1109(1).

1610. 1939   Greenwich, Conn., Fawcett Publications. *The living thoughts of Darwin.* 176 pp. As No. 1608. Presented by Julian Huxley, assisted by Thomas [sic] Fisher. Living Thoughts Series. A Premier Book. 1111(1).

1611. 1942   London, Cassell. *The living thoughts of Darwin.* 146 pp. As No. 1607, but second edition. 1110(1).

1612. 1946   London, Cassell. *The living thoughts of Darwin.* As No. 1611. T.

1613. [1956]   New York, Scribner. *The Darwin reader.* 8vo, ix + 470 pp. Edited by Marston Bates and Philip S. Humphrey. Contains No. 1305 at pp. 103–119. Also undated issues.

1614. 1957   London, Macmillan. *The Darwin reader.* 8vo, ix + 481 pp. British edition of No. 1613. Edited by Marston Bates and Philip S. Humphrey. Contains No. 1307 at pp. 103–119. C, L; T.   [380

1615. 1958   London, Cassell. *The living thoughts of Darwin.* As No. 1612.

1616. (1959) Greenwich, Conn., Fawcett Publications. *The living thoughts of Darwin.* As No. 1610. Premier Book D.82. 65–53520(1).

1617. (1959) Boston, Beacon Press. *Charles Darwin. Evolution by natural selection.* 8vo, 438 pp. Edited and with an introductory essay by Bert James Loewenberg. DLC.

1618. [1963]   New York, Viking Press. *Darwin for today: the essence of his works.* 8vo, viii + 435 pp. Introduced by Stanley Edgar Hyman. 63–17068.

1619. 1963   Greenwich, Conn., Fawcett Publications. As No. 1616. Second printing.

1620. 1966   London, Macdonald *What Darwin really said*. 124 pp.
                Edited by Benjamin Farrington.

1621. 1968   New York, Scribner. *The Darwin reader*. As No. 1613.

1622. (1968)   London, Jonathan Cape. *Darwin and evolution*. Card
                Wallet, 345 × 228 mm, containing facsimile and other
                material, including No. 373. Compiled by J. K. Crellin.
                Edited by Gerald Leach. Science Jackdaw S4. T.

1623. 1969   New York, Viking Press. *Darwin for today: the essence
                of his works*. As No. 1618.

1624. (1970)   New York, W. W. Norton & Co. *Darwin*. 8vo, xiii +
                674 pp. Edited by Philip Appleman. Contains No. 364
                at pp. 81–97. A Norton Critical Edition.

1625. 1971   New York, Viking Press. *Darwin for today, the essence
                of his works*. As No. 1623.

DANISH

1626. 1940   Copenhagen, Martin. *Darwins udødelige Tanker*. 176 pp.
                Translated by Kai Flor. Presented by Julian Huxley,
                assisted by James Fisher. From No. 1607.

1627. 1965   Copenhagen, Martin. *Darwin, I udtog ved og med
                indledning af Julian Huxley*. 189 pp. Translated by Kai
                Flor. From No. 1615.

DUTCH

1628. 1968   Assen, Born. *Inleidung tot het denken van Darwin*. 95 pp.
                Edited by D. Hillenius. Born-pockets Denkers No. 9.

FRENCH

1629. [1925]   Paris, La Renaissance du Livre. *Œuvres choisis* 204 pp.
                Translated by August Lameere.

1630. 1939   Paris, Corêa. *Les pages immortelles de Darwin*. 232 pp.
                Translated by M. Buchet. Selected by Julian Huxley.
                From No. 1607. Collection les Pages Imortelles. Printed
                on four different kinds of paper, three in limited editions.

1631. 1965   Paris, Editions Sociales. *Charles Darwin. Textes choisis*.
                166 pp. Introduced and with notes by H. Cluny. Col-
                lection les Classiques du Peuple.

1632. 1969   Paris, Presse Universitaire. *Théorie d'evolution*. 240 pp.
                Selected by Yvette Conry. College Superieur. Les
                grandes Textes.

GERMAN

1633.   1884   Leipzig, Thomas. *Charles Darwin und sein Lehre. Aphorismen gesammelt aus Darwin's eigenen Werken und Werken seiner Vorgänger und Zeitgenossen.* viii + 442 pp. T.

1634.   1906   Stuttgart, Greiner und Pfeiffer. *Charles Darwin. Auswahl aus seinen Schriften.* v + 213 pp. Edited by Paul Seliger.

1635.   1906   Heilbronn, E. Salzer, *Darwins Weltanschaung von ihm Selbst dargestellt.* xxiv + 219 pp. Selected by Bruno Wille.

1636.   [1965]   Bern und Stuttgart, Huber. *Charles Darwin. Ein Auswahl aus seinem Werke.* 155 pp. Commentary by Walter von Wyss. Klassiker der Medizin und der Naturwissenschaften Vol. 5. 67–106629(5).

1637.   1967   Munich, Goldman. *Ausgewählte Schriften.* 155 pp. Translated by Walter von Wyss.

ITALIAN

1638.   1920   Milan, Facchi. *Pagine scelte.* 248 pp. Translated by Gino Valori. Collezione di Pagine Immortali No. 3. 1195(1).

1639.   1967   Rome, Ubaldini. *Che nosa ha veramente detto Darwin.* 106 pp. Translation of No. 1620.

ADDENDUM

9a.   1975   Lawrence, Kansas, Society for the Study of Amphibians and Reptiles. 4to, 280 mm, vi + vi + 51 pp, portrait [of Darwin], 20 plain plates. Introduction by R. Donoso-Barros. Reduced facsimile of No. 9, part V.

PART 2 · PUBLICATIONS IN SERIALS

THERE are 166 publications in serials, Most of them are slight notes or queries, but several are important and a number were forerunners of his books. In this list, those which have also appeared as books, or contained in books, are entered here as well as in their book form in Part I. Some appeared, either complete or abridged, in continental abstracting serials: these have been ignored.

ENGLISH, FRENCH (1650) GERMAN (1654)

1640. 1836   A letter, containing remarks on the moral state of Tahiti, New Zealand &c. *S. Afr. Christian Recorder*, Vol. 2, No. 4, pp. 221–238. September. By Robert Fitzroy and Darwin, the latter's contributions being prefixed 'D.'. Dated 'At sea, 28 June 1836', i.e. between Cape Town and St Helena or Ascension.

1641. 1836   Extracts of letters from C. Darwin, Esq., to Prof. Henslow. Printed for private distribution. *Ent. Mag.*, Vol. 3, No. 5, Art. XLIII, pp. 457–460. = No. 2.

1642. 1836   Geological notes made during a survey of the east and west coasts of S. America, in the years 1832, 1833, 1834 and 1835, with an account of a transverse section of the Cordilleras of the Andes between Valparaiso and Mendoza. *Proc. geol. Soc.*, Vol. 2, pp. 210–212. Communicated by Prof. A. Sedgwick. Read Nov. 18, 1835. Described as by Francis Darwin but correctly indexed. = No. 3.

1643. 1837   [Notes on *Rhea americana* and *Rhea darwinii*.] *Proc. zool. Soc. Lond.*, Part V, No. 51, pp. 35–36. Follows John Gould's original description of *Rhea darwinii*. Read Mar. 14. In contents list, p. v, under Gould.

1644. 1837   [Remarks upon the habits of the genera *Geospiza*, *Camarhynchus*, *Cactornis* and *Certhidea* of Gould.] *Proc. zool. Soc. Lond.*, Part V, No. 53, p. 49. Title from contents list, p. iv. John Gould exhibited specimens on May 10. There are 4 other papers by Gould on Darwin's South American birds in Part V, but without direct comment by Darwin.

1645. 1837 Observations of proofs of recent elevation on the coast of Chile, made during the survey of His Majesty's Ship Beagle commanded by Capt. Fitzroy R.N. *Proc. geol. Soc.*, Vol. 2, pp. 446–449. Read Jan. 4.

1646. 1837 A sketch of the deposits containing extinct Mammalia in the neighbourhood of the Plata. *Proc. geol. Soc.*, Vol. 2, pp. 542–544. Read May 3.

1647. 1837 On certain areas of elevation and subsidence in the Pacific and Indian oceans, as deduced from the study of coral formations. *Proc. geol. Soc.*, Vol. 2, pp. 552–554. Read May 31. Reprinted in No. 271 etc.

1648. 1838 On the formation of mould. *Proc. geol. Soc.*, Vol. 2, pp. 574–576. Read Nov. 1, 1837. See also Nos 1655 & 1665.

1649. 1838 On the connexion of certain volcanic phænomena, and on the formation of mountain-chains and volcanoes as the effects of continental elevations. *Proc. geol. Soc.*, Vol. 2, pp. 654–660. Read Mar. 7. See also No. 1656.

1650. 1838 Sur trois espèce du genre *Felis*. *L'Institut*, Vol. 6, No. 235, pp. 210–211.

1651. 1838 [Origin of saliferous deposits. Salt lakes of Patagonia and La Plata.] *Jl. geol. Soc.*, Vol. 2, pp. 127–128. Miscellanea. An extract from No. 273 before publication.

1652. 1839 Note on a rock seen on an iceberg in 61° south latitude. *Jl. geogr. Soc.*, Vol. 9, pp. 528–529.

1653. 1839 Observations on the parallel roads of Glen Roy, and of other parts of Lochaber in Scotland, with an attempt to prove that they are of marine origin. *Phil. Trans.*, Vol. 129, pp. 39–81, 2 plates, 2 text figures. Read Feb. 7, 14, 28.

1654. 1839 Über der Luftshifferei der Spinnen. *Neue Notizen aus dem Gebiete der Natur- und Heilkunde*, Vol. 11, cols 23–24. Translated from pp. 187–188 of No. 11.

1655. 1840 On the formation of mould. *Trans. geol. Soc.*, Vol. 5, pp. 505–509. See also Nos 1648 & 1665.

1656. 1840 On the connection of certain volcanic phenomena in South America; and on the formation of mountain chains and volcanos as the effect of the same powers by which continents are elevated. *Trans. geol. Soc.*, Vol. 5, pp. 601–631, 1 text figure. See also No. 649.

1657. 1841 On the distribution of erratic boulders and on the contemporaneous unstratified deposits of South America. *Proc. geol. Soc.*, Vol. 3, pp. 425–430. Read 4 May. See also No. 1649.

1658. 1841   Humble-bees. *Gdnrs' Chronicle*, No. 34, p. 550. Aug. 21.

1659. 1841   On a remarkable bar of sandstone off Pernambuco, on the coast of Brazil. *Phil. Mag.*, Vol. 19, pp. 257–260. Oct. = No. 266.

1660. 1842   Notes on the effects produced by the ancient glaciers of Caernarvonshire, and on the boulders transported by floating ice. *Phil. Mag.*, Vol. 21, pp. 180–188. Sep.

1661. 1842   On the distribution of the erratic boulders and on the contemporaneous unstratified deposits of South America. *Trans. geol. Soc.*, pp. 415–431. Read Apr. 14. See also No. 1657.

1662. 1843   Remarks on the preceding paper in a letter from Charles Darwin, Esq. to Mr. Maclaren. *Edinb. new phil. Jl.*, Vol. 34, pp. 47–50. Jan. The preceding paper was 'On coral islands and reefs as described by Mr Darwin', by Charles Maclaren.

1663. 1843   Double flowers—their origin. *Gdnrs' Chronicle*, No. 36, p. 628. Sep. 9.

1664. 1844   Observations on the structure and propagation of the genus *Sagitta*. *Ann. Mag. nat. Hist.*, Vol. 13, pp. 1–6, 1 plate. Jan. Complete French translation in *Ann. Sci. nat. Zool.*, Vol. 1, pp. 360–365, 1 plate.

1665. 1844   On the origin of mould. [Correcting an error in No. 1648.] *Gdnrs' Chronicle*, No. 14, p. 218. Apr. 6.

1666. 1844   Manures and steeping seed. *Gdnrs' Chronicle*, No. 23, p. 380. Jun. 18.

1667. 1844   Variegated leaves. *Gdnrs' Chronicle*, No. 37, p. 621. Sep. 14.

1668. 1844   What is the action of common salt on carbonate of lime? *Gdnrs' Chronicle*, No. 37, pp. 628–629. Sep. 14.

1669. 1844   Brief descriptions of several terrestrial planariæ, and of some remarkable marine species, with an account of their habits. *Ann. Mag. nat. Hist.*, Vol. 14, pp. 241–251, 1 plate. Oct.

1670. 1845   Extracts from letters to the General Secretary, on the analogy of the structure of some volcanic rocks with that of glaciers. Specimens were exhibited. With observations on the same subject by Prof. Forbes. *Proc. Roy. Soc. Edinb.*, Vol. 2, pp. 17–18. Volume for 1844–

1850. Title page dated 1851. Communicated by E. Forbes. Feb. 3, 1845. Letters from Darwin to Forbes.

1671. 1845 [Extracts from Darwin's notes.] In Berkeley, M.J. On an edible fungus from Tierra del Fuego. *Trans. Linn. Soc. Lond.*, Vol. 19, pp. 37–43. Summary in *Proc. Linn. Soc. Lond.*, Vol. 1, pp. 97–98.

1672. 1846 An account of the fine dust which often falls on vessels in the Atlantic ocean. *Quart Jl geol. Soc. (Proc.)*, Vol. 2, pp. 26–30. Read Jun. 4, 1845.

1673. 1846 Origin of saliferous deposits. Salt lakes of Patagonia and La Plata. *Quart. Jl geol. Soc. (Proc.)*, Vol. 2, pp. 127–128. Reprinted from pp. 73–75 of *Geological observations on South America*, 1846, No. 273.

1674. 1846 On the geology of the Falkland Islands. *Quart. Jl geol. Soc. (Proc.)*, Vol. 2, pp. 267–279, 7 text figures. Read Mar. 25.

1675. 1847 [Unsigned review of] Waterhouse, George Robert *A natural history of the Mammalia*. Vol. 1, *Marsupialia*. London Baillière 1846. *Ann. Mag. nat. Hist.*, Vol. 19, pp. 53–56. Attributed to Darwin in *Life and letters*, Vol. 3, p. 367. The work was never finished, only Vol. 2, *Rodentia*, appearing in 1848.

1676. 1847 Salt. *Gdnrs' Chronicle* No. 10, pp. 157–158.

1677. 1848 On the transportal of erratic boulders from a lower to a higher level. *Quart. Jl geol. Soc. (Proc.)*, Vol. 4, pp. 315–323. Read Apr. 19.

1678. 1849 [Notes on Cirripedia.] In Hancock, Albany On the occurrence on the British coast of a burrowing barnacle, being a type of a new order of the Class Cirripedia. *Athenæum*, No. 1143, p. 966. Presented to the British Association for the Advancement of Science, 1849.

1679. 1850 On British fossil Lepadidae. *Quart. Jl geol. Soc. (Proc.)*, Vol. 6, pp. 439–440. Read Jun. 5. Abstract only. Darwin withdrew the paper with permission of the Council.

1680. 1852 Bucket ropes for wells. *Gdnrs' Chronicle*, No. 2, p. 22.

1681. 1855 On the power of icebergs to make rectilinear uniformly-directed grooves across a submarine undulatory surface. *Phil. Mag.*, Vol. 10, pp. 96–98. Aug.

1682. 1855 Does sea-water kill seeds? *Gdnrs' Chronicle*, No. 15, p. 242. Apr. 14. Note dated Apr. 11.

1683. 1855 Does sea-water kill seeds? *Gdnrs' Chronicle*, No. 21, pp. 356–357. May 26. Note dated May 21.

1684.   1855   Nectar-secreting organs of plants. *Gdnrs' Chronicle*, No. 29, p. 487. Jul. 21.

1685.   1855   Shell rain in the Isle of Wight. *Gdnrs' Chronicle*, No. 44, pp. 726–727. Nov. 3.

1686.   1855   Vitality of seeds. *Gdnrs' Chronicle*, No. 46, p. 758. Nov. 17.

1687.   1855   Effect of salt-water on the germination of seeds. *Gdnrs' Chronicle*, No. 47, p. 773. Nov. 24. Note dated Nov. 21.

1688.   1855   Effect of salt-water on the germination of seeds. *Gdnrs' Chronicle*, No. 48, p. 789. Dec. 1.

1689.   1855   Longevity of seeds. *Gdnrs' Chronicle*, No. 52, p. 854. Dec. 29.

1690.   1855   Seedling fruit trees. *Gdnrs' Chronicle*, No. 52, p. 854. Dec. 29.

1691.   1856   Cross breeding. *Gdnrs' Chronicle*, No. 49, p. 806. Dec. 6.

1692.   1856   Cross breeding. *Gdnrs' Chronicle*, No. 49, p. 812. Dec. 6.

1693.   1857   Hybrid *Dianthus*. *Gdnrs' Chronicle*, No. 10, p. 155. Mar. 8.

1694.   1857   On the action of sea-water on the germination of seeds. *Jl Proc. Linn. Soc. Lond.*, (*Bot.*) Vol. 1, pp. 130–140. Read May 6, 1856.

1695.   1857   Mouse-coloured breed of ponies. *Gdnrs' Chronicle*, No. 24, p. 427. Jun. 14.

1696.   1857   The subject of deep wells. *Gdnrs' Chronicle*, No. 30, p. 518. Jul. 26.

1697.   1857   Bees and the fertilisation of kidney beans. *Gdnrs' Chronicle*, No. 43, p. 725. Oct. 25. Note dated Oct. 18.

1698.   1857   Productiveness of foreign seed. *Gdnrs' Chronicle*, No. 46, p. 779. Nov. 13.

1699.   1858   On the tendency of species to form varieties, and on the perpetuation of varieties by natural means of selection. With Alfred [Russel] Wallace. *Jl Proc. Linn. Soc. Lond. Zool.*, Vol. 3, pp. 1–62. See Nos 346–364.

1700.   1858   Three papers on the tendency of species to form varieties; and on the perpetuation of varieties and species by natural means of selection. With Alfred [Russel] Wallace. *Zoologist*, Vol. 16, pp. 6263–6308. Reprinted from No. 1699. See No. 349.

1701.   1858   On the agency of bees in the fertilisation of papilionaceous flowers, and on the crossing of kidney beans. *Gdnrs' Chronicle*, No. 46, pp. 828–829. Nov. 13.

1702.   1858   Memorial [concerning public natural history collections]. *Gdnrs' Chronicle*, No. 48, p. 861. Nov. 27. Signed by Darwin and 8 others. = No. 372. See No. 371.

1703. 1859 [Records of beetles at Downe.] *Ent. Wkly Intelligencer*, Vol. 6. p. 99. Signed by Francis, Leonard & Horace Darwin who were 10, 8 & 7 years of age. See *Life and letters*, Vol. 2, p. 140.

1704. 1860 Cross-bred plants. *Gdnrs' Chronicle*, No. 3, p. 49. Jan. 21.

1705. 1860 Natural selection. *Gdnrs' Chronicle*, No. 16, pp. 362–363. Apr. 21.

1706. 1860 Fertilisation of British orchids by insect agency. *Gdnrs' Chronicle*, No. 23, p. 528. Jun. 9.

1707. 1860 Fertilisation of British orchids by insect agency. *Ent. Wkly Intelligencer*, Vol. 8, pp. 93–94, 102–103. Jul. 7, 14.

1708. 1860 Do the Tineina or other small moths suck flowers, and if so what flowers? *Ent. Wkly Intelligencer*, Vol. 8, p. 103. Jul. 14.

1709. 1861 Notes on the achenia of *Pumilio argyrolepis*. *Gdnrs' Chronicle*, No. 1, pp. 4–5. Jan. 5.

1710. 1861 Fertilisation of British orchids by insect agency. *Gdnrs' Chronicle*, No. 6, p. 122. Feb. 9.

1711. 1861 Fertilisation of vincas. *Gdnrs' Chronicle*, No. 37, p. 831. Sep. 14.

1712. 1861 Fertilisation of orchids. *Gdnrs' Chronicle*, No. 37, p. 831. Sep. 14.

1713. 1861 [Letter to D. Beaton.] in Beaton, D. Phenomena in the cross-breeding of plants. *Jl Hort.*, Vol. 1, pp. 112–113.

1714. 1861 Cross-breeding in plants. *Jl Hort.*, Vol. 1, p. 151.

1715. 1861 Cause of variation of flowers. *Jl Hort.*, Vol. 1, p. 211.

1716. 1861 Vincas. *Gdnrs' Chronicle*, No. 37, pp. 831–832. Sep. 14.

1717. 1862 On the two forms, or dimorphic condition, in the species of *Primula*, and on their remarkable sexual relations. *Jl Proc. Linn. Soc. Lond. (Bot.)*, Vol. 6, pp. 77–96. Read Nov. 21, 1861. For French translation see No. 1723.

1718. 1862 On the three remarkable sexual forms of *Catasetum tridentatum*, an orchid in the possession of the Linnean Society. *Jl Proc. Linn. Soc. Lond. (Bot.)*, Vol. 6, pp. 151–157, 2 text figures. Read Apr. 3. For French translation see No. 1723.

1719. 1862 Peas. *Gdnrs' Chronicle*, No. 45, p. 1052. Nov. 8.

1720. 1862 Cross-breeds of strawberries. *Jl Hort.*, Vol. 3, p. 672.

1721. 1862   Variations affected by cultivation. *Jl Hort.*, Vol. 3, p. 696.

1722. 1863   On the so-called 'auditory-sac' of cirripedes. *Nat. Hist. Rev.*, Vol. 3, pp. 115–116. Jan.

1723. 1863   On the existence of two forms, and on their reciprocal sexual relation, in several species of the genus *Linum. Jl Proc. Linn. Soc. Lond. (Bot.)*, Vol. 7, pp. 69–83, 1 text figure. Read Feb. 5. Volume dated 1864. French translation, with Nos 1717 & 1718, in *Ann. Sci. nat. Bot.*, Vol. 19, pp. 204–295, 1 plate.

1724. 1863   On the thickness of the Pampean formation near Buenos Ayres. *Quart. Jl geol. Soc. (Proc.)*, Vol. 19, pp. 68–71, 2 text figures. Read 3 Dec. 1862.

1725. 1863   [Unsigned review of] Bates, Henry Walter Contribution to an insect fauna of the Amazon valley. *Trans. Linn. Soc. Lond.*, Vol. 23, pp. 495–566, 2 col. plates. in *Nat. Hist. Rev.*, Vol. 3 pp. 219–224. Apr.

[1726. 1863   [Unsigned review of] Bates, Henry Walter. *The naturalist on the river Amazons—a record of adventures—habits of animals—sketches of Brazilian and Indian life, and aspects of nature under the equator during eleven years of travel.* in *Nat. Hist. Rev.*, Vol. 3, pp. 385–389. Jul. Not recorded as by Darwin in *Life and letters*, nor in John P. Anderson's list in G. T. Bettany's *Life of Charles Darwin*, 1887. First attributed to Darwin in Dent's Everyman edition of Bates' book, 1910 and later reprints; also given in the printed catalogue of the Department of Printed Books in the British Museum. Almost certainly not by Darwin.]

1727. 1863   Yellow Rain. *Gdnrs' Chronicle*, No. 28, p. 675. Jul. 18.

1728. 1863   Vermin and traps. *Gdnrs' Chronicle*, No. 35, pp. 821–822. Sep. 5.

1729. 1863   [Letter] The doctrine of heterogamy and the modification of species. *Athenæum*, No. 1852, pp. 554–555. Apr. 18.

1730. 1863   [Letter] Origin of species. *Athenæum*, No. 1854, p. 617. May 9.

1731. 1864   On the sexual relations of the three forms of *Lythrum salicaria. Jl Linn. Soc. Lond. (Bot.)*, Vol. 8, pp. 169–196. one text figure. Read Jun. 16. Volume dated 1865.

1732. 1864   Ancient gardening. *Gdnrs' Chronicle*, No. 41, p. 965. Aug. 6.

1733. 1865 On the movements and habits of climbing plants. *Jl Linn. Soc. (Bot.)*, Vol. 9, pp. 1–118, 13 text figures. Read Feb. 2. Volume dated 1867. = No. 833.

1734. 1865 Self-fertilization. *Hardwicke's Science Gossip*, Vol. 1, p. 114.

1735. 1866 Partial change in sex in unisexual flowers. *Gdnrs' Chronicle*, No. 6, p. 127. Feb. 10.

1736. 1866 *Oxalis bowei. Gdnrs' Chronicle*, No. 32, p. 756. Aug. 4.

1737. 1866 The common broom (*Cytisus scoparius*) *Jl Linn. Soc. Lond. (Bot.)*, Vol. 9, p. 358. Read Apr. 19 by George Henslow in relation to his paper "Note on the structure of *Indigofera*, as apparently offering facilities for the intercrossing of distinct flowers. [With additional notice of Dr Hildebrand's paper on *Medicago*, *Indigofera*, and *Cytisus*, in the *Botanische Zeitung*, March 1866; and a communication from Mr Darwin on the common broom (*Cytisus scoparius*).] *Ibid.*, pp. 355–358. Volume dated 1867.

1738. 1867 Fertilisation of cypripediums. *Gdnrs' Chronicle*, No. 14, p. 350. Apr. 6.

1739. 1867 Queries about expression in S[winhoe], R[obert] Signs of emotion amongst the Chinese. *Notes and Queries on China and Japan*, No. 8, p. 105. Aug. 31. Darwin's queries anonymous. = No. 872.

1740. 1867 Hedgehogs. *Hardwicke's Science Gossip*, Vol. 3, p. 280.

1741. 1868 Queries about expression for anthropological enquiry. *Rep. Smithson. Instn*, for 1867, p. 324. = No. 874.

1742. 1868 On the character and hybrid-like nature of the offspring from the illegitimate unions of dimorphic and trimorphic plants. *Jl Linn. Soc. Lond. (Bot.)*, Vol. 10, pp. 393–437. Read Feb. 20. Volume dated 1869.

1743. 1868 [Inquiry about sex ratios in domestic animals.] *Gdnrs' Chronicle*, No. 7, p. 160. Feb. 22.

1744. 1868 On the specific differences between *Primula veris*, Brit. Fl. (var. *officinalis*, of Linn.), *P. vulgaris*, Brit. Fl. (var. *acaulis*, Linn.) and *P. elatior*, Jacq.; and on the hybrid nature of the common oxslip. With supplementary remarks on naturally produced hybrids in the genus *Verbascum. Jl Linn. Soc. Lond. (Bot.)*, Vol. 10, pp. 437–454. Read Mar. 19. Volume dated 1869.

1745. 1869 The formation of mould by worms. *Gdnrs' Chronicle*, No. 20, p. 530. May 15.

1746. 1869   [Letter] Origin of species [On reproductive potential of elephants]. *Athenæum*, No. 2174, p. 861. June 26. Letter dated Jun. 19.

1747. 1869   [Letter] Origin of species [On reproductive potential of elephants]. *Athenæum*, No. 2177, p. 82. Jul. 7. Letter dated Jun. 7 [= Jul. 7].

1748. 1869   Notes on the fertilization of orchids. *Ann. Mag. nat. Hist.*, Vol. 4, pp. 141–159. Sep. 21. Notes begin with a letter from Darwin explaining that they are being inserted in the French edition of *On the fertilisation of orchids*, No. 818, which was published in 1870.

1749. 1870   In Elliot, *Sir* Walter Opening address by the President. *Trans. bot. Soc. Edinb.*, Vol. 11, pp. 1–42, for 1870–1874. Content of Darwin's discourse to the Plinian Society in 1827, footnote p. 17. = No. 935. See No. 1764.

1750. 1870   Notes on the habits of the pampas woodpecker (*Colaptes campestris*). *Proc. zool. Soc. Lond.*, No. 47, pp. 705–706. Read Nov. 1.

1751. 1871   Pangenesis. *Nature*, Lond., Vol. 3, pp. 502–503. Apr. 27. Undated letter criticising a paper by Francis Galton read to the Royal Society on Mar. 30, 1871, published in *Proc. Roy. Soc.*, Vol. 19, pp. 393–410, 4 figures.

1752. 1871   The descent of man. *Hardwicke's Science Gossip*, Vol. 7, p. 112.

1753. 1871   A letter from Mr Darwin. *Index*, Vol. 2, p. 404.

1754. 1871   A new view of Darwinism. *Nature*, Lond., Vol. 4, pp. 180–181. Jul. 6. Letter dated Jul. 1, referring to a letter by Henry B. Howorth of same title, *ibid.*, pp. 161–162. Jun. 29.

1755. 1871   Fertilisation of *Leschenaultia*. *Gdnrs' Chronicle*, No. 36, p. 1116. Sep. 9. Note replying to query in No. 34, p. 110. Aug. 26.

1756. 1872   Bree on Darwinism. *Nature*, Lond., Vol. 6, p. 279. Aug. 8. Letter dated Aug. 3. Relating to a review by A. R. Wallace entitled 'The last attack on Darwinism' *ibid.* pp. 237–239, of Charles Robert Bree *An exposition of the fallacies in the hypothesis of Mr. Darwin*. London, Longman 1872. Reprinted in *Life and letters*, Vol. 3, p. 167.

1757. 1873   Inherited instinct. *Nature*, Lond., Vol. 7, p. 281. Feb. 13. Undated letter introducing one, without title, from William Huggins, *ibid.*, pp. 281–282.

1758. 1873 Natural selection. *Spectator*, Vol. 46, p. 76.

1759. 1873 Perception in the lower animals. *Nature*, Lond., Vol. 7, p. 360. Mar. 13. Undated letter supporting one from A. R. Wallace entitled 'Inherited feeling', *ibid.*, p. 303. Darwin's letter not indexed. *Zoologist*, Vol. 8, pp. 3488–3489.

1760. 1873 Origin of certain instincts. *Nature*, Lond., Vol. 7, pp. 417–418. Apr. 3.

1761. 1873 Habits of ants. *Nature*, Lond., Vol. 8, p. 244. Jul. 24. Undated letter introducing one from James D. Hague, *ibid.*, p. 244.

1762. 1873 On the males and complemental males of certain cirripedes, and on rudimentary structures. *Nature*, Lond., Vol. 8, pp. 431–432. Sep. 25. Communication dated Sep. 20.

1763. 1873 Variations of organs. *Nature*, Lond., Vol. 8, p. 505. Oct. 16. Contribution dated Oct. 4. The paper is by George H. Darwin, but gives his father's views.

1764. 1873 [Footnote to article on local natural history societies, giving titles of Darwin's two papers to the Plinian Society of Edinburgh, Mar. 27, 1827.] *Nature*, Lond., Vol. 9, p. 38. Nov. 20. See Darwin's *Journal*, No. 1573, p. 5; also J. H. Ashworth Charles Darwin as a student in Edinburgh. *Proc. Roy. Soc. Edinb.*, Vol. 55, pp. 97–113, especially pp. 103–104, 1935; also P. Helveg Jesperson Charles Darwin and Dr Grant. *Lychnos*, 1949, pp. 159–167. See also No. 935 & 1749.

1765. 1873 Aeronaut spiders. *Gdnrs' Chronicle*, No. 40, p. 1437. Oct. 4.

1766. 1873 In letter from P. L. Sclater entitled: Transfer of the South Kensington Museum, containing 'Copy of a memorial presented to the Right Hon. the Chancellor of the Exchequer [Benjamin Disraeli]' dated May 14 1866, signed by Darwin and twenty-four others. *Nature*, Lond., Vol. 9, p. 41. Nov. 20. = No. 870.

1767. 1874 [Irritability of *Pinguicula*.] *Gdnrs' Chronicle*, Vol. 2, p. 15.

1768. 1874 Recent researches on termites and honey-bees. *Nature*, Lond., Vol. 9, pp. 308–309. Feb. 19. Letter dated Feb. 11, introducing a letter from Fritz Müller, *ibid.*, p. 309.

1769. 1874 Fertilisation of the Fumariaceae. *Nature*, Lond., Vol. 9, p. 460. Apr. 16. Letter dated Apr. 6, referring to a letter from J. Traherne Moggridge, *ibid.*, p. 423.

1770. 1874 Flowers of the primrose destroyed by birds. *Nature*, Lond., Vol. 9, p. 482. Apr. 23. Letter dated Apr. 18. See No. 1771.

1771. 1874 Flowers of the primrose destroyed by birds. *Nature*, Lond., Vol. 10, pp. 24–25. May 14. Letter dated May 7, with postscript [May 11]. See No. 1770.

1772. 1876 Cherry blossoms. *Nature*, Lond., Vol. 14, p. 28. May 11. Letter dated May 6, referring to a letter from R. A. Pryor, *ibid.*, p. 10.

1773. 1876 Sexual selection in relation to monkeys. *Nature*, Lond., Vol. 15, pp. 18–19. Nov. 2. Quotes from work by Johan von Fischer, partly published in *Der zool. Garten*. Apr. 1876. Reprinted in *The descent of man*, 12th thousand, 1877, No. 948, and later printings.

1774. 1877 Holly berries. *Gdnrs' Chronicle*, Vol. 7, No. 159, p. 19. Jan. 6.

1775. 1877 [The scarcity of holly berries and bees.] *Gdnrs' Chronicle*, Vol. 7, No. 160, p. 83. Jan. 20. Reply dated Jan. 17 to a communication from D. T. Fish, replying to No. 1774.

1776. 1877 [Letter of thanks, without title, dated Feb. 12.] In Harting, P. Testimonial to Mr Darwin—Evolution in the Netherlands. *Nature*, Lond., Vol. 15, pp. 410–412. Mar. 8. Letter dated Feb. 20, and containing a letter from A. A. Bemmelen and H. T. Veth, dated Feb. 6, presenting an album of photographic portraits of Dutch scientists in commemoration of Darwin's 68th birthday [Feb. 12]. Darwin's letter addressed to Bemmelen and Veth.

1777. 1877 Note to Mr Francis Darwin's paper. *Quart. Jl micr. Sci.*, Vol. 17, p. 272. Francis Darwin's paper entitled: On the protrusion of protoplasmic filaments from the glandular hairs on the leaves of the common teasel (*Dipsacus sylvestris*). *ibid.*, pp. 245–272, 1 plate. See No. 1778.

1778. 1877 The contractile filaments of the teasel. *Nature*, Lond., Vol. 16, p. 339. Aug. 23. Letter dated Aug. 15, supporting a paper by Francis Darwin, No. 1777, and with extracts from a letter from Prof. Cohn.

1779. 1877 A biographical sketch of an infant. *Mind*, Vol. 2, pp. 285–294. Jul. = No. 1305.

1780. 1877 Fertilisation of plants. *Gdnrs' Chronicle*, Vol. 7, p. 246. Feb. 24. Reply to a note by G. Henslow, *ibid.*, p. 203.

1781.   1877   Fritz Müller on flowers and insects. *Nature*, Lond., Vol. 17, p. 78. Nov. 29. Letter dated Nov. 21 introducing a letter from Müller, *ibid.*, pp. 78–79.

1782.   1877   Growth under difficulties. *Gdnrs' Chronicle*, Vol. 8, p. 805.

1783.   1878   Transplantation of shells. *Nature*, Lond., Vol. 18, pp. 120–121. May 30. Introducing a letter from Arthur H. Gray, *ibid.*, p. 120.

1784.   1879   Fritz Müller on a frog having eggs on its back—on the abortion of the hairs on the legs of certain caddis-flies, etc. *Nature*, Lond., Vol. 19, pp. 462–463, Mar. 20. Introducing a letter from Müller, *ibid.*, pp. 463–464.

1785.   1879   Rats and water casks. *Nature*, Lond., Vol. 19, p. 481. Mar. 27. Undated letter in support of a letter from Arthur Nicols, *ibid.*, p. 433.

1786.   1880   Fertility of hybrids from the common and Chinese goose. *Nature*, Lond., Vol. 21, p. 207. Jan. 1. Dated Dec. 15, 1879.

1787.   1880   The sexual colours of certain butterflies. *Nature*, Lond., Vol. 21, p. 237. Jan. 8. Dated Dec. 16, 1879.

1788.   1880   The Omori shell mounds. *Nature*, Lond., Vol. 21, p. 561. Apr. 15. Letter dated Apr. 9, introducing one from Edward S. Morse, *ibid.*, pp. 561–562 which refers to a review of Morse's work entitled Shell mounds of Omori, in *Mem. Sci. Dep. U. Tokio*, Vol. 1, part 1, 2539 [= 1879]. Reprinted in *Amer. Nat.*, Sep. 1880. The review, by Frederick V. Dickens, entitled Prehistoric man in Japan, *Nature*, Lond., Vol. 21, p. 350.

1789.   1880   Sir Wyville Thomson and natural selection. *Nature*, Lond., Vol. 23, p. 32. Nov. 11. Letter dated Nov. 5, referring to Thomson's introduction to the *Challenger Reports*. Reprinted in *More letters*, Vol. 1, pp. 388–389, with an additional paragraph.

1790.   1880   Black sheep. *Nature*, Lond., Vol. 23, p. 193. Undated letter containing extracts from a letter from 'Mr Sanderson'.

1791.   1881   Movements of plants. *Nature*, Lond., Vol. 23, p. 409. Mar. 3. Letter dated Feb. 22, on observations in a mss letter from Fritz Müller. See also No. 1794.

1792.   1881   Letter to Frithiof Holmgren [on vivisection]. *The Times*, Apr. 18. *Brit. Med. Jl*, Vol. 1, p. 660. *Nature*, Lond., Vol. 23, p. 583. Apr. 21. = Nos 1352–1354.

1793. 1881   Darwin on vivisection. *The Times*, Apr. 22. Reprinted in *Life and letters*, Vol. 3, pp. 207–208.

1794. 1881   The movements of leaves. *Nature*, Lond., Vol. 23, pp. 603–604. Apr. 28. Letter dated Apr. 14 on further observations in a mss letter from Fritz Müller. See also No. 1791.

1795. 1881   Inheritance. *Nature*, Lond., Vol. 24, p. 257. Jul. 21.

1796. 1881   Leaves injured at night by free radiation. *Nature*, Lond., Vol. 24, p. 459. Sep. 15. Undated letter with observations by Fritz Müller.

1797. 1881   [On the bodily and mental development of infants.] *Nature*, Lond., Vol. 24, p. 565. Oct. 13. Report of a letter from Darwin to a social science meeting at Saratoga [N.Y.].

1798. 1881   The parasitic habits of *Molothrus*. *Nature*, Lond., Vol. 25, pp. 51–52. Nov. 17. Letter dated Nov. 7 referring to a mss letter from W. Nation.

1799. 1881   Mr Darwin and the defence of science. *Brit. med. Jl*, Vol. 2, p. 917.

1800. 1882   The action of carbonate of ammonia on the roots of certain plants. *Jl Linn. Soc. Lond. (Bot.)*, Vol. 19, pp. 239–261, 2 text figures. Read [by Francis Darwin] Mar. 16, Jun. 26. See also No. 1801.

1801. 1882   The action of carbonate of ammonia on chlorophyll bodies. *Jl Linn. Soc. Lond. (Bot.)*, Vol. 19, pp. 262–284, 3 text figures. Read [by Francis Darwin] Mar. 6, Aug. 28. Abstract by Francis Darwin, with No. 1800, entitled The action of ammonia on the roots of certain plants and on chlorophyll bodies, *Nature*, Lond., Vol. 25, pp. 489–90. Mar. 23.

1802. 1882   On the dispersal of freshwater bivalves. *Nature*, Lond., Vol. 25. pp. 529–530. Information from W. D. Crick and F. Norgate.

1803. 1882   On the modification of a race of Syrian street-dogs by means of sexual selection. By Dr [W.] Van Dyck, with a preliminary notice by Charles Darwin. *Proc. zool. Soc. Lond.*, No. 25, pp. 367–370. Read Apr. 18 [by the Secretary, P. L. Sclater]. [Darwin died on Apr. 19.]

1804. 1883   The late Mr Darwin on instinct. *Nature*, Lond., Vol. 29, pp. 128–129. Dec. 6. Summary, with last 3 paragraphs in full, of a communication by J. G. Romanes to the Linnean Society of London on Dec. 6, but not published by the Society. Published in full in No. 1434, pp. [355]–384 and index pp. 405–411. See also No. 1583.

1805. 1886 Darwin, Francis On the relation between the 'bloom' on leaves and the distribution of the stomata. *Jl Linn. Soc. Bot.*, Vol. XXII, pp. 99–116. Read Feb. 4. Published Apr. 14. Volume dated 1887. 'The results obtained were worked out in the year 1878, and it was intended to publish them in a work of my father's to be devoted to the subject of bloom'—p. 101. The work was carried out by F. D. at Kew, working as his father's research assistant. *Life and letters*, Vol. III, p. 339—'He amassed a quantity of notes on the subject, part of which I hope to publish at no distant date' with footnote 'A small instalment [i.e. this paper] . . . has appeared'.

INDEX

Numbers in roman refer to pages; numbers in italic to individual entries. London and New York are not entered because the number of entries would be too large to be meaningful.